Boys in the Field

A CHAMPIONSHIP JOURNEY FROM RED LAND TO WILLIAMSPORT

Thank you for believing in these boys!

Scott Slayton

DAVID SCOTT SLAYTON
Assisted by JEANETTE SLAYTON AND NANCY ZIMMERMAN

Published by
Orison Publishers, Inc.
PO Box 188
Grantham, PA 17027
www.OrisonPublishers.com

DEDICATION

To Trey, Riley, and BayBay
The three best teammates a man could ask for.
Always keep a foot in your field.

And to Kelly, the Captain of our Team,
Whose love, patience, and kindness has made our team a family.

Team/Mgr:	MID-ATLANTIC / PEIFER
Opponent:	MID-WEST

Game #: 8 Date: AUG 20, 2015 Time: 8:00 AM Home: ☐ Visitor: ☒

ORDER	#	STARTER	POS	SUBSTITUTE	POS	INN
1	4	BRADEN KOLMANSBERGER	4			
2	22	COLE WAGNER	3			
3	12	JADEN HENLINE	1			
4	19	ETHAN PHILLIPS	7			
5	25	CHAYTON KRAUSS	6			
6	18	DYLAN RODENHABER	5			
7	7	JAKE CUBBLER	9			
8	16	KADEN PEIFER	2			
9	10	ADAM CRAMER	8			

#	PLAYER AVAILABLE	#	PLAYER AVAILABLE
3	CAMDEN WALTER	9	BAILEY WIRT
13	ZACK SOOY		
14	JARRETT WISMAN		

CONTENTS

PROLOGUE

It started with Braden Kolmansberger. It always seemed to start with BK. He was their "leadoff" man, so it only made sense. What he initiated quickly spread down the line to his teammates. The eight-year-old little leaguers refused to turn around and show their faces to the cameras. They had participated in all the "appropriate things" good sportsmanship demanded, but they just could not face the group waiting to greet them.

They kept their backs toward the third base line where the cameras awaited their faces, their smiles—but those smiles would never appear. To turn and face their parents, to capture this moment on film, and worse—to *smile*, would mean to accept second place, and they didn't, they *couldn't*, accept defeat—not even a little bit. In their minds and in their hearts, *they* should have won this tournament, and they were angry with themselves for not meeting their own expectations. Therefore, they kept their backs turned to their parents—not out of contempt, but because of that uneasy *feeling* they had deep in their gut. They lined up as a team as they were asked, but they would not turn around.

"We can't even see the trophy!" shouted one parent to the group of kids who now stood unified behind this decision of perceived defiance. They stood together, refusing to salvage even an ounce of satisfaction from their runner-up status.

Braden (BK) Kolmansberger, the keeper of this symbol of shame and leader of this small rebellion, held up the trophy without ever turning around. He placed it on top of his head and gave the small crowd of amateur photographers what they seemed to be craving...a photo opportunity—of their backs.

Click.

The trophy could now be seen just as clearly as the last names on all their jerseys—Kolmansberger, Peifer, Walter, Rodenhaber, Cramer, Cubbler, Wirt and all the way down the line—not one face was photographed. Finally, when all the cameras were securely put away, the boys turned around, walked to their parents' vehicles, and started the journey home.

It was only then, in the privacy of the ride home, that their anger, their humiliation, their frustration softened to what they were *truly* feeling in their eight-year-old hearts—sorrow, disappointment, and failure. Soon thereafter, came the tears. Fathers would tell them to "toughen up" and "remember this moment." Moms watched helplessly as they saw their little boys' hearts breaking. They wanted to hug their sons and tell them that "everything will be all right." Both were correct.

The kids had no idea exactly *what* they were feeling, they just knew they did not like it, and they never wanted to feel that way again.

Their competitive fire had been ignited. In fact, this second place finish, in a game and tournament they so desperately wanted to win, served as the catalyst for what would become an inferno. That spirit, that fire, would be stoked, rekindled, prodded and would ultimately drive these boys for the next four years toward becoming the 2015 Little League National Champions.

What the thousands of supporters who traveled to Williamsport, Pennsylvania, and the millions of Americans who watched on ESPN witnessed August of 2015 was the result of what that tournament loss and those competitive flames produced. Long before their dominance, their precision, their raw displays of power (both offensively at the plate and defensively on the mound), these boys spent thousands of hours refining the skills of their chosen craft—baseball.

They started merely as boys. They developed into a team.

And then, they became…*Champions.*

◆◆◆◆

This is the story of thirteen kids who dared to chase a dream, a dream they shared as ballplayers, and the men who guided them each step of the way. They came together—worked hard together, aspired together—and **together,** in the summer of 2015, they formed a team that captured the hearts and imaginations of people everywhere.

From the headlines of National newspapers, to the highlights on sports broadcasts, these kids with their unbridled enthusiasm and their contagious smiles seized the attention of the American public for two magical weeks—but their journey started long before that. Despite the overwhelming attention they received, these kids played the Great

American Pastime with the same joy as children at recess, and the purity of a son just having a catch with his dad in the backyard.

What started in front of a few dozen parents on the fields of Lewisberry, Pennsylvania, concluded in front of 45,000 frenzied admirers in Howard J. Lamade Stadium and millions of others glued to their television sets. However, the journey that these kids, this team, and their coaches made, and allowed America to take with them, took them much farther than the ninety-seven miles between Lewisberry and Williamsport.

Through sacrifice, struggle, and the building of relationships between fathers who had to harden their sons, and mothers who had to comfort them, this group of individuals became unified to one purpose. As a result, boys became friends, friends became teammates, and working together, they became champions.

Throughout this entire experience, a small community simply known as Red Land, which is nothing more than an eclectic collection of even smaller towns, came together to not only stand behind these boys, but to walk beside them every step of the way. Soon, it was not only their small hometown that was supporting them, but small towns all across America, and America itself. That is one of the pure beauties of this country—its citizens unabashedly embrace those causes that lift their spirits. There is something intrinsically uplifting about being able to support a team whose players still believe in Santa Claus and like to be tucked in at night. These kids restored the common man's faith—not just in baseball, but in humanity, and they made watching the News tolerable.

Cole Wagner enamored baseball purists everywhere with his skill and dominance. Jaden Henline became America's sweetheart with his brilliant smile and bona fide charisma. Adam Cramer personified the "Carpe Diem" mentality with his brilliant performance in front of a prime time, national TV audience. And America…America fell in love with this team, and with these boys.

1

"MOM, WE CAN PLAY HERE"

Parents all across Pennsylvania have made Williamsport one of their summertime traditions. For Jody and Stephanie Henline, it was one of the highlights of their summer. Each August, Jody and Stephanie Henline would pack up their car and three boys, Colton, Jaden, and Landon, and the family would spend the day in Williamsport, Pennsylvania, watching as many games as they could in Volunteer and Lamade Stadium. In the summer of 2013, it was the exact remedy for their dejected ten-year-old son, Jaden, who had just suffered a heart-wrenching blow on the ball field.

◆◆◆◆

After working their way through the districts and sectionals, and ultimately becoming the ten-year-old State Champions of Pennsylvania, the team moved on to Regionals in Rhode Island where they would compete against other state champions from New York, New Jersey, and other teams from the New England area. In a tournament for which they almost did not qualify, they played really well and ended up in a three-way tie for the final spot in the teams who would be playing for the Regional Championship (there were four).

In full celebratory mode, the team headed to the bowling alley to celebrate their victories and the fact that they were in The Final Four. While there, they received a call from the Little League officials telling them there was a mistake with the calculations for who would be the fourth team to make the Championship Bracket. Red Land was led to believe that "Runs Scored" broke any ties and would decide who moved on. They were clearly ahead in that category.

The other two teams who were tied with Red Land for that coveted fourth spot believed that to be the criteria as well, so they headed home. Upon further review, tournament officials realized that the ultimate deciding factor in breaking ties was actually "Runs

Against", which meant the team from New Jersey would actually be the team who had won the tiebreaker. The problem was, they were halfway home—on a turnpike somewhere in New York. The other problem was Red Land had already been told that they would be playing the next day—Jaden was told by his coach that he would be pitching—and all the families extended their hotel reservations. With a free night before they played, coaches and parents decided to go bowling, but then they got the call.

Quickly, the parents returned to the hotel and prepared for a meeting in the lobby with a representative from Little League. The boys, completely unaware of what was taking place, were more upset by their game of bowling being cut short than any potential news that would be forthcoming.

As the Henlines returned to their hotel room before the meeting, Jaden began his nightly ritual of laying out his uniform—hat, jersey, pants, socks, shoes. He did it the night before *every* game. "Why don't you wait to do that, honey?" his mom suggested.

"I can't. I have to get to bed early. I'm pitching tomorrow. Mom, I think we can win this," affirmed Jaden—determined, regimented, logical.

In the lobby, the coaches, parents, and players gathered—and waited. When the tournament officials arrived (with security "just in case"), they explained to the team that a mistake had been made and had to be corrected. Red Land was **not** the fourth team, they would **not** be playing tomorrow, instead, New Jersey would. They had already been notified, they were turning around and en route back to the tournament.

"We're very sorry. We are quite embarrassed. We apologize for the confusion." With that, their tournament, and their summer of baseball was over. The families, infuriated, went back to their hotel rooms, packed everything on the spot, and left. They drove home angry, unsatisfied, and empty handed—no trophy, no championship—just a heart full of unfulfilled hopes and dreams, and above all—disappointment, again.

◆◆◆◆

Jaden's mom had no idea if her son would want anything to do with baseball after that, but he came to her shortly thereafter and asked if they would be going to Williamsport again that summer.

"If you still want to."

"I do. Can I bring Jake [Cubbler]?"

"Sure, honey."

So once again, the family loaded up the car and headed to the Little League World Series, but this time, it was different. The two friends were not really going as mere *observers*, it was almost as if they were going as *scouts*. They watched the boys play, they saw how they pitched, hit, and fielded. They looked at how big they were and noticed that these players were not that different from themselves.

While they sat out on the lower hill in right field watching the game, Jaden turned to his mother. "Mom, I can do this. *We* can play here." "I'm serious. The next time we come back to Williamsport, I want you to be sitting over there." He pointed to the grandstands. Then he pointed to the field and said, "And I want to be out there."

She smiled. She knew he meant every word.

Later that day, she took her son and his friend to a "Photo Booth" that was set up behind the main grandstand. There, they had all the jerseys for all the international teams: Japan, the Caribbean, Australia, and Canada. They also had all of the regions for the United States: the West, Southwest, New England, and the Mid-Atlantic. The boys picked the jerseys they wanted to wear for the photo. Nobody touched the Mid- Atlantic jersey.

Stephanie prodded her son and his friend, "Come on, somebody's gotta wear the Mid-Atlantic one!"

"Nope," her son immediately retorted. "The only time I'll wear that jersey is when I earn it."

"Come on, it's our region!" she declared.

"Mom, I'm serious, I won't wear that jersey. I have to *earn* it. And I will."

He never forgot the goal he had set for himself that day. The following year, after Red Land's 2014 team lost to Collier, he refused to go to Williamsport and watch other teams play. The first thing he said to his mom when he got in the car after they lost in the state tournament was, "We got one shot left to get to Williamsport. One shot. We can't blow it."

2

"GOD HAD A BIGGER PLAN..."

It was the only job that Tom Peifer ever wanted. As a student-athlete at Red Land High School, he hoped that, eventually, his calling in life would bring him back to the high school from which he graduated and grew to love—Red Land.

However, the path he followed, as happens with so many, was not the path he envisioned. Tom experienced more success on the football field than he did on the baseball diamond in high school, so as he moved onto college at Lycoming, it was on the gridiron rather than the diamond.

Simply hoping to make the team and have a positive impact, Tom Peifer swallowed his ego and focused on the non-glory job of blocking for the Warriors' lead back, only occasionally getting to actually carry the ball, which was fine with Tom. He found his niche, and the coaches noticed. He was a grunt, a grinder, and he savored the opportunity to be the team's silent, reliable yeoman. The three touchdowns that he actually scored in college were much more an anomaly than a pattern. "I always knew my role, always knew where I could fit in, and it's always bothered me when other guys refused to accept theirs," said Peifer.

Therefore, he kept plugging away. He never outwardly complained, never demanded a meeting with the coaching staff so he could plead for a more glorified role on the team. Tom Peifer played then as he coached now, ego-free and team-oriented. He did what the coaches asked and filled the needs of the team any way he could. That was always enough for him.

Tom had visions for what he thought his role was going to be when his playing days were over. For the four years he wore pads and a helmet, he also wore another uniform, that of a Registered Nurse, which meant an all white shirt, white pants, and white shoes. He was the first player ever to play football while enrolled in Lycoming's prestigious and demanding nursing program.

Nurse Peifer caught plenty of grief from his teammates, he recalls. "Oh yeah, the white lab coat, the white sneakers. They were ruthless.

They used to ask me all the time if I was going to give them a sponge bath after practice. What could I say, I just took it." It takes a tremendous amount of confidence, a great deal of maturity, and a reservoir of patience to be able to endure the constant verbal hazing of teammates in the locker room. In addition, it took something else, something that would benefit Tom for the rest of his professional life—it took a laser-like precision focus.

Tom became the first football player to graduate from Lycoming College and receive his nursing degree. After earning his diploma, he received his first assignment in the Surgical Intensive Care Unit at Hershey Medical Center. In this unit, the most elite nurses worked with the sickest patients in need of the most critical care—heart and kidney transplants, those recovering from open heart surgery, and trauma patients. To say the experience was *extreme* would be an understatement.

Tom would regularly deal with trauma patients who were rushed in from car accidents, gun shot wounds, or any other circumstance that would require immediate, emergency care. The circumstances that Tom would witness on a daily basis would allow him to develop a kind of grace under pressure, a stability, that could truly only be understood by someone who has seen the urgency of life and death situations. He says, "Yeah, it was intense, but I loved it."

What he did not love were the hours he put in so he could pursue his other love, which was coaching. While working in the ICU, he was also splitting his time between coaching JV baseball at Cedar Cliff and freshmen football at Red Land. "It was crazy, but I was young. I would work my eight hour shift overnight, go home and try to sleep, and then wake up for practice. That was pretty much my existence. It was nuts. But all of that was before Kaden."

Somewhere between the chaos of nursing and coaching, Tom fell in love with being a coach and knew it was something he wanted to do for the rest of his life. He dreamed of becoming the head football coach at Red Land, but the demands of his full time profession stood in his way. Working under the demands of the Intensive Care Unit made that impossibly difficult. Most nurses worked twelve-hour shifts, he could not. Most coaches had time away from the practice field to attend to their coaching responsibilities, Tom didn't.

Because of that, Tom went back to school. He originally planned to become a history teacher, but then he was presented an opportunity to get his School Nursing Certificate. In less than a year, Tom was able to complete the required classes and became certified to be a school nurse.

He continued to pay his dues as a coach and a school nurse, moving from assignment to assignment over the course of three years. Then, lifelong friend Kyle Wagner became Red Land's varsity baseball coach, and he chose Tom to become his assistant. After moving through seven different nursing assignments in the West Shore School District, he was hired as Red Land's full time school nurse. Slowly, but steadily, Tom's professional puzzle was starting to come together—he was now a full time Patriot.

In April of 2003, Tom and his wife, Amy, were blessed with a baby boy. Tom was needed at home. No longer could he be just Nurse Peifer and Coach Peifer, he also needed to be Daddy. "I had to make a choice—football or baseball—because realistically, I knew I couldn't continue to do both." No surprise, Tom chose football.

In his first season as Offensive Coordinator, Red Land won the 2006 AAA District Championship. A few short years later, the head coach moved on, and suddenly, the job that Tom once dreamed of having was vacant. Tom applied.

"That was why I did what I did. That is why I chose football. Why I became a school nurse. It was all a part of what I thought was my ideal plan. If that job became vacant, I wanted to be in the absolute best position to get it. I feel I put myself in that position." Tom was the logical choice. He was certainly qualified. Tom was wildly optimistic about his chances. "It just felt like everything was falling into place, but then …"

But then, Tom Peifer was not the choice of the West Shore School District to be the next football coach at Red Land High School.

"I was crushed. Absolutely crushed. Devastated, in fact. It was the biggest disappointment of my life."

"God had a bigger plan…" his wife interjected. "He just had a *bigger* plan. But that was one of the hardest times of our marriage, the hardest time of our life…it was tough. It was awful."

"It still stings," Tom admitted. "Probably always will."

Red Land hired another, more recent alum, Chad Weaver. Chad, a phenomenal student-athlete known for his work ethic, positive attitude, and leadership on every team he had ever played on, was a member of the Class of 2000. Chad had earned the respect of every coach he ever had played for, and his demeanor was so good-natured that it was hard to find anybody who did not get along with Chad Weaver.

Still, it was a surprising choice given how much longer Tom had been involved in the program and how much more experience Tom had in coaching. Chad was not a *bad* choice, it just wasn't what was expected—most of all by Tom Peifer. "There may have been more coaches who were more qualified from outside our program, but not from inside. When they hired somebody else from the inside, that was tough. Really, really, tough."

However, Chad is and always has been a unifier; he is the consummate teammate and professional. When Chad offered Tom the position to serve as his Offensive Coordinator, it was one of the most difficult decisions that Tom had ever had to make professionally. "Uhhh, that was such a tough call. If it was anybody else other than Chad, I would have never even considered it, but it was Chad." Anybody who has known Chad Weaver understood what that meant. Chad is just that good of a person and impossible not to like and respect.

Eventually, his love for Red Land, for working with the players that he helped develop through the years, for the seniors who would be returning and would need help in transitioning from Coach Gay to Coach Weaver, and, ultimately, because of his respect for Chad, Tom allowed himself to swallow just a bit of his pride and remain on the staff.

What it also allowed him to do, without the mantle of endless responsibilities that come from being the Head Coach of any Varsity team, was to be involved in his own son's primary sports experience, in particular, with his Little League baseball team. He continued to coach Kaden's teams all the way up through the ranks. In doing so, he enhanced his own skills as a baseball manager to compliment the natural ability he already had to be a head coach.

The West Shore School District may have passed over Peifer, but nobody else seemed to want to. Kyle Wagner immediately scooped up Tom to take the lead with the eight and up age group at his newly formed Green Light Hitting Academy. The concept of loyalty was never lost on any of the teammates from the 1990 State Championship team. He never forgot the bond they had formed as teammates or in the dugout when they coached together, and Kyle knew the ability that Tom possessed to lead teams.

The Red Land Little League Board was all too eager to have Coach Peifer involved in their program as well. The Board selected Tom to be on the coaching staff for their youngest All Star Team. Tom, Nate Ebbert, and Mitch Kaufman would all share coaching duties in leading their sons' teams to four District Championships, three Sectional Championships, and a State Championship as nine and ten-year-olds in 2013.

After an agonizing defeat in the State Championship to Mountville in 2014 as ten and eleven-year-olds, the stage was set for the summer of 2015. In addition to all the Little League glory, Tom was leading travel teams against some of the most elite teams from across the country in some of the most prestigious tournaments in the nation, such as Ripken Experience Tournament in Aberdeen, Maryland, and Cooperstown, New York, home of the Baseball Hall of Fame and the Cooperstown Dream Park.

Peifer served as the mastermind behind all their progress and all their success, and he did it by allowing his kids to be pushed hard, but never without a clear understanding of the purpose behind the prodding. He delegated, never allowing his ego to get in the way of instruction, regardless from whom or where it came. And he allowed his kids, his son and the twelve others that he metaphorically adopted, to be…kids. "You can't play baseball with a football state of mind," said Peifer. "We had a loose group. They had a great personality, and we had to let that come out." He did. They loved him for it.

In 2015, when it came time to name the coach for the Red Land All Star team that would lead the charge to Williamsport, there was not much debate. Everybody involved in Red Land Little League Baseball, from President Scott Sozanski to the members of the board, knew exactly what was at stake, and they had to have the perfect person to take charge of this team, which was so loaded with potential. Tom Peifer was their irrefutable choice to be manager. *They* would not let him slip away, and their instincts would soon be validated.

Being called "Coach" is something special. There is a certain level of trust, respect, and loyalty that comes from such a title. It is earned. However, Coach Peifer was more than just a coach to so many of these kids, and he had proven that through the years of working with this group of players. As special as the title of Coach is, and will always be, in sports—there truly is no other relationship in the world quite like that of a player with his coach—it didn't capture the essence of just how these kids felt about their mentor.

So, to many of the kids, he was Uncle Tom. Yes, he was Coach Peifer, there was no doubt with any of them who was in charge, who would make the final decisions, who would instill the discipline and hold them accountable for their performances on the field, but *Coach* didn't capture the affection that so many of the boys had for him. Uncle Tom did. Only in Little League, only with boys with a purity in their souls and innocence in their hearts, with young men who are indeed still children, could a term like that mean so much. Uncle Tom. What the Little League had decided, the players themselves overwhelmingly approved. Tom Peifer was the man to lead this team to the World Series.

Each progressive championship allowed them to move on to the next step, first in Newville, then in Bristol, and finally in Williamsport. Coach Peifer was able to validate his ability to take a group of kids to an extraordinarily high championship level. Suddenly, the man who was deemed unworthy to be head coach material was granted the opportunity to coach for a National Championship. It was the perfect validation, not that anyone who knew Tom needed any. And not only was he able to do it with *his* team, which consisted of *his* players, whom he dearly loved, he was able to experience all of it, every single step of the way, with *his* own son, and that meant more to him than being the Head Coach of a high school football team—even if it was his alma mater.

"God had a bigger plan...." His wife tried to finish her sentence, but the tears made that difficult. "He just had a bigger plan. Maybe, just maybe, this summer was part of it."

However, in order for that plan to come together, he had to turn his son into an elite catcher and formalize his coaching staff.

3

"KEEP THE
GOOD WORK GOING"

When it came to putting together a coaching staff, Tom Peifer knew where to start. Through childhood, he had access to some of the absolute best baseball minds in the area. That knowledge was not coincidental, and it did not come from just playing the game, it was passed down through four generations of Wagners who were all baptized in the waters of the Great American Pastime.

The story of twins Bret and Kyle Wagner would not be complete without telling the story of the Wagner family. Small towns all across America have a way of creating mythical sports heroes that are born from stories that are passed down from grandfathers to fathers, fathers to sons. And these stories, which are part folklore and part truth, become every bit a part of the history of a community as the banners that hang from the rafters the subjects of those stories helped to hang. Carlisle has the Owens and the Lebos, Hickory, Indiana, had Jimmy Chitwood, Red Land has Bret and Kyle Wagner. The background of these baseball men was formed in a family where the only thing that comes close to their love for each other is their love for this game—and for competing. That passion has been passed down from Harold to Butch, Butch to Bret and Kyle, and from Bret and Kyle to their sons Cole and Luke. The Wagners' singular obsession for baseball, to perfect their craft, coupled by their passion to compete, has enabled this family to secure their identity in the fabric of the Red Land community. But it all started with Harold, better known as "Great Pap."

Harold Wagner was as old school as bricks and mortar themselves. He grew up in Beavertown and dropped out of school in 8th grade because his father would not let him do a school project. The project was to raise a pig at home. Harold's father did not see the need for such a frivolous assignment, so he made his son drop out of school.

Harold went onto serve in World War II, became a catcher for his US Marine Corps team, and later taught himself to become an electrician. An avid baseball player, Pap served as President of the West Branch League, which included teams from Northumberland, Mifflinburg, Watsontown, and a team from the Lewisburg State

Penitentiary. Men would work their jobs during the day, and then work even harder at their positions at night for their town's baseball team. The competitive nature of that league was legendary. After all, the pride of an entire community was at stake each and every time the men laced up their cleats.

And the rivalry was not limited to just the men on the field. Once, in a championship game against their bitter rivals from Middleburg, Frances Wagner (Harold's wife) did as much to help the team as anything her husband did. Facing the 'Burgs best pitcher, Frances Wagner, who was in every other circumstance a quiet and dignified housewife, immediately declared verbal warfare against the Middleburg Ace. As he continued to doctor and claw at the rubber with the heel of his cleat, she lambasted him with an onslaught of chatter, "What's the matter, pitch, that rubber not good enough for ya? It worked just fine for the last guy! He didn't have any problems with it! What's yours?"

After hearing enough, the pitcher sent an obscene gesture her way and the umpire immediately threw the man out of the game and her out of the stadium. Having taken care of the heckler in the stands, and the distributor of vulgarity on the mound, the umpire brushed off the plate, ordered a new pitcher be brought in, and barked, "Play Ball!" Middleburg's ace never got to throw a pitch! Beavertown won in a landslide.

"That was Great Grandma's claim to fame. She kinda helped them win a championship that year," proudly explains Linda Wagner, Bret and Kyle's mother.

Harold excelled in the West Branch League. He would lead the league in home runs and hitting multiple times, so much so that one year the league refused to give him the batting title because, as they put it, "It wouldn't be right for one man to win both, and you've got enough already." Harold never really thought of baseball as a way to earn a living though. When the St. Louis Cardinals came calling in the 1940's, Harold turned them down, electing, instead, to maintain his position at Middleswarth Potato Chips—the money was better and more stable.

And the whole time he played, his son Butch served as the team's bat boy and caught the same competitive spirit that drove his father to excel in this tough, hard-nosed brand of baseball, where fights were every bit as common as home runs. When Butch was old enough to play in the league, Harold had long since hung up his cleats, but with the prodding of the younger players, who both encouraged, challenged, and questioned if Harold could still play, Great Pap came out of retirement at age 50.

The biggest difference between the game that Pap knew and the game that he was returning to was that new guys wore helmets when they came up to bat. After being forced to wear one in his first at bat ("I don't need one of these things"), Pap was drilled in the head as a welcome back from his rivals who had heard the stories of his heroics in younger days. In his second at bat, Pap was still adjusting the speed of the game and the velocity of the much younger pitcher. The first balls he made contact with were foul ball screamers down the right field line.

"Too quick for ya old timer? Need us to slow it up for ya just a bit?" came the calls from not only from the opposing players, but also from his son Butch and his cronies in the dugout. It was a game at Northumberland. The pitcher was a college kid, some thirty years younger than Harold, who was really bringing some heat. A man of very few words, Harold stepped out of the box, spit in his hands, and launched the very next pitch into the trees far beyond the centerfield wall. "Did you see that one go? Did you see how far that one went… or did it leave the park too quick for you young ones?!" He laughed all the way around the bases. The Wagners were just born to hit baseballs.

And to catch.

"My first baseball glove was a catcher's mitt!" says Harold's grandson Kyle, now an adult. "That's a lousy gift to give a kid. I mean, a catcher's glove at age five for goodness sake! That's lousy! But that was Pap. I remember him saying, 'You're gonna make a great catcher someday, might as well get started now.' I countered with, 'Yeah, but Pap, it's tee-ball! But that didn't get me anywhere.'"

Kyle's twin, Bret, did not have to endure such a "thoughtless" gift because he was born a lefty. That meant he would be a pitcher. And Bret turned himself into one of the finest young pitchers there was—at least that's what he was led to believe by college recruiters and big league scouts—because he could throw really hard and was accurate, but he never intended to make it to the next level from the mound. He was too good of an athlete to "just be a pitcher," and Bret Wagner could punish the baseball when he was at the plate.

Bret and his brother Kyle took their playing careers to Wake Forest University—Bret as a pitcher, who continued to play centerfield on his non-pitching days, and Kyle was predictably the team's (ahem) catcher. There, they fine-tuned their skills at their given positions, and after his junior year, Bret was the 19th player drafted in the first round by the St. Louis Cardinals, as a pitcher. The problem was he did not really know *how* to pitch. He knew how to throw hard (unbelievably hard), and location was never a problem for Bret, but he never really learned the art of pitching—he never had to—he was dominant with the stuff he had.

After two seasons within the Cardinals minor league system, the team traded Bret to the Oakland A's organization. The trade hurt Bret's progression. The Cardinals were more nurturing, more understanding of Bret's needs, his insecurities. The A's were not as patient. He became increasingly insecure about his ability to ever make it to the major leagues. "The A's thought they were getting a finished product, but I still needed to learn how to *pitch*. I needed a change up. I needed a breaking ball. I was drafted on potential—I threw really hard, and I had good command of my fastball—but that only takes you so far. I really didn't know how to pitch; I just knew how to throw hard. I didn't know how to change speeds. Nobody ever taught me *how* to be a pitcher!"

In his first full season with the A's, Bret went 8-8 in 27 games with an ERA of 4.23. In 134 innings, he gave up 125 hits and walked 77 batters. His WHIP was at an all time high of 1.50, and for the first time in his pitching life, Bret was failing. "I got hit, then I got moved to the bullpen. I wasn't mentally tough enough to deal with failure."

The following season, after only 2 2/3 innings, Bret Wagner was even more discouraged. His ERA was over 20. In those 2 2/3 innings, he had given up seven hits, walked six batters, and had surrendered eleven runs.

On a hot summer night in 1997, outside of a locker room in some nameless minor league town that did not matter, Bret Wagner walked away from the game of baseball forever. At least as a player. "I just never learned how to deal with failure or how to be a *pitcher*."

◆◆◆◆

Tom Peifer knew that. He knew Bret would never allow that same thing to happen to any of the pitchers he would have on his team. He knew Bret would not only be able to call a great game from the dugout, but he would teach his pitchers to *pitch*, not just throw. He had to have Bret on his staff.

"When Tom asked me to be on the staff, I wasn't going to let what happened to me happen to any of my guys, especially a guy like Adam, who already knew what he was doing up there on the bump. I knew Cole could throw hard and that would probably be enough for him, but I still wanted him and Adam and Jaden to learn what it meant to actually pitch."

Half of Tom Peifer's "Wagner Mission" was completed, but he still had to secure Bret's twin, Kyle, as an extended member of the coaching staff. His involvement would be vital in not only his development of Kaden as a catcher, but for the philosophy he wanted his hitters to have as well.

◆◆◆◆

Harold Wagner would live to see his great grandson (Cole) coached by his grandson (Bret) and the two make it all the way to Williamsport. He took a tremendous amount of pride in all of his grandkids and great-grandkids for all of their accomplishments, and he never missed a chance to call and give them a birthday wish or just to leave them a message. And at the end of every conversation or message, he would close with, "I love you. Keep the good work going!"

He cherished the 2015 run the team made and came to all of the games but one—the final game against Japan. He would bask in the attention that Cole and the rest of team would shower upon him after every win. He and Lou, the stuffed dugout Minion, became their unofficial good luck charms. The only game Pap did not attend was the game they lost.

As he progressed through his years and milestones, weddings, births and graduations, he would make the girls jewelry boxes and the boys trophies for their various performances in tournaments. He was very much aware of his own mortality and wanted to give them as many keepsakes as possible. But before he passed, he did have one final baseball wish.

"He always said that the one last thing he wanted to see was Cole and Luke play together on 'the big field,'" explained Kyle. Many years prior, he thought Bret and Kyle would be the last ones that he would get to see do that, but now, the Lord blessed him with additional memories that he never thought he would get to make. It broke his heart that Luke was too old to be on the team that made it to Williamsport, so what he really wanted was to see the boys play together, one last time. Conversations would come up that the two would play together in high school, but Great Pap knew the math did not really work in his favor to make that goal a reality, so this became his final ambition.

On the final day of Harold Wagner's life, the Lord bestowed upon him one last answered prayer.

After the Little League World Series was over and Fall Ball began, that wish became a reality. Both Luke and Cole played for the Lumberjacks, a *travel team, and for the first time, his two great grandchildren would be playing on a big field, together. "I'm going to enjoy that," Harold told the family the week leading to the tournament.*

"A 50/70 field [where the pitcher's mound is fifty feet away from home plate and the bases are seventy feet apart] is real baseball," explained Bret. "The fences are farther away, you've got to deal with base runners, fielding comes more into play. It's just more like real baseball. And Pap couldn't wait to see it."

On Sunday, September 27, 2015, Harold was able to see his two great grandchildren play on a regulation baseball field for the first time ever. On a beautiful fall day, he got to watch his great-grandsons play—and win—a 14U Future Stars baseball tournament. He was a happy and satisfied man.

After the game, he hugged his children, his grandchildren, and his great-children for the last time. He told them he loved them and to "keep the good work going." On his drive home to Beavertown from Harrisburg, he pulled into the path of an oncoming vehicle, and ultimately lost his life. Pap was 88 years old. He will forever be remembered with love and affection as his family remembers to keep their good work going.

4

FROM THE ABYSS OF A HITTING DOLDRUM

The offensive philosophy that provided the infrastructure for the offensive juggernaut that became the 2015 Little League National Champions was conceived in the abyss of Kyle Wagner's hitting doldrums in a hotel room in Winter Park, Florida, in 1995 before any of the members of that team were born. "The whole concept for Green Light hitting came about because I couldn't hit like my identical twin brother. I knew if I wanted to have a chance to play Major League Baseball, I had to be a better hitter. I begged for help—from somebody, anybody, but nobody could help me. I knew I had the genes to be a great hitter, but I wasn't. And I didn't know what to do to make myself better, and neither did anybody else. So, I sat helplessly in my hotel room, and cried. Pain is our greatest teacher, and I made a decision that day that if I couldn't find help for myself, I was going to figure out a way that I could help others become better hitters. And that's where my quest began."

Kyle was born with a relentless work ethic. The accolades he earned throughout his baseball career were a direct result of his unquenchable thirst to earn them. He did not have the natural talent that his brother Bret did; Kyle had to meticulously and habitually craft his trade of hitting and catching. Finding the desire to do that was never a problem. He burned to be able to hit like his brother. He knew hitting was in his genes, heck, his twin did it without even thinking, and that gave Kyle all the motivation he would ever need.

The stories of the battles the two would have against each other were as epic as the battles the two of them would have against their rivals. "I always hated guarding him in basketball," Bret said, "cause it always ended up in a fight. Anytime we went to play somewhere, we always ended up guarding each other cause nobody else could stop the other, so we'd end up saying, 'I'll guard him!' But I hated guarding him; I would go and play with other people so I didn't *have* to guard him. If I wanted to just battle with my brother, we could do that in our driveway! But nobody else could do it, so I'd end up having to try." As Bret pushed Kyle, Bret was pushed equally as hard by Kyle, because he would not dare give any ground to his brother. That created an unbreakable bond between them.

Out of Red Land High School, the Houston Astros drafted Kyle in the 27th round of the 1991 Major League Baseball Amateur Draft. That was not good enough for him, so Kyle joined Bret at Wake Forest University in Winston-Salem, North Carolina. Together, the two created a dynamic pitcher-catcher tandem. After his junior year, Kyle once again entered the MLB Amateur Draft, and the St. Louis Cardinals, who had selected his brother in the first round, drafted him in the 21st round. He was still not satisfied that he would get a legitimate chance to play professional baseball, and wanting to give himself the absolute best opportunity to make it to the big league, Kyle returned for his senior year and earned his degree in Mathematics.

At the conclusion of his college playing career at Wake Forest, Kyle amassed a very respectable .289 batting average and was named to the All-ACC 2nd Team behind future big-leaguer and two-time World Series Champion, Jason Varitek. By 1995, Kyle continued to work his way up the Major League Draft Chart and for the third time was drafted by a major league team. This time, it was in the 12th round by the California Angels.

However, Kyle knew if he did not improve his hitting, he really did not have a chance of ever playing on a major league ball field. His minor league career took him to the Boise Hawks in the Northwest League for the Class A Short Season, and in 78 official at bats, Kyle accumulated a modest .141 batting average, but earned the respect of his teammates, coaches, and the entire Angels organization for the manner in which he not only conducted himself as a catcher, but as a leader in the clubhouse.

Following the season, Kyle was told that he would always have a place in the minor league system. The Angels loved the way he worked with their pitchers, but the chances of him ever actually making a big league roster were minimal. Knowing how daunting and realistically futile his chances were, Kyle closed the chapter on his baseball career as a player. "When my career was through, I hurt all over. Part of the success of that 2015 team was created from my own failure. I didn't want people, particularly kids, to ever be as frustrated as I was."

From that season in Boise, from that hotel room near Rollins College, the foundation of his future in baseball and the ideology that would serve as the foundation for 2015 US Little League National Champions was firmly established—but that wasn't the team for whom this completely unrestrained form of hitting was originally intended to help.

◆◆◆◆

"Just hit the ball, Luke—like you do when you're with me." Kyle was coaching his son who was playing organized baseball for the very first time.

"I can't," his son responded. "When I'm with you, I just hit. But when I play baseball, I have to wait to see if it's a strike." From that simple conversation, Kyle knew what he wanted to do to be able to teach his son to think less and hit more. When they played in the backyard, Luke clobbered baseballs. His favorite game to play with dad was "basefootball."

The purpose of this game was for Luke to hit the ball as far as he could and then run the bases as fast as he could. As Kyle had to retrieve the ball, giggles and screams would come from the toddler's voice as he raced around the bases towards home. Always one for the dramatic, Kyle would retrieve the ball and make a diving attempt to tackle his son before he made it to home plate. The result, successful or unsuccessful for little Luke, always resulted in glorious fun. Luke quickly realized that the farther he hit the ball, the better his chances were to score, so his swings grew in intensity with the hopes of generating as much power as a six-year-old could create.

As time passed, Kyle noticed that Luke was not hitting the same way in his Little League games as he would in the backyard, so he asked his son why. "I have to *wait* to see if it's a strike and then decide if I'm going to swing." From that moment forward, Green Light Hitting had its mission statement, as Kyle would have none of that self-deprecating, traditional hitting philosophy to permeate into his son's approach to hitting a baseball when he was at the plate.

Together, brothers Kyle and Bret, along with Bob Gorinski, formed the GoWags Baseball Facility in Camp Hill, Pennsylvania, which served as the home of the Green Light Hitting Academy. Soon, Kyle, along with coaches like Mitch Kaufman, and others who believed in his approach, began to implement the Green Light Hitting philosophy. These principles allowed players to be completely unrestricted in the batter's box and unleash their maximum potential when hitting. It replaced traditional terms like "Strike Zone" with more dynamic terms like "Smash Zone" and encouraged hitters to be far more aggressive at the plate.

Players that worked with them would not be slowed down by overanalyzing and making paralyzing decisions while in the batter's box. "There's no yellow, no caution, no *waiting*. When our hitters are at the plate, their lights are green, neon green! I never want there to be any constraint at all on our hitters. When they don't swing, we want aggressive takes, because I want them to love hitting baseballs."

Another crucial concept to their mindset is demolishing the notion of a 'strike zone.' "There's no such thing as a ball and a strike in our world, just a ball we can hit or a ball we can't. If you can hit, we want our guys to try to hit it as far as they can by swinging as hard as they can. We want our kids to swing as hard as they can every time because 100% is easy to replicate. ¾ speed isn't. Everybody understands 'as hard as I can.' It's the varying degrees of effort that complicates things, so we take that out of the equation. 100%. All the time. Full Reps. That is the Green Light hitting approach. And if you can't get to a pitch, if it's outside of your smash zone, you instantly flip your mental switch to red, but not until the last possible moment. There is no such thing as yellow, no caution. Just green...until we flip to red at the last possible second. So even our takes are extraordinarily aggressive."

The brilliance behind the simplicity radiates to every hitter that successfully goes through their academy. Green Light hitters do not just beat pitchers with their athleticism, they bludgeon them. Their ravenous approach to hitting creates a free moving, uninterrupted athlete who savors the opportunity to punish even a well-located fastball or a perfectly timed breaking ball. Individuality is celebrated at the academy, where phrases such as *"Unique Does Not Mean Wrong"* are uttered with regularity.

Harold Wagner and his son Butch were good ballplayers. Butch's sons Kyle and Bret "were even better because they matched their baseball instincts with great natural athletic ability. But [next generation] Cole and Luke, they had all of that, plus they have been able to refine their talent with all of this technical training," explained Linda Wagner, Kyle and Bret's mother.

As Luke got older, the results continued to be validated, not just by Luke and the other ballplayers that made up the many travel teams associated with GoWags, who consistently pummeled their opponents from around the country, but by all the kids who were going through the Academy—many of whom made up the 2014 eleven and twelve-year-old All Star team from Red Land, who hoped to be the first in the area to represent Red Land in the Little League World Series.

Kyle's methodical hitting structure was designed with THAT group of kids in mind. *They* were the ones that he chose to begin implementing his systematic method of hitting a baseball as early as they were able to swing a bat. THAT was the team that he (and others) envisioned being the first in Red Land history to make it to Williamsport. You see, before THIS team made it to the Little League World Series in 2015, THAT team started the process for them in the spring and summer of 2014.

◆◆◆◆

Mitch Kaufman was the head coach of that team in the spring of 2014. Kyle Wagner served as his assistant. That team had one goal in mind—to be the group that made it to the Mecca of Little League Baseball. As notorious as the 2015 Patriots were for punishing baseballs, the 2014 team hit only three fewer dingers, despite the fact that the majority of the fields *they* played on had fences that were 25 feet deeper than the ones the boys of 2015 would clear. Luke Wagner was every bit as dominant on the mound as his cousin Cole, in fact, some would argue he was an even better hitter than the larger-than-life figure that Cole became. Cole would not contend that suggestion.

The model that Luke and his team cast for the 2015 Patriots was one that allowed them to strive for such greatness. More specifically, the shadow that was cast by Luke Wagner on his younger cousin Cole was one that drove this eleven-year-old to become even better. Luke was the best Little League baseball player that Cole had ever seen. If he could become as good as Luke, then maybe he, too, could consider himself an elite baseball player—but that was a daunting task. Cole admired Luke and the way he could dominate a baseball game on the mound AND at the plate.

Luke once had a tournament in Cooperstown, New York, against some of the most elite teams in the country where he reached base an absurd 23 times in 25 at bats. Before Cole could even imagine becoming one of the best Little League players in the country, he first had to try to be the best player in his family, and when he was eleven, the sentiment wasn't even feasible. The magnitude of that discrepancy was never more evident than on an early Saturday morning in the spring of 2015 when Luke's father took Luke and Cole to Bob Evans before a game.

As the boys finished their breakfast and walked to the car in full uniform, an elderly gentleman benignly asked them while passing, "Which of you is better?" Without any hesitation, Cole immediately pointed to his cousin and said, "Him." Luke, who shyly put his head down as if he anticipated his cousin's response, simply chuckled in hopes of deflecting the question and allowing the moment to pass. And that was that. There was no argument. In the early spring of 2015, Luke was better, and both boys knew it.

Luke's father, on the other hand, took exception to the fact that his nephew capitulated so quickly to his son. When the three of them got in the car, Kyle instantly turned to his son and said, "This has nothing to do with you, don't think that this is anything *against* you," and then he turned his attention to Cole. "Listen to me, Cole, from this day forward, don't be so quick to concede to him, you understand me? Just don't. You want to be as good as him, work at it, and it will happen. But only if you work at it." With that, he turned around, started the car, and the three of them drove away in silence.

As Bret once did for Kyle, Luke was now doing for Cole. And as his Uncle Kyle had, Cole had an unrelenting work ethic.

The challenge had been set, the foundation was laid, and soon the work would begin. "Cole was always in catch up mode, just trying to be as good as Luke, and never believing he was," Kyle explained. "It was an amazing source of motivation for him just trying to be as good as his cousin was. But he pursued it with an unwavering determination."

In the same manner Kyle once marveled and pursued his brother Bret's abilities, Cole would now emulate his cousin Luke, and so did the rest of the 2015 Patriots, who would arduously work to exceed the accomplishments of the trailblazing ballplayers that came a year before them. "That environment created a level of competitive stress that soon became the norm, and that gave 2015 a huge advantage over us because we didn't have anybody pushing us like that," said Kyle. "All those other Pennsylvania teams stagnated after their 2014 runs. We didn't. We helped that 2015 team prepare with a sense of urgency, not to win the Little League World Series, but to win the state of Pennsylvania. Our boys hardened those boys." He scoffs as he comes back to one of his favorite sayings, "Pain is our greatest teacher." The pain that the 2014 team went through cut deep, but it was not for naught.

When the 2014 Red Land Little League team was eliminated from the Pennsylvania State Playoffs, thereby dashing their hopes, visions, and dreams of being the first to ever make it to Williamsport, their pain would become the greatest teacher the 2015 team would have. As the twelve-year-olds on that team had to watch the summer of 2014 become the summer of Mo'ne Davis, they knew they would never get the opportunity to go to Williamsport again.

When the 2014 Red Land team lost their final game to Collier, the eleven-year-olds on that team (Cole, Jaden, and Chayton) never forgot the devastation they saw in the eyes of their teammates. They knew they never wanted to feel that way themselves. *They* had another chance, *they* could still play the following year, but for every other boy on that team, including Luke, their window of opportunity to play in Williamsport was permanently closed.

"I don't think Luke was ever jealous of Cole and the success he experienced in the Little League World Series," explained Kyle, "but I'm sure he was envious of the *opportunity*."

The moment that team lost to Collier, the 2015 team began their mission to get to Williamsport and make sure they would not feel the same way the team that preceded them felt. However, what *was* reinforced out of that, albeit heartbreaking, campaign in 2014 was validation of the Green Light Hitting principles and the building of a tangible standard for the 2015 team to aspire to. "There is no doubt that those guys (the 2014 team) created a culture for these guys (the 2015 team)," said Kaufman, the Head Coach of the 2014 team. "That winning culture was vital.

"We didn't have that. We were creating the culture. Once that level of excellence was established, they just had to try to match it, even try to beat it. It drove them. We didn't have that, and it was a huge advantage for them. They were the hunter. In a way, we were their prey. Before the 2015 team was ever trying to win the Little League World Series, they were trying to be as good as the team that came before them. That was a big enough challenge for them, because in their mind, they weren't."

During that entire time, coaches Tom Peifer, along with future assistants JK Kolmansberger and Bret Wagner watched, learned, and waited for their chance. Bret served with his brother Kyle as an assistant to Mitch and saw firsthand all that was involved in making a championship push at this level, while Tom started to create their own blueprint for the team he wanted to create when it was time to make *their* run. "Tom did an unbelievable job with the 2015 team. He was like a conductor of an orchestra. He had a 5-6 year plan, and he executed it beautifully," said JK Kolmansberger, who would be by Tom's side for every practice, audition, and concert.

Slowly, the margin began to shrink between the 2014 version of the Patriots, who in the spring of 2015 were a year older, stronger, and battle-tested. Gradually, the group that would follow them began to show signs of narrowing the gap. And people noticed.

Steadily, crucial factors began to fall into place. There were no soft spots in their batting order, and they had a much deeper pitching staff led by a genuine ace in Cole Wagner, who knew how to conserve pitches. That was imperative to being successful, especially with the unwavering restrictions set forth by Little League.

What the coaching staff did best, and to the players' credit they accepted, was to define what each boy's responsibility was if they were going to be successful. "There was no learning curve for our kids" said JK, "we just switched hats and jerseys, but everybody knew what their role was."

Bret Wagner had a front row seat for every game played by both teams. He said, "Our 2014 team had great *players*, but that 2015 group was a great *team*."

"Yeah," said Kyle to Mitch a year after their run was finished, "when we started to make our run, we were still trying to figure out exactly where everybody fit in. *They* had already done that."

The coaches learned from each other as well. Manager Tom Peifer moved into the dugout so he could better manage the game, working out the requirements that Little League demanded of each kid getting at least one at bat and controlling the pitch counts so the danger of "burning pitches" never became a reality.

They mirrored Mitch's strategy to move their left and right fielders depending on the batter's tendencies. They would move their stronger fielder to right field when Cole pitched to right handed batters, playing the percentages that more kids would not be able to pull the ball against his velocity—and the kids not only accepted this, but embraced it! That cannot be understated. In a world where ego many times trumps logic, the kids from Red Land consistently simply did what was best for the team.

Now, when it is asked to Luke and Cole, Cole is not nearly as willing to concede as he was that morning outside of Bob Evans. And Tom knew he wanted the Wagners fully invested in *this* team—with Cole as a player, Bret as his assistant, and Kyle as a "consultant." With the Wagners secured as members of his staff, Coach Peifer had only one hole to fill, and he knew the perfect person to be able to do just that.

5

THE CEO

Jim Kolmansberger's day would usually start at 5:00 am. He would wake up, head into his office, and attack the day. The work he could do at that time not only allowed him to be productive for himself and the tasks that he had to complete, but it also allowed him to create the environment that would enable his employees to flourish. For him, the climate he created in the offices he built around the world superseded any business strategy that he followed. Tom Peifer wanted that same climate, that same culture, created for his baseball team.

He knew that Bret and Kyle Wagner would provide all of the technical baseball knowledge that the team would need, but he also knew that was only one part of the equation. He fully understood that the game was only a fraction of the day, and that if his team was going to make it to Williamsport, the atmosphere around the team was going to be every bit as important as their baseball skill. Fortunately for him, he had access to a coach who not only knew baseball, but also possessed a wealth of knowledge about cultivating that kind of successful culture. So Tom pursued Braden's father, JK, as diligently as he had pursued the Wagners—to him he was the final piece of the puzzle.

What Coach Peifer was to managing the baseball games and operations, and Coach Bret was to the pitching staff, JK was for the overall *mindset* of the team. He kept them grounded, kept them focused, kept them loose. "We knew they'd be okay, both the kids and the coaches, as long as JK was involved." Amy Peifer first said it, but it was echoed by just about every mother who was sending her son away for 22 days without any of the comforts of home. Not only would JK's stability, wisdom, and guidance provide comfort for the boys, he would serve as a calming force for the coaching staff as well as the pressure continued to build. After all, JK saw his entire childhood not only through the eyes of the player he was, but as the son of a coach who worked with such legendary coaches as Bob Knight and Mike Krzyzewski. His father had worked for the Hall of Fame Bob Knight in the earlier stages of "The General's" career while he was still earning his stripes at West Point. His roommate in those days was Coach K, who, for those who do not follow basketball, went on to win five NCAA Championships, twelve Final Fours, and multiple Olympic gold medals as an assistant to the Dream Team in '92 and as the Head Coach in 2008 and 2012. Jim Kolmansberger I and Jim Kolmansberger II both knew sports, and they knew it from every angle.

As a child, JK would sit in on every practice, every coaches meeting, and he would accompany his father on every scouting trip. He heard how his father dealt with every parental problem, every cut night, and heard the rationale behind every decision his father ever had to make. As a three-sport athlete, JK came to know the physical demands of football, the intensity of basketball, and the nuances of baseball. What he learned most was not just the strategies behind each game, but also the philosophy behind motivating players. He quickly learned that the morale and culture of a team far superseded strategy, and that could give a team some kind of tactical advantage. Hitters went into slumps, as do shooters. Running backs, quarterbacks, wide receivers, and linemen consistently find themselves less than 100% due to the physical nature of football, but *culture* can be sustained. It is consistent, it endures. Positive energy and chemistry provide amazing resiliency, and that kind of growth mindset radiated from JK. He did not want to just get the most out of a *play*; he wanted to get the most out of his *players*. Tom Peifer certainly wanted an asset like that with him in the dugout.

That mentality did not end when JK hung up his high tops and cleats during his freshmen year at Bloomsburg. He knew he did not have a future in playing baseball, so he focused on his academics, earning his bachelor's degree from Bloomsburg and then his MBA from Baltimore's Merrick School of Business. Along the way, his business mentor of 27 years, Uncle Joe, helped him sharpen his business sense with the many projects they embarked upon and the risks they took together. He never stopped wanting to achieve. He labels himself as an entrepreneurial visionary and admits to loving the energy of a start up business.

In 2009, he, along with Brian Robertson and Rich Waller, founded his fourth and most successful business, VisiQuate, a company that specializes in big data analysis for healthcare professionals. In his company, JK serves as the President. He is the integral force behind the innovative culture, which emanates a positive energy where all of his employees—from the CEO to the janitor—feel a part of the creative genius that is implemented daily. Employees are given company stock so they have a true sense of ownership in the business, and they flourish under the leadership and direction that JK, Brian and Rich provide.

His "common man" approach to business, one that dictates he travel in Seat 13C of coach rather than first class, despite his overwhelming success, complimented perfectly to the culture that Coach Tom Peifer was trying to build with this team. The results—the celebrations at home plate for teammates' success, the productive, lively atmosphere that surrounded everything the team did, the ego-free climate that is so rare in sports today, which Tom exuded himself better than anybody—was anything but coincidental. It was the result of a premeditated and meticulously manicured environment where every member of the team felt valued.

Tom Peifer oversaw the daily baseball operations. Bret Wagner's area of expertise was pitching. But it was JK's responsibility to cultivate the spirit of the team, and that was every bit as vital—maybe even more so—when dealing with boys away from home on a stage as grand as the one on which they were playing. He, along with his wife Kristie, who was the youngest executive in a Baltimore Healthcare Company and well on her way to becoming a CEO herself before she gave it all up to become a full time mom (JK says, "Her ambition wasn't to be the President of a company, it was to be a MOM.") had been able to pass these characteristics onto their children. Their daughter, Hollis, started her own business at age fourteen, and BK was the epitome of a leadoff hitter because when he got on base, there was no doubt he was going to find a way to get to home plate. Now JK just had to pass these characteristics on to his team. As he sat in the dugout on the warm summer mornings, those were the musings that rolled through his head as he reveled in all that the team had already accomplished.

Once in Williamsport, nothing changed. Jim Kolmansberger's day would start at 5:00 a.m. JK would wake up early, pick up a morning cup of coffee, and walk the fields of the historic grounds of Williamsport. "There's something nostalgic about Little League baseball," said Coach JK, "and I couldn't believe all that our kids were getting to experience. There is no other event in the world that captures the essence of sports and youth better than the Little League World Series. And now our kids were a part of that history."

On game days, he would head up to the South Entrance on Montgomery Street and interact with the fans that were already in line with optimistic hopes of getting a spot on the hill so they could be a part of the *Red Sea* that engulfed the outfield. He talked to the locals who, despite having thousands of people swarm their otherwise peaceful town every summer, still found themselves caught up in the excitement that was generated each August. He would mingle with the locals from back home who would tell of their experiences while watching his team play from the outfield, an entirely different perspective from the one JK had from the dugout and in the first base coaches box. It gave him chills and a tremendous sense of pride to feel the passion the Red Land fans had as the boys continued to progress through the tournament. It also was quite humbling.

Finally, JK would head down to the field and sit in the dugout that looked onto the field where his team was making all of these memories possible for so many—memories that would last an entire lifetime. "It was like going to church," he said. "It was so peaceful. It really helped me savor all that was happening—and I wanted the boys to be able to savor all of it as well."

There will always be success throughout the Kolmansberger family. Theirs is a rare blend of grit and drive, passion and integrity. From a mother who walked away from a promising career to volunteer to work fostering her husband's new professional mission because, as she told him, "I believe in you" to a husband and father who once walked away from the security of being an employee because he

39

knew he wanted to be his own boss, those words were the greatest assets he had. The family has grit. Their children have learned quickly that with an insatiable work ethic and with uncomfortably high self-standards, greatness can be achieved. Now, he just had to help pass that belief system on to the players that made up the Red Land Little League team of 2015.

6

"YOU EVER HEAR OF TY COBB?"

Some kids have natural talents that are evident from a very early age. They dominate youth sports from the day they first put on a uniform. Psychologists call them prodigies. Formally defined, they are individuals who at a very young age produce meaningful output in some domain to the level of an adult expert performer. Examples of such defined prodigies would include Mozart, Picasso, and Bobby Fischer (the American Grandmaster chess player at the age of thirteen). The sports world is no different. Some kids just develop physically and mentally faster than other kids do. The game seems to slow down for them, and they can see plays evolve sooner than their peers do and because of that, they flourish.

Camden Walter was not that kind of player.

He was "Every Man." His smile was as big as his heart, and the love of his life was baseball. He was born into it, hence his mother and father naming him after the home ballpark of the Baltimore Orioles. His father played at Red Land High School but graduated in 1989—just one year too soon to be a part of the never to be forgotten State Championship baseball team. The disappointment from not being a part of that gold medal team still resonates with Aaron Walter, Cam's dad, today. He never wanted his son to have to experience that kind of anguish, but he was worried that that was exactly what was inevitably going to happen.

Walt noticed that his son was struggling at the plate early in the spring of 2015. Due to a ruptured spleen in a snowboarding accident over the winter, Camden was limited for eight weeks to very little, if any, physical activity. When he expressed his concern to the doctor about being able to play baseball, the doctor responded, "Son, you're bleeding internally, right now that's more important than baseball."

As a result, as the early season was underway, Cam was behind. This was not just a slump, his timing was off, his swing path was flawed, and his strength just was not where it needed to be. To make matters worse, try-outs were coming up for the 2015 Little League All Star team, and Walt knew that Cam would not make the team with the way he was playing. It pained him immensely to watch his son futilely grind away day after day with no progress of which to speak. To make matters worse, Walt knew that this Little League team had a realistic chance to compete for a National and possibly World Championship, and the thought of his son having to watch his friends celebrate their accomplishments seemed all too familiar, so something needed to be done.

◆◆◆◆

In high school, when Aaron needed answers, he turned to his catcher, Kyle Wagner. His senior year, "Walt" was struggling as a pitcher. Having aspirations of pitching well not only for his high school, but also in college, Walt sought guidance for how to improve. "I was never a hard throwing pitcher. I had a decent curve ball, but I just needed something else to consistently get hitters out." He sought out the advice of his Coach, Brandt Cook, and his catcher, Kyle Wagner. Together they watched a video and decided to develop a split finger fastball. "Kyle told me, it's not going to be pretty trying to learn how to throw it. It's gonna hit the dirt and you're gonna look silly, but I'll figure out how to catch it. I'll handle it. So we went to work."

Walt used the confidence he gained from that pitch not for his senior year at Red Land, but in a try-out at the University of Delaware. "I promised my dad I would try out. There were about forty dudes, and they took all the pitchers down to the bullpen and luckily that day the split was working. When the tryout was over, the pitching coach came up to me and said, 'There's something to that pitch I like.' Lo and behold, I made the team."

He did more than just make the team. What started out as just being able to come to fall workouts turned into a college career that ended in the NCAA Regionals in Miami, where Delaware lost to NC State and Notre Dame. Prior to entering the NCAA tournament, Aaron started his only game for the Blue Hens vs. Georgetown. It was the culmination of all the work Walt had put in through the years: recovering from injuries with his rotator cuff, overcoming an accident in an automobile that left him with two broken feet and a broken jaw, fulfilling a promise he had made to his father, and a tribute to his former catcher. "That pitch certainly revived my career. When it was all over," Walt grins, "I retired as the winningest pitcher in Delaware history!" Walt was 1-0.

But now, Walt was not looking for answers for himself. The answers he was seeking, and the sense of urgency with which he was probing for those answers, was far greater than anything he ever wanted for himself. These were for his son. So once again, he turned to Kyle Wagner.

◆◆◆◆

"Have you ever heard of Ty Cobb?" Kyle asked Cam.

"Sure."

"What I want to do to help you isn't just about hitting, it's also a matter of if you have the personal courage to do it in a public forum. Are you willing to step to the plate with a five or six inch split grip [hands separated rather than the traditional way of having them together at the handle of the bat] knowing it'll help you, but also knowing that people will talk about it?"

It was a simple question, but in the world of a middle school aged kid, where being accepted is sometimes the absolute most important element of his entire existence, it certainly had to be considered.

"It'll only work, though, Cam, if you fully embrace it."

To baseball purists, Ty Cobb is arguably the greatest hitter that ever played the game. His career .366 batting average, twelve batting titles in thirteen seasons (nine of which came consecutively), and having three times batted over .400 certainly make for a somewhat irrefutable argument. It is also known, and old photographs will verify, that Ty Cobb did, indeed, bat with his hands separated at the handle of the bat. If it worked for "The Georgia Peach," could it be possible that it would work for young Cam Walter?

"To his credit," said Kyle, "he immediately responded very matter of factly, 'I'll do anything to get better at the plate and help the team.' So we went to work. And the impact was instantaneous." Never considered a power threat, Cam saw results that spring that earned Kyle instant credibility in the young ballplayer's eyes. As his confidence continued to grow, so did the results.

In early June of 2015, before official try-outs and the Red Land Little League roster being set, a team consisting of many of the future members of the 2015 Mid-Atlantic Champions, traveled to Cooperstown, New York, for the Cooperstown Dreams Park Tournament. Camden was on that team. As his father took the ten hour round-trip journey daily to see his son play as often as he could (his job as Guidance Counselor at Red Land High School was still in session for the school year), he was able to make the Monday morning game vs. Stetson Hills, Arizona.

As Cam came to the plate with the bases loaded, he was utilizing the split grip that had revived not only his confidence at the plate, but his entire value on the team.

As the ball cleared the fence and Camden Walter rounded the bases, the excitement in that smile was a culmination of months and months of frustration and fear that he may never experience a moment like this again on a baseball field anywhere. Those emotions were paled by the swelling of pride his father felt while up in the stands, weary from the five hour morning drive from Pennsylvania, but suddenly invigorated for the five hour ride back home. "You can't fake joy like that," Walt said. "Cam was always the first kid out of the dugout greeting whoever hit the home run with a smile. Now here he was on the other end of that. You just can't fake joy like that in a kid."

◆◆◆◆

Cam, however, was not the only one who was on a mission to make this team. Many of the kids went into the tryouts for this elite group knowing they were going to have to prove themselves and continue to have to overcome their weaknesses and difficulties to secure a spot on the roster. Jake Cubbler was another one of those boys.

Jake was a grinder, a hard-working, blue-collar player that any old school ball player would be proud of. When he was eight, he tried out for his first "travel team," the team that would eventually come in second place and refuse to acknowledge their accomplishment. While at a birthday party after the try-outs, many of the boys who had tried out for the team were also in attendance. Jake was convinced he had not made the team. He was not able to enjoy himself and take part in the activities as the other boys were. He did not like that feeling.

When the team was selected, Jake was on the roster, not so much for his baseball ability, but for his intense competitive spirit and his willingness to do anything asked of him. Still, on a team of twelve, he was the twelfth boy selected. As a nine-year-old, he was not selected for the 9/10 team when five others of his nine-year-old teammates were. Cole, Jaden, BK, Dylan, and Kaden all made the team. Jake did not. He was clearly falling behind in terms of being able to keep up with the rest of the players, but he loved baseball, and loved being with his teammates. He went to all the games, tried to help with "scouting reports" for the teams they would be playing, and tried to be as involved as he could—but he wasn't on the team. In terms of baseball, Jake Cubbler was clearly at a crossroads.

His father, Scott, knew how ultracompetitive his son was and had taken note of this many times over the course of his son's life. "I've kept a journal since the day he was born, and I can't tell you how many times I've written in it, 'I'm worried about just how competitive Jake seems to be.'" Therefore, he challenged his son. He explained the circumstances and logically showed his son that if he wanted to continue down the path of elite baseball, he had to drastically improve his skills. It was a tough talk for a father to have with his son, but he had it. "Jake, if you want this, than you have to fully commit to becoming a better baseball player."

"Jake's always been a thinker," said his mom. "If you explain to him a situation completely, he'll be able to make his own decision based on his own logic. And we wanted Jake to understand just how much hard work it was going to be to become a better baseball player."

Jake was willing to put in that hard work. He was already a good soccer player, but that came more naturally for him. He did not have to work nearly as hard to be really good at soccer as he did to just be pretty good at baseball. It was the same with school. Jake was naturally smart, so good grades were not something that he really had to work at. Same with music—he had a natural propensity for picking up his instrument and being able to just naturally play. However, baseball was different. Baseball required that Jake put in the work, but he was willing to do it—and his parents were delighted that he was.

"Baseball has taught him some phenomenal life lessons, the biggest being, that if you want to be really good at something, you've got to be willing to work really hard. You've got to enjoy the process. And for him to see that connection, to see all that hard work pay off in such a big way, he wouldn't have learned that from anything else—from soccer, from music, from school. He learned it from baseball. And for him to learn that about life, at such an early age, well, I think that's any parent's wish for their child."

As he continued to progress, and see the dividends paying off, Jake's skills drastically improved. He was a part of the 2014 State Runner-Up team and felt confident about his chances of making the team going into the spring of 2015, until one ill-fated trip to Sky Zone resulted in a broken ankle and hindered Jake's preparation going into the spring tryouts. When he finally got the walking cast off after six weeks, he struggled to return to the form that he was before the injury. His timing was off, his power was not quite the same, and everything seemed to be labored.

Again, Jake tapped into the work ethic that he had developed over the course of the past three years, which he never even knew existed.

47

Slowly, small signs started to reveal themselves that Jake belonged on this team, and though the entire summer of 2015 would still be very much a test of endurance for Jake, he passed a big one when the roster was announced. Jake was able to enjoy the fact that his name, deservedly so, was on it—not because he was a competitor, and not because he was naturally gifted, but because through his hard work, he had become a baseball player.

◆◆◆◆

All the boys who were not a lock to make the team approached the tryouts with tremendous anxiety. Though all of them at one point in their careers knew exactly what it felt like to be "the star," on *this* team, they were going to be role players, and that, for some kids, is a tremendous adjustment that they are never able to make.

On their regular teams, they bat leadoff, or cleanup, or somewhere near the top of the batting order to make sure they get as many at bats as possible. They hit home runs, triples, play shortstop, pitch, and basically serve as the foundation for whatever the team is trying to accomplish, but instead of demanding to be the star, each just wanted to be a good teammate—a rarity in today's sports arena. These boys acquiesced and were genuinely satisfied when told their "roles" would be limited to coming off the bench for possibly only one at bat per game, serving as a pinch runner, or as a defensive specialist late in the game. Each one of them knew exactly what they were signing up for—they wanted to be a part of something "bigger" than themselves. "Bailey is the consummate teammate," his father stated. "He would love to be a starter, knows he has the skill to be, but understands that there was a ton of talent on that team. He did not pout or complain. He just stood, or in more literal terms, *sat* behind his teammates. I was proud of him for that."

However, before they could even think about contributing, kids like Cam, Jake, Zack Sooy, Bailey Wirt, and Jarrett Wisman just had to make the team. For them, that was even more important than being able to have visions of making a contribution—and they all knew what was at stake when it came to try-outs.

"Oh yeah, I was nervous," admitted Bailey. "I knew I wasn't a lock, far from it, so I had to perform well—really well." Things worked out. Each of the boys excelled in their own way on their own team, both in recreation ball and on various All-Star and travel teams. But *this* team was even more elite than even the most advanced All-Star team, and when it came to selecting the last few players on the team, a kid's attitude and mental approach was just as important as how fast he could pitch, how far he could hit, or any of his other baseball skills.

"I just wanted to be able to help the team anyway I could," said Zack Sooy. "I knew I wasn't going to start, knew I would only get a limited number of at bats, but I didn't care. I just wanted to be on the team and be able to help any way I could. My contribution came on defense." It surely did! Twice his glove and arm helped extinguish rallies that were brewing on their way to a US Championship.

"It was because of my speed. I knew my role," explained Cam. "I knew I would be coming in to run for Chayton or Ethan, and my job was to advance around the bases so someone could hit me in. So I stayed ready."

They all did. Bailey and Jarrett knew they would be called upon to add a little pop to an already potent batting order, they just didn't know when that would be, or what the game situations would be like—but they stayed ready. Early on, Jarrett was called upon to hit for Kaden Peifer in a 2-2 game vs. Camp Hill in the Semi-Finals of Districts. With two on, Jarrett blasted a home run that kick started an otherwise dormant Red Land offense and shook the Patriots from their slumber on their way to an eventual 9-2 win. It was the closest game they would have before arriving in Williamsport.

To their teammates' credit, they never felt as an inferior part of the team—most likely because they were not. Whether it was in the field, at the plate, or on the bases, each was able to have a moment where his presence on the team was validated. When both Zack Sooy and Bailey Wirt were selected for ESPN's Top Ten Plays of the Night, their status in the locker room quickly increased. Cam's three runs scored put him behind only BK, Cole, Jaden, and Adam Cramer, boys who had at least twice as many plate appearances as he had.

That kind of unselfishness—the ego-free way of playing—has become even more rare in the "Look at Me," self-promoting, bat-flipping, jersey popping sports world that has become all too common today. "I didn't care if anyone knew who I was, I loved being on the team because I loved my teammates. I was willing to do anything I could to make us better," explained Cam Walter almost a full year removed from Williamsport.

The other boys agreed. "We still got asked to sign autographs, though. That was pretty cool!" added Bailey Wirt. That sent the other boys into a roar of laughter, which showed they had nothing but positive memories about the entire experience.

7

"I'M GOING HOME WITH MOM!"

The role of a mother can never really be celebrated enough. One day a year doesn't seem to do it justice for all the roles a mom has to play—counselor, nutritionist, equipment manager, comforter, organizer, and unconditional supporter—nothing worth remembering ever happens in a traditional American family (and who knows what qualifies as traditional anymore) without a mother's touch. And though the summer of 2015 was filled with many nights of laughter, joy, and celebration, there were also nights in the spring of 2015 where frustration, annoyance, and resentment permeated the surroundings. Practices where father and son weren't quite in complete harmony, games where an *0 for whatever* lingered on the car ride home rather than being buried in the fields of competition. **Nobody** felt that more than the moms of the team, especially Amy Peifer. "The two slam nights were the worst. I would hear SLAM!" said Amy, "then I would just wait and, low and behold, five or ten seconds later, there would be a second SLAM! Those were the nights I knew were going to be challenging."

Though other players got more attention, nobody had a more significant role on the team than their catcher, Kaden Peifer. It was simple logic: If they couldn't develop somebody who would be able to consistently catch the 75 mile per hour lasers that Cole Wagner was blistering past batters, then they wouldn't be able to utilize what was quite possibly their greatest defensive asset—Cole's left arm. It was not sophisticated logic: without a catcher behind the plate who could secure pitch after pitch, having the fire-balling left-hander on the mound would become self-deprecating. Even those batters who would strike out would reach first base while the catcher was frantically running down passed balls, which would career off backstops and ricochet in any direction. Once on first, runners would certainly advance around the bases at will if the intended receiver did not regularly secure pitches.

Kaden Peifer was that intended somebody.

To make the task even more formidable, Kaden not only had to have the toughness and presence to be able to catch Cole, he had to know the art of catching in order to be able to catch someone with the craftsmanship of Adam Cramer. Whereas Cole seldom, if ever, threw a pitch at less than 70 mph, Adam rarely, if ever, came even close to the 70 mph benchmark. In addition to their drastically different styles, they were left-handed, which meant the ball would have a completely different release and spin from pitchers like Jaden Henline and Chayton Krauss, both of whom were right-handed. In short, Kaden had to *master* the position. So, Coach Peifer, Coach Bret, Coach JK, and Coach Kyle Wagner all went to work on Kaden. RELENTLESSLY.

Night after night, practice after practice; the men did everything they could to turn young Kaden Peifer (the only 6th grader on the team) into an elite catcher who had the ability to compliment the elite talent that was on the mound. Some practices, as is the case with all players, went better than others did; some did not go well at all.

"You gotta catch that, Kaden!"

"Kaden, you gotta catch that ball!"

It was a line the twelve-year-old heard often. So much so, that his nightmares were not about monsters or thunderstorms, they were about passed balls and wild pitches. The biggest difference between Cole Wagner as an eleven year old and the Cole Wagner, who was now twelve, was the fact that Cole could now throw strikes with amazing precision—that helped. If Cole were wild at 75 mph, *nobody* would be able to catch his pitches; but being inaccurate was not a viable excuse for not being able to catch a pitch from Cole anymore. Now, Kaden just had to brace himself pitch after pitch for the explosion that detonated inside of his glove each time Cole uncoiled one of his fastballs. With Adam, it was a matter of being able to thrust his body in front of the ball that would consistently dive into the dirt just inches before it reached the plate—which invariably made the pitch unhittable, and to a certain extent, uncatchable. The best the guy behind the plate could do would be to serve as a backstop so he could smother the ball and have it rest softly in front of him. What made this all possible was Kaden's willingness to become that guy. He *wanted* to be pushed, he *wanted* to be coached hard, and he *embraced* the feedback that came night after night, practice after practice, and repetition after repetition. He longed to fill the void that the team so desperately had to fill.

So, the men and their catcher went to work.

"If I can't be a catcher, I can always be a water slide tester. That's a real job, you know. It would be great," Kaden explained one day with his trademark grin. "I'd rather be a catcher for the Dodgers, but if that doesn't work out, the water slide thing would be awesome!" For now, the contingency plans could wait. The team needed a catcher, and the men had their willing student.

To expedite the process for Kaden, the coaches would have Kaden catching *all* batting practice sessions *as well as* catching the pitches of Cole, Jaden, Adam, Chayton, and every other pitcher on the team. He caught the pitches of Aaron Walter, the High School team's pitching coach, who admitted he had never thrown pitches to his high school kids as hard as he was throwing to these eleven and twelve-year-olds. He caught pitches by former big leaguer Bret Wagner, who peppered fastball after fastball, trying to improve their batters as much as he was trying to get Kaden accustomed to dealing with that kind of velocity. He would catch pitches from "Iron Mike," the machine that would mechanically fire pitch after pitch usually intended for hitters, but there was no reason why there had to be a batter in the box all the time, right?

"You gotta catch those, Kaden, you just gotta catch those." He heard it repeatedly, not only when it was said, but also even when it was not—in his *head,* on pitches that he did not get cleanly. When the coaches wanted to give him a pass, he still heard it. It was a phrase he could not escape. Those were the nights when Kaden's mom (and Tom's wife) would hear two slams, the nights when Coach Peifer and Coach Wagner could not be Dad or Uncle Bret, they had to make him a catcher. Sometimes that required a kind of tough love that was heavier on the *tough* and lighter on the *love.* But as the rest of the team was being put together piece-by-piece at eight other positions with twelve other boys, this was the one position that really only had one option, and there was one kid that was going to fit there. Kaden. He quite simply had to become a National Championship caliber catcher. Hence, "You gotta catch that, Kaden!"

Coach Peifer allowed his son to be coached hard, much harsher than he would have ever coached somebody else's son, which is usually the case with coaches' children. It is why many times relationships are soured and the entire experience is seen much less fulfilling than outsiders think by the individuals who are actually involved. But Tom trusted that the coaching staff would make Kaden better, would turn him into what Coach Peifer needed, and he trusted the process that his son had to go through because he understood the reasoning behind it. Most competitors can tolerate the *how* if they understand the *why*; Tom understood that completely, and to a certain extent, so did Kaden, which is why he kept grinding away.

After practice, Tom would comfort his son at home, but that was usually preceded by a silent car ride home. The really tough nights were the ones after a game or practice when Tom's critique was just a little bit more than what Kaden wanted. Those were the times when Kaden would seek out his mother and declare, "I'm going home with Mom!" Those were the toughest moments for Tom Peifer, the father. At those times, he would question if it were all worth it. Would the end result be an elite catcher who would forever be bitter at his father, who wouldn't look back on the whole experience and be able to remember it fondly? Tom certainly did not want that to happen on *any* level. He earned a lot of credibility with parents by the manner in which he treated his own son. Favoritism was never an issue; nobody suspected Coach Peifer was favoring his own son. He was more demanding, more critical, and less patient with Kaden than with any other player wearing a uniform—and then he took at bats away from him in games to make sure other kids got theirs. It was a delicate balance in a situation that really did not have the luxury of being handled delicately.

However, the longer the process progressed, the more frequently the glove would pop. There is no sound in baseball as crisp as a fastball that snaps cleanly into the glove that awaits it behind home plate. POP! SNAP! It is alluring. It is like a perfect swish in basketball or the crunch of a collision of pads on a clean hit in football. There is just nothing like it. It certainly superseded the THUD! that would be heard when the ball sailed to the backstop instead of at its intended target. The thud was always followed by those five dreaded words, "You gotta catch that, Kaden!"

Kaden was not hearing that as often anymore, though. At home, he had a tennis ball that he would throw against the wall, or he would have his mom, dad, or sister, throw him "dirt balls" so he could work on blocking the ball down into the rug. He had turned a corner and wanted to keep going. On family road trips, he would quiz his sister in the back seat on the signs he would use with the pitchers to indicate what type of pitch Coach Bret called. It was an all-consuming process, but Kaden's thirst to become better seemed unquenchable.

"There were plenty of sessions that I remember looking at Kaden and seeing tears behind that mask. His hand would be killing him. But he wouldn't...he wouldn't take that mask off and let anyone see those tears," said Bret, who was not only coaching Kaden, but was also coaching the pitchers, trying to keep their velocity high while maintaining control. When he or Walt were pitching, they would put themselves on the gun, making sure the ball was moving at 70+ miles per hour, not only so the hitters would get used to the velocity they were going to see in Bristol or Williamsport, but also so it would become second nature for Kaden to catch these types of pitches. In addition, just to keep him honest, there was always the occasional ball in the dirt.

Soon, with a closer, unabated look at the catcher, the men saw more than just tears. Below those tears was a snarl, a curled lip that served as an undeniable symbol of a fire burning in this young warrior's soul that not only wanted to give this team and these coaches what they so desperately needed to fill the void and validate their championship potential, but also the natural desire for a son to want to please his father. He was succeeding at both.

As the coaches took note of how comfortable the batters were progressively getting accustomed to the smoldering fastballs that they continued to see, they also became enamored by the development of their catcher. POP! POP! POP! The only time they did not hear it was when they heard the PING! of an Easton bat inflicting damage on one of those baseballs—and the coaches liked that sound, too.

As the tournament began in Williamsport, Kaden had solidified his spot behind home plate as securely as Cole, Jaden, Adam, and Chayton secured their roles just 46 feet away atop the mound. Kaden would be thrown over 450 pitches, 170 of which were thrown by Cole Wagner—only two of those pitched balls ever reached the backstop. For every other pitch that was not hit or fouled off, it was "POP!" "POP!" "POP!" followed by, "Atta boy, Kaden!" or "Nice Stop, Kaden!" Those two sounds became euphoric not only to young Kaden Peifer, but to his mother as well, who remembered all too well the other two sounds of doors slamming while Kaden was paying the dues that every elite catcher ultimately has to pay.

8

I'VE NEVER EVEN SEEN ANYBODY HIT THE ROAD!

With the coaching staff and team selected, it was time to allow the boys to do what they did best—wreak havoc on the opposition with their barbaric strength. It did not take long for them to do that. The mere statistical numbers themselves jump off the page. As a *team*, they batted .462. Of their 212 hits, almost 40% of them (80) were home runs. When Cole Wagner got a hit (which he did 67% of the time he stepped to the plate), 65% of the time, it was a home run. Home runs made up over 40% of the hits that Chayton Krauss, Jaden Henline, Dylan Rodenhaber, and Jarrett Wisman accumulated over the course of the sixteen game campaign that led this team to the Little League World Series in Williamsport.

A Red Land player hit a home run every 5.8 at bats, and the reason why Red Land insisted on being the away team every time they had the option was because so often they "10 or 15 run ruled" their opponents so often, it gave their players extra at-bats before they inevitably mercy-ruled their opponents.

And their pitching statistics were every bit as remarkable. For their season, the Red Land pitchers struck out 175 batters in 107 innings and opponents batted a mere .166 against them. They were a multi-faceted machine that could dispense their devastation from anywhere on the field—and sometimes even beyond that.

Because of their capacity to punish baseballs, the surrounding areas of the ballparks had to be altered whenever they could. Cars could no longer park where locals were accustomed to parking for baseball games. People could not safely sit under trees that were normally considered unreachable. Parents who normally allowed their toddlers to play in the deep shaded areas beyond the outfield fences had to be on constant guard whenever Red Land came up to bat. Nobody knew that better than Roger and JeriLynn Mease from Fredericksburg, PA.

Roger Mease grew up in his home on Lions Drive, and when his mother passed away, he and his wife JeriLynn moved into the house in which he was raised. The Mease home has always sat safely across from Lions Park in Bethel Township, Pennsylvania, for many years, but this summer, the Meases found themselves in the crosshairs of a number of Patriot long balls. Over the course of his close to sixty years, Roger has witnessed countless Little League games played on the field across the street from his ranch home. "But I've never seen a team like that Red Land team. I've been here my whole life, and I ain't never seen anything like what those boys could do to a baseball!"

The Mease's love for baseball has always run deep. In 1999, Roger proposed to JeriLynn on opening day as they watched their beloved Cleveland Indians take on the California Angels. Though the Indians lost 6-5, there was plenty of consolation for Roger when JeriLynn accepted his proposal. And though their hearts will truly always belong to the Cleveland Indians, the boys from Red Land certainly won at least a temporary spot there in the summer of 2015.

"We could just tell they were ballplayers," said Roger. "The very first time I saw them, I just knew this team was special." His eyes glimmered as if he were talking about his own children.

"I haven't seen Roger that excited about Little League baseball since his own son was playing."

His own son was an entirely different kind of special. Chase had a pre-natal stroke that left him unable to fully function on the right side of his body. "To pick up a phone for him with his right hand would be a struggle. But he loved baseball. And nothing was going to stop him from playing." Chase was a pitcher, and much like Jim Abbott, who the world marveled at as pitcher for not only the University of Michigan, but also for the Yankees, Angels, White Sox, and Brewers. (Jim was born without a right hand, but with an insatiable amount of persistence and an unrelenting work ethic, he made it all the way to the major leagues as a left-handed pitcher. His baseball career would span more than ten years, and on September 4, 1993, he even threw a no-hitter—as a Yankee—against Roger's beloved Indians.)

"Chase was just like Abbott. He'd rest the glove on his right hand, throw with his left, and quickly put the glove back on his left so he could field." Chase would become so skilled as a pitcher that he pitched the first game ever in Fredericksburg's now famous Earl Wenger Field when it opened in 1996. "Yeah, when he was 13, he pitched the first ever game there, a Legion game. 1-0 victory over Chambersburg," Roger reflects with a tremendous amount of pride. "But *he* didn't face any hitters like *these* boys. No way!"

"I've never had children of my own," interjected JeriLynn, "but those boys sure felt like mine. They were so polite, so kind, and really all of them from Red Land—the parents, everybody, were just so nice to us. The first time I met them was when Dylan's (Rodenhaber) daddy came over to our house to apologize for his son hitting my house with a home run ball and I told him, 'Shoot, you don't have to be sorry! I think it was wonderful!'" After the game, Dylan came over to personally apologize and JeriLynn told him he could make it up to her by signing the ball. Dylan thought that was pretty cool. Soon, all of his teammates were racing over to see the damage the powerful third baseman had done to the home across the street.

"That is so cool!" said one of them. "I mean, I'm sorry it happened to your house, but it is kinda cool."

"It's not *kinda* cool," corrected JeriLynn, "it's *really* cool!"

Instantly, so, too, did JeriLynn and Roger Mease reach epic "Cool" status in the eyes of the Red Land players.

The damage done to their home is now a badge of honor. JeriLynn laments the fact that the red markings of the laces have worn off with the passage of time.

"I've seen plenty of home runs hit over there on that field, but nothing like the ones that they hit. Heck, I've never even seen anybody hit the road, nonetheless come close to hitting my house! And these boys seemed to hit it all the time!" Roger boasted with a hearty laugh.

Red Land quickly became not only a favorite of the Meases, but also a favorite with many of the locals that lived across from the field on Lions Drive and N. Mechanic St. When the boys were not playing, they would hang out in the Mease's yard and watch some of the other teams play. Roger would fire up the grill and cook for the boys, and JeriLynn would provide them with endless treats. When the boys were playing, the Mease house became "the place to be."

"I counted one night," Roger recalled. "We had 41 people lined up in lawn chairs right here in the yard. Those kids were the biggest thing to hit this area in a long, long time. I couldn't make enough hamburgers and hot dogs fast enough to keep everybody happy. It was fun, though, watching those boys with everybody. It was an event."

Just as quickly as the Meases took to the boys, the boys took to the Meases. The kids could interact with the Meases in their yard, unlike what they would be able to do once they moved onto bigger, more publicized tournaments. By the time they got to Williamsport, they would not be able to walk from one side of the stadium to another without a designated escort. "They were special people," said many of the kids and parents from Red Land, who made the Meases feel like they were a part of the Red Land family. "They were one of us, there was no doubt about that."

When the boys won the District 6 Championship, upon receiving their championship banner, parents and siblings were allowed to come down onto the field for pictures with the team holding their banner. As the photo session concluded, the boys insisted on taking two more pictures with two more important "members" of the team—Lou, their stuffed Minion mascot, and JeriLynn.

"It was crazy," said JeriLynn with a smile that showed just how fond she was of these boys and the joy they brought into her life following the death of her dog Grady (named after her all time favorite Indian player Grady Sizemore). "Here they were telling me to come down there with them, and I wasn't even from Red Land. Those boys were so nice to me, to both of us. I don't know why. And they don't know what they did for me. When I lost Grady, I lost *everything*. I just felt so sad all the time. I never had any children of my own, but I had Grady. But then, I lost him, and it felt like I had nothing. He died on June 16. These boys showed up on June 26." As tears began to form in her eyes, she murmured, "God works in mysterious ways!"

JeriLynn refused to go down onto the field. In her mind, it just was not her place— that was an honor reserved for family only. "Then," Roger broke in, starting to fight back tears himself, "they started to jump the fence one by one, and they started to come over into our yard, and they brought the banner to us and made us take a picture with them. Those boys were special..." He trailed off, fighting back the lump that was clearly forming in his throat.

"They were *special*," echoed JeriLynn. "And baseball is only part of the reason."

9

THE WALK OFF

To say that Cole Wagner was in a zone would be a colossal understatement. In the first five games of the district playoffs, he was producing at an absurd Babe Ruthian type rate. In 15 at bats, Cole had 13 hits and 25 RBIs. Of those 13 hits, 10 were home runs—none of which were the type that were only slightly clearing the fences that stood 200 feet from home plate. No, the titanic blasts that Cole was sending into orbit were the type where the outfielder wouldn't turn and run, thinking he might have a play, instead, he would simply turn and marvel at the distance the ball actually traveled into the Pennsylvania sky before it actually landed. As was the case with most of the blasts that Cole hit, it was not a matter of "if," it was more a matter of "how far." However, this streak was even more brilliant than the normal high expectations that those familiar with Red Land baseball had come to expect from Cole Wagner.

Practice on most days came with the usual banter and heckling between coaches and players, but the best lines always came from Aaron Walter. Walt was crucial in being able to deliver live batting practice with the same velocity and movement that the boys would see as their competition continued to get better and better. Once Cam secured a spot on the roster, Tom Peifer quickly took advantage of Walt's pitching background and made him, like Kyle Wagner, an unofficial member of the coaching staff. "It's amazing what can be accomplished when nobody cares who gets the credit," explained Tom. His leadership style was the perfect ego-free temperament that allowed the team to flourish and was so inviting to so many different personalities.

What Walt brought to the team, in addition to a solid right pitching arm with velocity was an air of brevity that allowed the kids to relax and constantly reminded them that this was just a game. What he could do better than any twelve-year-old was chatter, talk trash, and play mind games. In those departments, Walt was in the big leagues. His target on this particular day was Cole Wagner. "You ain't facing no little leaguers today, Cole. Today you're getting my best stuff!"

Cole smirked. Quiet and determined, he let Coach Walt have his fun. "Might want to tell Coach Peifer to give you the day off, cause the last thing I want to do is shake your confidence. But that's the risk you take if you get in that box today."

Though outwardly Cole would not engage, his competitive fire was slowly igniting.

As the boys took their turns in the box, the chatter continued. "I'm feeling good tonight, boys. Not sure you're gonna be able to get around on the stuff I'm throwing tonight." Walt was having fun. They all were. This was a loose group, and they had been playing their best baseball of the summer. Through those five games, Red Land destroyed their competition 105-4! Statistics like that were almost inhumane.

Walt would readily admit that he had never thrown this consistently hard to his high school players, but these boys, all of these boys, were able to routinely make solid contact with the pitches that he continued to throw.

Then, Cole stepped into the box.

The typical Red Land practice would consist of three different hitting groups. Coach Peifer or Coach Bret would text the team before practice and let them know what color shirt to wear for that day—red, white, or blue. As the groups hit, each player would get twelve swings. Scores were kept varying from home run derby, three team baseball, or other drill type activities that the coaches would have them do. It was not atypical to have a team hitting, a team in the outfield, and another team on the other side of the fence trying to keep balls from flying into the woods. Coach Walt was hoping that group was not going to be needed for Cole's at bat.

As Cole dug in, so did his coach.

The first pitch had maybe just a little bit more gas on it than the young man anticipated. He swung. He missed. A roar of "Ohhhhhhhhhhh!" came from the boys in the outfield.

"Come on, Cole! We're getting bored out here! Hit us a ball!"

They laughed. So did he. It was a great time to be a player on the Red Land Little League team. Their team was composed of absolute juggernauts, and they had every reason in the world to be as confident, as carefree, and to be having as much fun as they clearly were.

"0 and 1," said Walt from the mound, and then he laughed. So did Cole. So did everybody else who could hear it on the field, in the dugout, and on the bleachers.

"*0-1? It's BP, what does he mean by 0-1?*" the phenom thought to himself. "*All right, I'll play along. 0-1.*"

He dug in a little deeper. As he did, he started a little conversation with himself. *I'll end this little game quick.* "Pitch!" he said out loud.

This time, Walt took a little bit off. He saw Cole digging in, ready to catapult his next offering not only over the fence, but off the complex, perhaps maybe to the other side of the Mason-Dixon line, a trifling 34 miles or so away.

Another swing and miss.

"OHHHHHHHHHHHHHHHHH!!!!!" It was twice as loud now from the guys on both sides of the fence. Cole probably had not swung and missed two times in a row all summer. This now had the potential to be a somewhat historical event, at least locally.

As surprised as the boys in the field were that they were not on the receiving end of a laser being shot in their direction, so, too, was Coach Walter, who now was in the middle of the ring of this spontaneous prizefight.

Now Cole was fully engaged. Walt, on the other hand, tried to somewhat diffuse the situation, but it was much too late for that. "Pitch!"

Suddenly, the circumstance and tension on Giant Field at the Newberry Complex could only be matched by that fictional, mystical aura described by Ernest Thayer in "Casey at the Bat."

Ten thousand eyes were on him as he rubbed his hands with dirt;
Five thousand tongues applauded when he wiped them on his shirt;
Then while the writing pitcher ground the ball into his hip,
Defiance flashed in Casey's eye, a sneer curled Casey's lip.

There were far less than ten thousand eyes watching what was taking place that day, and the look on young Wagner's face was much more of a grin than a sneer. But there was drama, even if it was more fabricated than real, and it made an otherwise banal Wednesday night practice all that more intriguing. And the kids absolutely loved every second of it.

"COME ON, COLE!!! HIT ONE ALREADY!!!"

The sneer is gone from Casey's lip, his teeth are clenched in hate,
He pounds with cruel violence his bat upon the plate;

Around the field, all the players looked on with the anticipation of a kid on his birthday, waiting to open up the biggest box in the bunch. And really, they were not sure of the outcome they wanted most. Should Coach Walt complete the trifecta, or should Cole unload a moon shot of epic proportion? Either way, they would all be winners. Being fully aware of the audience, whose attention was now completely undivided, both characters in this three act play—the thirteen-year-old boy and the 44-year-old "boy"—stood in their respective spotlights at center stage.

And now the pitcher holds the ball, and now he lets it go,
And now the air is shattered by the force of Casey's blow.

If you tried to make this stuff up, nobody would believe it—everybody would say it was too far-fetched. Casey at the Bat is one of the greatest American poems ever written; it permanently harbors in the nostalgic heart of anyone who has ever read it. It is every bit a part of baseball as Cracker Jacks and hot dogs—but it's just a story, a tale of a time when an overmatched pitcher was victorious in a face-to-face battle with a larger than life batter. However, there was one major difference between how the poem and this scenario ended.

Oh, somewhere in the favoured land the sun is shining bright,
The band is playing somewhere, and somewhere hearts are light;
And somewhere men are laughing, and somewhere children shout,
But there is no joy in Mudville—mighty Casey has struck out.

As Walt fired the final pitch of the at bat over the plate, Cole Wagner unleashed a swing as hard as anything Babe Ruth, Hank Aaron, or Paul Bunyan ever discharged.

And like mighty Casey, he missed.

The difference was the joy, the exasperation, the amusement, and the unfiltered bliss that came from everybody that witnessed the event. It was as captivating and refreshing as any moment that had occurred to that point all summer. The howls, laughter, and good-natured heckling that came from his teammates had them all rolling in the grass. Even Cole had to smile.

Coach Walt, as only he could do, soaked up every moment. Lisa Cubbler had once said that Walt was as much of a twelve-year-old as any of the boys, "I guess that's why they love him so much." It was here, at what seemed like the perfect time, Walt let that 12-year-boy who was still within him, come out to play. There on the mound, in true Greco-Roman Wrestling style, he tossed aside his glove and began to untie his cleats, first one, then the other. Laces undone, he removed his shoes from his feet, laid them on top of his glove right in the center of the mound...and began to walk off the field.

"I'm done!"

"Let me hit!!! I want to hit!!!" They all wanted a piece of Coach Walt. Every one of them—Dylan and Jarrett and Chayton and Bailey. Every one of them wanted to be the one who got the next hit off the guy who struck out Cole—but none of them would get their chance.

"I'm done!" Walt hollered as he walked off the field in his socks, leaving his shoes and glove lying on the mound as Rulon Gardner once did after winning a bronze medal in the 2004 Olympics in Greece. (Gardner became a part of American sports folklore when he defeated then undefeated and unconquerable "Alexander the Great" from Russia to become the first American to win a gold medal in Greco-Roman wrestling with a full field of international competitors.) Now Walt wanted to mimic his dramatic exit.

And although Walt would be back tomorrow or the next day to be the sacrificial lamb that had to throw to this pack of wolves with Louisville Sluggers and Easton bats, for one night at least, he had thrown his last pitch and would walk off the mound a winner.

And the boys in the field, even the one left standing at the plate, loved every single moment about it.

10

"SOMEBODY'S GOTTA GO TO WILLIAMSPORT"

The goal was never to win the Little League World Series, at least not for the moms. The goal for them was to win the State Championship. "Cole was never on a state championship team before. That was really exciting," explained his mother, Colleen.

"Yep. State Championship, That's all we wanted," claimed Kristie Kolmansberger, mother of BK and wife of JK. "Everything else was icing on the cake."

With that, *"Icing on the Cake"* was written on a piece of paper. "We could use that for the back of the tee shirts!" exclaimed Kristie.

"Yeah, that might work," responded Amy Peifer.

The coaches and their families had gathered for a BBQ on a typical Monday night, and the conversation quickly turned to the State Championship that their sons had just won and the trip to Bristol, Connecticut, that they were about to make in four days. What waited for them in Bristol was a chance to play for a Mid-Atlantic Championship and represent that region in Williamsport, Pennsylvania, at the Little League World Series. They could hardly wait.

The excitement was growing for not only the parents and their children, but around the area as well, since this was one step further than any team from Red Land had made since the 1970's. People around the area wanted to show their support and share in the excitement in what was quickly becoming a rage around the mid-state. "Where do we get a shirt?" was a question the coaching staff was asked as often as "Who, When, and Where do you play next?" Hoping to seize the opportunity, the parents started generating ideas about designing t-shirts as a way of raising funds—not only for Red Land Little League, but also for the charities with which they were becoming associated. After a thorough lesson from the teenagers in attendance (and having to review those lessons multiple times) on the art, science, and all around "coolness" of #hashtagging, the parents quickly decided that they needed something that was going to create a buzz. Why limit the impact to just the Red Land area, why not go viral? If the boys actually DID make it to Williamsport, it would be on ESPN—this could go national!

Still, the question was asked, and re-asked, "What's a hashtag?"

"You'll see."

"Icing on the Cake!" Kristie offered.

"No, too girly. This is baseball, not softball," refuted one of the men in the group. "We need something tough—like our boys!"

"How 'bout Buckle Up. That's tough. O's used that one. If it's good enough for them, it'd be good enough for us," reasoned Aaron Walter, a lifetime Orioles fan, hoping to incorporate a little bit of that *Oriole Magic* into this group as well.

"No. We need something original. No plagiarism." The group agreed. They had to have something that was going to be their own creation. They did not want to recycle some clichéd expression that did not have special meaning to *their* team.

"Well, they have to be red." Yes, they all agreed that they *had* to be red. This was progress. While the adults continued to brainstorm ideas for the saying on the back of the shirts, sixteen-year-old Hollis Kolmansberger started designing the front of them. Creating a visually appealing shirt was a lot easier than getting all the adults to agree on what would go on the back.

The night went on, the ideas flowed, and a good time was being had, but there was a certain sense of importance to be able to finalize a plan of action. The music played.

The music played...

"How about *Running Down a Dream*?" Tom Petty was speaking to the group. Not bad, a little better.

"How about *Dream On*?"

"Oh, I like that! *Dream On*!"

"I like the idea of dreaming!" The group was getting excited, progress was being made. Still, the idea, those expressions, were not their own.

"How about #FullReps?" Bret Wagner offered. "It's what we break huddle with at GoWags. Full reps, baby, go hard. No shortcuts. Go Big or Go Home. All of them speak to the way we want to play—the way we want to *work*." It is almost as if he were giving himself his own pep talk. He was ready to sprint out of the locker room, burst onto the field, and run for 100 yards, or hit someone who was trying. Bret Wagner may have been a baseball player for most of his life, but he still had a football mentality.

Eventually, #LookAtMeNow took a commanding lead and appeared to have the consensus of the group. However, there was something about the word "me" that did not sit well with the group. There was no *me* with this team. That was the beauty of them. The boys meshed unlike any other unit that had ever been put together in all of their youth sports. These boys had been friends since the day they were able to have play dates as toddlers. Like the coaches, they were not just teammates, they were comrades. The fact that they were now winning on the highest level offered to their age group only solidified the bond that had long since been created. For road trips, kids never traveled with the same families—not by instruction, by choice. Guys played catch with different partners before every practice. The dorms had a feeling of the world's greatest sleepover—not just with one or two of your best friends, but with twelve of your brothers.

So did the parents. "Parents can absolutely tear a team apart. I've seen it," explained Kristie Kolmansberger. "But it wasn't like that with this team. I loved going to games not only because I got to watch the kids play, but I got to spend time with people who became dear friends."

Then, with the creative juices flowing even more, someone suggested that they change the spelling of the word Look to LOUK in honor of the team's adopted mascot, Lou the Minion. The boys loved their little stuffed minion they named Lou (after Lou Gehrig) and he had become a valuable symbol of the team's unity. Though Cole's little sister Emma dearly missed him, she understood that Lou had a greater calling at the moment than serving as a decoration on her bed.

Still, the "Louk at Me" mentality, no matter how it was spelled, just did not seem to resonate with the group. Although it was dubbed the default front-runner, it was far from being declared the victor. As the discussion continued and started to meander toward the potential for these shirts—who would buy them, and how many would need to be ordered—somebody asked, "Do you really think we can do it? I mean, seriously? Do you really think it could be *us* playing on ESPN in the Little League World Series?"

Though every coach sitting on that patio wanted to vault from his chair and exclaim at the top of his lungs, "Absolutely!" none of them dared to express what they all truly believed was a very practical notion. They truly believed they could. They would not go as far as to say they *should*, but they liked their chances. "I didn't know if we could win it, but I knew we could compete. I knew we wouldn't embarrass ourselves," said Coach JK.

There are just too many factors involved for one to really be able to accurately access the reality of an objective that grand: pitch counts, injuries, weather, bad hops, errors, the intangible factors are simply immeasurable. But those men, those coaches, believed that in three weeks time, their team, their sons, their boys, would be playing baseball on the fields of North Central Pennsylvania. It was Head Coach Tom Peifer who broke the silence. "Well, somebody's gotta go to Williamsport, why not us?"

Just like that, the brainstorming session ended. What followed was just silence. There was no more discussion about slogans, no more votes, no further input was needed. The slogan was born, the mantra was set, #WhyNotUs was the unanimous winner.

"But, I still don't get it, what's a #hashtag?"

When that was settled, the production of the t-shirt firestorm was put into action. What became a little project for 100 shirts or so, quickly outgrew even the grandest of plans that were conceived that night. The wheels of production were put into high gear, and in four days, Nate Ebbert's EbeXpress churned out 5000 shirts! The demand quickly superseded what Nate could produce, so a second source was utilized (KD Graphics) to keep up with the quantity needed to fill all the requests.

That Friday at the send off, thousands of locals, hoping to get their hands on anything connected to this team, showed up at the Newberry Complex where Scott Sozanski, the President of Red Land Little League and suddenly a man whose volunteer position became exponentially more significant with each passing day, was thrust into the role of marketer, distributor, and organizer of the whirlwind atmosphere that had been created.

As Amy Peifer pulled up to the complex behind Newberry Elementary, she noticed the fire trucks, the police, and the crowd of people that had formed in the gravel parking lot behind the school. Her heart sank and a feeling of panic overtook her. "I thought, 'Oh, my God, the concession stand is on fire, the fields are going up in flames!' So I asked an officer who was directing traffic, 'What's going on?'"

The officer, not knowing who he was speaking to, responded, 'It's the Little League team, they're selling t-shirts! Isn't this great!' It's when I first started to realize just how big this thing was getting. And then I just cried... because I knew it was only the beginning."

Small town folks across America do not need a real reason to congregate on humid summer nights. It is every bit as traditional as sparklers and lemonade. On this night, the town came together to send their local team to New England to stake their claim as one of the eight American teams playing for a United States Little League Championship. "I remember getting the invitation," recalled Lisa Cubbler, "and thinking, 'Who the heck is gonna come to this?' Nobody came when we left for Rhode Island when we won two years earlier; who the heck was gonna come now? Boy, was I wrong."

The townspeople, completely caught up in the growing hysteria, came by the hundreds. Local officials came just to be seen with their constituents, quickly found themselves immersed in the atmosphere and delirium, and just as quickly forgot that they were *supposed* to be there—now they *wanted* to be a part of it all. US Congressman Scott Perry came and spoke to the group. He reflected on his own days of being a Little Leaguer but admitted, "I never experienced anything like this!"

"He was so genuine, so enthusiastic. He was just so happy for our boys," said Lisa. "I hate politicians, but I loved that guy!"

JeriLynn and Roger Mease came to deliver care packages to each of the boys. "I had to do something," JeriLynn explained. "They gave me so much, I had to give them something to thank them." In each of their bags, she gave them the typical care package items for a baseball player—gum, sunflower seeds, candy. She also gave each of them a toothbrush and a Sharpie. "When they opened up their bags, they loved all the candy and birdseed as they called it, but they kept asking me 'What are the markers for?' 'What do we need these for?' 'We're not artists!' But I knew they were going to do great things. I knew a lot of people were going to fall in love with them just like we did. I knew it was just a matter of time before they were going to need those Sharpies. And I was right."

Perhaps the highlight of the night was the last Red Land Little League State Championship team—the 1974 team. Robin Summey Sr. came, wore his state championship jacket, and talked to the boys about how these memories would last them an entire lifetime. He knew the ones he made as a boy still held a special place in his heart. The boys played, they listened, they signed autographs, and they started to realize how much their team meant to some people—many people.

Carmella Walter summed it up best, "My husband always said that people want to be a part of something great, and here were all these people that were doing anything they could to be connected with this team. People sensed it. They sensed it early. They were a really special group of kids."

They were. And they played for a community that consisted of special people. And on this night, they all came together as one, and they would stay together, united in a cause for the next 22 days. The bond they would create, however, would last for a lot longer than that.

11

BRISTOL.

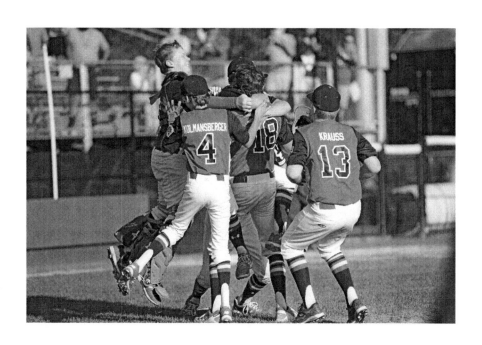

Tom Peifer described the pressure at the Mid-Atlantic Regional in Bristol best when he said, "The difference between first and second place is bigger there than anywhere else in the world. If you win, you're going to have a once in a lifetime experience in the historic Little League World Series in Williamsport, PA, playing on ESPN in front of 1000's of people—for us it would be tens of thousands! But if you lose, well, you go home and dream about what could have been for the rest of your life. There is nothing like it anywhere else in sports. Bristol is *intense*. Bristol is *pressure*. Bristol is *brutal*. Period."

"I could sense the tension and stress in the coaches," explained Fred Sanders, grandfather of Kaden Peifer. "None of the coaches were really themselves. Tom especially wasn't the same. He was just a ball of nerves. We couldn't get him to loosen up even a little, he just stayed to himself, stay focused. He wouldn't talk to anybody." Then he added with a laugh, "Once Bristol was over and he and the team got to Williamsport, you couldn't get him to shut up!"

As is the case so often with youth sports, the intensity and pressure on the field carried over into the stands where the parents and fans of each team seemed to live and die not only on every game, but every inning, and with every pitch. "It was fierce. The tension was so palpable in the stands," explained Jake Cubbler's father, Scott. "We all knew what was at stake. We tried to disguise it in front of the kids, but there was no way you could do it. It was everything you could do from keeping it from becoming to cut throat."

The magnitude of the situation was accentuated by the fact that the Red Land coaching staff now had the burden of soaring expectations. As the team arrived in Bristol, Connecticut, on August 10, they were overly familiar with their competition. Assistant Coach Bret Wagner explained, "We knew the other teams and we knew we were the ones who everybody expected to go to Williamsport. We were the ones who were *supposed* to go. None of us on the staff would say that out loud to each other, but we all knew. And I have to admit it weighed on our minds a little bit." Being the best on paper never amounts to anything in sports—ask the 1980 Russian Hockey team who were on the losing end of the "Miracle on Ice", ask Clyde Drexler and Hakeem Olajuwon from the 1983 Houston Cougars basketball team (who lost to Jimmy Valvano's Wolfpack), or the 1969 NFL Baltimore Colts who lost to Joe Namath's Jets—in sports, things don't always go the way they are *supposed* to go.

In addition to wearing the yoke of being the favorite, Red Land was trying to inconspicuously deal with the suddenly temperamental left arm of their prized pitcher. "We had no idea if he was going to be able to pitch at all. None," stated his father who resorted to purchasing an ultrasound machine and put Cole on a treatment program similar to the one he utilized while working his way through the minor league systems into the big leagues. "I told him, 'Cole, it'll work. It always worked for me. You've got to do this—consistently.'"

"Every time I saw him," added Coach Peifer, "I asked him, 'You doing what you need to do? You using the ultrasound?'" He was. Cole wanted to be on the hill as badly as his coaches and teammates needed him to be there. The signs were there for anybody that bothered to look for them. He did not pitch an inning in districts. Not one. His arm was too sore. In Sectionals, his appearances were sporadic, ranging from a nine pitch outing vs. Big Valley on July 21 to a four-inning no-hitter seven days later. "Every time he took the mound," said Peifer, "it was 50/50. If he felt good, we let him go. It was all or nothing with Cole. People thought we were crazy not pulling him up 20-0 and saving him, but with him, it was all or nothing. He needed complete rest between starts, so if he was feeling good, we let him pitch his limit. If he wasn't, there wasn't anything we could do. Our biggest question going into that tournament in Bristol was 'What if he isn't healthy enough to pitch?'"

Fortunately, for the coaching staff, the way the kids played eased many of their worries. In the first game at Bart Giamatti Field in Bristol, Connecticut, located a mere 4.5 miles from the ESPN Headquarters, the home run barrage that began in their home state of Pennsylvania continued as they tackled the fields of New England. With home runs from Cole, Jaden, Ethan, and Jarrett, Red Land and their "Herculian Feats of Strength" were once again on full display. Giving the coaching staff further peace of mind was the 44 pitch, three inning, no hit outing Cole was able to put together in the first game. The boys cruised to an 11-3 victory over a team from Maine that displayed both their power at the plate and their dominance on the mound.

As the boys settled in after their first win in Bristol, there were no signs of the stress that their coaches were undoubtedly grappling with. In the dorms, the "Aunts" as they were known (surrogate moms who stayed with the boys in the dorm and served as chaperones), pulled the Red Land Coaching staff aside and gave them perhaps the best off-field advice they received throughout the summer.

Coach Peifer explained that upon their arrival, the ladies gathered the coaches together and told them very matter of factly that, "No team whose coach didn't take the boys cell phones every night has ever won in Bristol. If you want to win here, you've got to collect the boys' cell phones every night—that way they actually go to sleep." The coaching staff heeded the advice and would continue to collect the phones at the end of every day. It became one of the two pre-bed routines that the team would do every night from that first night in Bristol until the last night in Williamsport. The other was to provide an agenda for the following day. The significance of both of these moments will never truly be known.

With distractions removed and another win under their belt, their 14th of the summer, the boys drifted off to sleep, undoubtedly dreaming of the opportunities that were becoming more and more realistic with each passing day—and with each victory.

Two days later, Red Land went against a team from Jackson, New Jersey, who was riding the wave of momentum after dramatically hitting a walk off home run to win the New Jersey State Championship and the right to come to the Mid-Atlantic Regionals. They then defeated a very athletic team out of the District of Columbia area in their opening game. On this late Thursday afternoon affair, Red Land, once again electing to bat first, jumped out early with their usual combination of getting leadoff batter Braden Kolmansberger on base, moving him over, and then letting the big dogs hit him in. BK was well aware of his role. "My job is to get on base somehow—a walk, a hit, an error, a passed ball on a strikeout. Somehow, I have to get on base. Then, I have to figure out a way to get to third base with less than two outs. From there, the guys just have to hit me in. It's pretty simple."

After a single up the middle by Kolmansberger, he moved to second base on a wild pitch, and then a blast to dead center field by Cole Wagner (a harbinger of what was to come), and the Patriots were up 2-0. Surprisingly, the bats were silent for Red Land in the next inning, and after they allowed an unearned run in the bottom of the 2nd, the Patriots found themselves in a hotly contested 2-1 battle. The pressure grew and there was concern that the pressure the coaches had been trying to shield the players from was starting to be felt by the kids themselves. However, once again, the beauty of this *team* would allow those who felt they had to carry the burden to lighten the load that they bore.

In the next two innings, Ethan Phillips would knock in a run with a double to left, Chayton Krauss would blast a deep home run to left-center, and Braden Kolmansberger would knock in a run (in addition to scoring yet another one). This gave the Patriots a little breathing room before they completely broke the game open in the 6th with a grand slam from Ethan Phillips and a two-run homer by Dylan Rodenhaber. Though challenged early, the steady left-right combination of Adam Cramer and Jaden Henline kept the New Jersey hitters off balance, and after a 13-2 victory, the Patriots found themselves just one game away from returning to Pennsylvania, not to go home, but to serve as the hosts of one of the most memorable and historic Little League World Series in Williamsport.

That feeling that the pressure was rising just a little bit in the second inning was enough to make Coach Peifer want the boys to be able to release it. And there was no better way to be able to do just that than by getting away from baseball for just a little bit, and that is exactly what

Coach Peifer ordered for Friday, August 14th, one day after the boys clinched their spot in the Mid-Atlantic Regional Championship and two days before they would play for it. The rules were simple: no baseball, no media—just parents, grandparents, siblings, and other family members. Wiffle Ball was allowed, but games could not become too competitive.

Two days prior, the boys were given a VIP type tour of the ESPN studios, where they sat in the same seats as Mike Greenberg and Mike Golic of "Mike and Mike in the Morning," stood on the field of the "Baseball Tonight" studio, and even got to listen to Ryen Rusillo host his afternoon Sportstalk show. As good as that trip was, the day with family was even better—sometimes twelve-year-old boys don't need to be catered to as minor celebrities, they just need to be comforted by their moms. Knowing this is what they needed most, Coach Peifer allowed them the opportunity to feel that they were not just baseball players trying to get to Williamsport; they were kids on summer vacation. So, in the midst of all of the hype that surrounded them, for one afternoon anyway, they were allowed to be just that. Then it was back to work.

"By far the longest day of my life!" said Peifer, and immediately reinforced by Coach JK and Coach Bret.

"Longest day of all of our lives," the two men agreed. The Mid-Atlantic Championship game was slated for late in the afternoon, and there was not enough TV, dining hall time, or warm ups to keep the clock moving toward 4:00. The day just seemed to linger like a curve ball that has no break.

When game time finally arrived, the coaches monitored Cole Wagner's pre-game warm up with the precision and care of nurses in an Intensive Care Unit.

"He's ready," Coach Bret said to his manager and friend, letting him know that their ace, his son, felt no pain as he started to unleash himself and his velocity began to slowly increase. "He'll be fine," he said, more to himself than to anyone else.

"Pop!"
"Pop!"
"Pop!"

Kaden Peifer could feel the sting in his hand as the two warmed up. He took off his glove. He shock his hand a little bit to try to give it a little relief, to get some of the feeling back. "He's ready," Kaden said to his coach. "He's humming the ball. Really humming it."

"Okay. Let's go," the manager said, as he walked away from the pen and prepared for the biggest game of his life.

The first five innings went by as slow and almost as uneventful as the morning and day had gone. In the first inning, Red Land was able to plate a run on two walks, an error, and Dylan Rodenhaber getting drilled by a pitch. Another error plated a second run in the third. In the 4th, a perfectly placed bunt by Cam Walter, a fielder's choice, a wild pitch, and single by Jaden Henline that scored BK again showed why Coach Peifer made the right decision to put Kolmansberger back at the top of the batting order. "The boy just has a nose for home plate," said a proud father and logical assistant coach when asked about his son's seemingly innate ability to get on, get over, and get in. In the fifth, another error put Jake Cubbler on base, and when pinch runner Cam Walter was able to score on Adam Cramer's single, the Patriots had scratched out a 4-0 lead heading to the bottom of the fifth.

If the four runs the Patriots put across the plate seemed unremarkable, than the three hits Jackson was able to produce over the course of the first four innings must have seemed near comatose. However, in the fifth, a small rally had to be stifled when the team from New Jersey put together back-to-back two out singles. It was the first time Cole Wagner had given up back-to-back hits all summer. The very next pitch produced nothing more than a dribbler back to the mound, and as quickly as a rally was started, the rally was squashed.

In the top of the 6th, Red Land continued to patiently pound away at everything Jackson tried to throw at them. Singles by Cole Wagner and Jaden Henline to start the inning allowed Ethan Phillips to finish the Regional tournament with an astounding .700 batting average and eleven RBI's in three games. When the dust settled at the end of the 6th inning, Red Land had a commanding 12-0 lead, and Williamsport, which in reality was 273 miles away, suddenly seemed like it was right around the corner.

If the morning and early afternoon were eternal, and the first five innings seemed to be indistinguishable from that, then time stood still while the final three outs were accumulated. All the kids, including the three that were managing the team, wanted to do was celebrate with each other and make it official, but first, they had to finish the job. Possibly caught up in the anticipation of the imminent celebration, Cole's first two pitches caught too much of the middle of the plate and were both hit for singles. Quickly looking to extinguish even a flint of hope, he struck out the next batter on three pitches, got the next batter to ground into a fielder's choice, and fittingly struck out the final batter—looking.

Then the mayhem ensued. The celebration was like the grand finale of a fireworks display without the ten-minute build up. The pure elation as the boys converged on each other was marked as some of their favorite moments of the entire summer. "I loved those dog piles," said Jake Cubbler. "They were always the best because it meant we won something—something big. That one in Bristol was awesome. We were all so happy, so relieved to be actually going to Williamsport."

Anytime Tom Peifer tries to talk about it, he never gets very far without becoming overwhelmed with emotion, but he tries. "Before you dream of winning in Williamsport, you dream of getting *to* Williamsport. And we were going. I've never been so happy for a group of kids in my life than I was that day in Bristol. It was the culmination of everything we worked for, everything we did, everything we tried to do. All the sweat, all the tears, all the pushing, moments that nobody would ever know about, the nights of kids wanting to quit, the tough decisions we had to make, the setbacks, all of it became *worth it*. We were going to Williamsport. Our dream was now becoming a reality. That level of happiness, the feeling of satisfaction, it's just completely indescribable."

Immediately after the game, a bus was waiting for the kids to take them to Williamsport. They would travel together with the team from New England, and the three-hour journey would become a complete blur. "We were texting, making phone calls, singing, cheering. It was overwhelming. I don't even remember much about it—but I know I was happy. We all were. We were going to Williamsport. Just saying the words brings a smile to my face!" And a tear to his eye. Tom Peifer will never be able to talk about the accomplishments of his team, of his boys, without having that small token of overwhelming emotion reveal itself.

12

"GOOD NIGHT, BOYS."

A fter the very first night in Bristol, the coaches quickly realized that the sooner they came up with a very regimented schedule, the better it would be for everybody involved. This was true not only for the players, who undoubtedly would be tempted to get into mischief if there was too much free time, but also for the parents, who were constantly wondering when they might get an opportunity to be with their sons. Time spent with mom and dad became greatly cherished, as it was extremely limited while the boys were in Bristol and Williamsport. Outside of a selected few scheduled events with the parents, their interaction was minimal.

To alleviate many questions parents had as to what the boys would be doing each day, the coaching staff would create daily agendas, and at the end of every day right before bed, Coach Kolmansberger (or Coach Peifer or Wagner) would read the boys the daily agenda for the following day. It became known as their bedtime story.

A typical non-game day agenda would be:

9:00 Wake Up / Breakfast

10:00 Clean Up Room, Make Bed, Dress for Practice or Morning Activity

10:30 Practice on Designated Field (A, B, C, D) or Morning Activity
Morning Activity could include a Photo Shoot with ESPN
A Special Breakfast (with parents, with Williamsport officials)

Noon Lunch

1:00 Practice Time and / or Cage Work

3:30 Showers / Prepare for Afternoon Activity
Meeting with ESPN, Other Media Requests
Baseball Tonight / Local Newscasts
Williamsport Officials

               Day Trip (Penn State / ESPN)
               All Formal Trips required khaki shorts and jerseys
               Attend Another Game Being Played
               Meet with Rep. for Oakley for Sunglasses /
               Easton for bats

5:00   Dinner
               Off Site Dinner (BW's)
               Picnic / Parade / Dinner with Parents

6:30   Team Meeting / Free Time in Dorm / Ping Pong / Swim

8:30   Pizza in the Room

9:30   Clean Room Again / Prepare for Bed / Call Home
               There was always a reminder to call home, not that the
               boys would forget, but sometimes it's nice to be reminded
               how much your mom and dad actually miss you.

10:00 In Room

10:30 Lights Out

As the boys settled into their bunks, Coach Kolmansberger, Coach Peifer, or Coach Wagner would sit on a bucket in the middle of the room, collect the cell phones from the boys (still following the advice of the "Aunts" in Bristol), and answer any questions the boys might have about the events from earlier in the day or what was going to happen the next day. It quickly became a part of their routine, and one of the favorites of the coaches. It was their respite, their sanctuary.

There were no cameras, there was no pressure, and there were no fans (as great as they were to always have around). It was just the boys and their coaches. It was peaceful, and if the boys would have known what the word meant, they would have said, it was "cathartic." The coaches knew, however, and for them, it was. Finally, when Coach JK would finish answering all the questions and reading the next day's agenda, each father would give his son a hug and start to head out the room.

"Good night, boys. Good night, Braden." He hesitated for a moment and wanted to add, "I love you" to the sentence but did not want to embarrass his son in front of his teammates. Instead, he turned and walked away.

"Good night, Dad, I love you." Jim Kolmansberger was floored. His instinct was to turn and hug his son right there on the spot. Inwardly, he was as proud of his son as he had ever been in his life. Here was his son, without any hesitation at all, unabashedly telling his father he loved him— in front of his teammates—when only seconds earlier JK had hesitated, ever so briefly, not wanting to make his son feel… awkward. For a moment, he was speechless—perhaps it was due to the lump that had formed in his throat. Shortly, he was able to muster up enough of his voice to respond, "I love you, too, Braden."

Then, there was another short pause as Coach Kolmansberger flipped off the lights and walked out the door. Not more than a second after he closed the door behind him, he heard the whooping of twelve other boys shouting, "I love you, too, Coach!"

"Me, too, Coach. I love you!"

"Yeah, Coach, *I* love ya!"

"Yep. Same here, Coach!"

Then, almost in unison he heard what sounded like thirteen voices calling, "We all love you, Coach JK! We all love you!"

All that could be heard after that was thunderous laughter. Coach JK could not help but laugh and smile to himself. And why wouldn't he? When thirteen teenage boys declare their love for you in public, you must be doing something right. There was no doubt whatsoever why this was truly one of his favorite times of the day.

"Good night, boys," he whispered to himself. "I love you guys, too."

13

97 MILES

As idealistic as it is watching children play baseball, the drive to Williamsport is every bit as wistful. The 97-mile trip from Lewisberry to the home of Little League Baseball extends north along the Susquehanna River through small towns like Duncannon, Selinsgrove, Sunbury, and Lewisburg. A traveler can stop for a bite to eat at The Whistle Stop, The Red Rabbit Drive-In, Lumberjack's Kitchen, or Dreamers Ice Cream & Subs. And, of course, a first timer's trip to Williamsport would never be complete without a visit to Clyde Peeling's Reptile Land, where tourists can see creatures such as a Komodo Dragon, a Cuban Rock Iguana, an Australian Emu, or even Snowflake, the Albino Alligator, better known as the Ghost of the Bayou.

The preparation for a trip to Williamsport is every bit as crucial for the fans as batting practice is for the players. When one approaches Williamsport from the southern end of the state, there are no major highways to travel. The interstate systems (Routes 11,15, and 22) are the paths of choice. Commuters can pass the time by challenging themselves to find a stretch of road where either the Susquehanna River or a railroad track is not in plain view. As one descends upon Williamsport, the mountainous region paints the pristine backdrop for an event such as this. When one gets close enough, the magnitude of the ceremonies becomes evident as the Goodyear Blimp hovers over the stadium and serves as a beacon for one's final destination.

The experienced journeyman will no doubt find refuge in a local driveway across from the main complex, where locals are all too happy to assist fans for a $5 parking fee. "$5?" asks one driver. "You guys could get five times that amount for the crowds that'll be coming this year!"

"Yeah, we probably could," agreed the resident. "But $5 is enough for us."

As the commuters unload their belongings for the day, it becomes irrefutable who is the novice and who is the expert by their choice of a seat for the hills that await them inside the complex. There are two levels of hills outside the outfield walls in Howard J Lamade Stadium.

The first is the one easily seen on television and was filled within an hour of the gates being opened. The upper hill is behind a walkway that encircles the field, a line of concession tents, and the centerfield scoreboard. This hill poses quite the challenge for those less physically capable of maintaining their balance on a ridge of this slope. As much of an obstacle that this degree of inclination provides for spectators, it provides countless hours of recreation for those children with the proper foresight (or just good fortune) to find the perfect piece of cardboard to serve as a sled. By late August, after a summer of stifling Pennsylvania heat, most of the grass is hay, and this makes for a perfect way to pass the idle hours between (or during) pitches.

The steepness of the hill also makes traditional lawn chairs utterly worthless. A true pilgrim of Williamsport knows this and will have properly cut off the back legs of a plastic lawn chair to make for a perfectly level seat up on the hill. That insight proves to be invaluable (though chairs of this type have been rumored to sell for up to $40 during this particular week) as hours on the hill squatting or fighting gravity prove to be exhausting.

For these warm August days, members of the *Red Sea*, Red Land's official cheering section, arrived early to stake their claim behind the right field fence to cheer on their young heroes. The first arrivals left Etters as early as 4:00 am to assure themselves they would be first to the gate when it opened at 8:00. Upon arrival at 6:00 am, they were disappointed to learn that on most days, others were already there. By the time 8:00 am rolled around and the gates opened up, the lines stretched far beyond the view of those fortunate enough to be in the front. Some quick maneuvering to the "Fast Lane" allowed those without bags to be checked to rush through security and sprint to their designated spot on the lower hill and spread out as many blankets as they could to secure their sacred ground.

Only then, would they even contemplate breakfast. As the team continued to win, and the crowd continued to grow, loyalists like Ben Green and Palmer Rodenhaber, whose younger brother played on the team, were worried about the system they had in place. "We actually texted Chayton and asked him if he could wake up early and set our blankets out there," said Ben. "But he said Coach wouldn't let him. We were all right, though, we had a pretty good system. I could carry six blankets myself, and when we ran down that hill, we had the whole place to ourselves. But that didn't last long."

As the popularity of the team continued to grow, so did the popularity of the *Red Sea*. Jaymee Sire quickly became an honorary member of *The Sea* and even partook in their famous "Roller Coaster" cheer during the championship game vs. Japan. "Yeah," said Palmer, "she loved us. She even tweeted about us. She hung out with us for about 15-20 minutes just talking before the cameras were ever even on." Soon, the nation seemed to fall in love with *The Sea* almost as much as they fell in love with the team. The mechanical arm that ESPN positioned in the outfield became the *Red Sea* Cam that focused in on the reactions and cheers that came out of right field as often as it showed the action on the field itself. Little kids would walk in front of *The Sea* and have their pictures taken with some of the captains. Some of the more daring ones attempted to start a chant like, "Let's Go, Red Land!" during random times in the game. "We even had our own security guard to prevent people from running in front of us during the game," explained Dylan.

After the National Championship, many of the members of *The Sea* planned on camping out overnight so they could be first in line the next morning to see the boys battle Japan. Not one time over the course of the entire two-week period did any of the high schoolers that filled the hill ever once think they were "too cool" or "too old" for something like Little League Baseball.

"No way," responded Ben when asked, "what those kids did was awesome! It was a once in a lifetime experience for them—but it was for us, too. I'm proud to say I was a part of it. It brought our whole community together! It gave us an identity that we could be proud of. People always rip Red Land for whatever reason—but nobody was ripping us anymore. People *wanted* to be a part of what was going on. It was something I'll never forget, and neither will they."

And that was never more evident than when the "WE ARE" / "RED LAND" chants would echo through the peaks and valleys that make up the landscape of the West Bank of the Susquehanna River. "It was just cool." Dylan paused. "For two weeks that whole place was just booming. With Pride. With Red Land Pride. I never really knew what that meant before, to be proud of where you were from, but for the first time in my life, I was *proud* to be a part of it. I *got* it. Those kids helped me *get it*."

For those that could not make the trip, they filled the local restaurants back home unlike any sporting event has ever done. Places like Kokomos, Hogans, and The Fieldhouse all became rallying points for fans to gather whenever the games were on. On days before games, Darrenkamps Market became a "headquarters" for fans to stock up on snacks, beverages, and apparel. Nearly a quarter of a million dollars worth of t-shirts were sold out of the hometown grocery store. Darrenkamps fully embraced the spirit of the journey the boys were on.

It was as if the whole town just stopped—just so they could be a part of what these kids were about to embark upon. What had already been done was impressive, what they were currently doing was remarkable, but what they were *trying* to do would be...*historic*. Everybody could recognize just how big of a deal this really was. However, the impact that these boys were having on their community was an even *bigger* deal.

And the journey was only beginning.

14

THE ANTICIPATION OF AN IMPENDING STORM

They came with all of the anticipation, apprehension, and potential of an impending storm. As sixteen teams and over 200 Little Leaguers from all over the world converged upon Williamsport, Pennsylvania, for the 69th version of this tournament, each team had only one goal in mind—to leave as champions. For the team from Lewisberry, Pennsylvania, that meant winning the United States Championship first—a World Championship would be a fortuitous afterthought. When the coaches spoke to their players before ever throwing a pitch at Lamade Stadium, their message was irrefutable: "Win a Championship!" Therefore, as the thirteen players, three coaches, support staff, and literally tens of thousands of admirers congregated in the small town nestled along the West Bank of the Susquehanna River, their intentions were unified—and a storm was brewing.

Following the rainout on day one, the officials decided to make Day One a historic event by having all sixteen teams play—and the results did not disappoint. Games began at 10:00 am on Friday, August 21, and as the day progressed, teams from Europe, Africa, Latin America, Oregon, Australia, Kentucky, China, and Lewisberry, PA, did battle in Volunteer and Lamade Stadiums in front of thousands of adoring fans.

Before the day was done, fans were treated to a second straight no hitter by Alex Edmondson (the first coming in the Southeast Regional Championship) and a 16 strikeout performance in five innings by Matthew Wilkinson of Canada (who had the benefit of striking out four batters in the fifth inning when a third strike was dropped by the catcher and allowed the batter to reach first base).

Amazingly, Wilkinson's effort, as exceptional as striking out 16 players in five innings when only 15 outs were needed was, it wasn't quite enough. Mexico was able to walk off with a win in the bottom of the 6th when Canada was forced to go to their bullpen. Wilkinson had hit the 85-pitch limit set by Little League Baseball.

Day One also saw the team representing the West Region from the Sweetwater Valley Little League in Bonita, California, the third team to come out of San Diego County in the past seven years and eleventh overall, launch a record six home runs in their lopsided 14-2 victory over the team from the Great Lakes Region. But none of those six home runs generated as much commotion as the herculean blast that came off of the bat of Terrence Gist from South Carolina that spectators (and ESPN announcers) reported actually cleared a light tower in left-center field, which stands at 100 feet tall.

The crowd continued to grow over the course of the day from a respectable 10,423 for the 11:00 am Texas-Oregon game, to an astounding 32,634 people when the team from Pennsylvania took the field at 8:00 pm. Throughout the day, fans would bounce back and forth between Volunteer Stadium and Lamade, but when the Pennsylvania boys took the field, the seats on Terrace hill became permanent. And those kids had no intention of sending their fans home disappointed!

Pennsylvania came averaging a daunting 15.3 runs per game and had launched 80 home runs. Their .452 batting average meant that they were getting a base hit almost half the time their players came to the plate, and when they did get a hit, they had as good a chance to hit a home run, triple, or double (they hit 106) as they did a single (also 106). This team not only loved to hit, they loved to smash baseballs.

When they stepped into the batter's box, their intentions were to inflict damage upon any baseball that dared to enter into the reach of their swings— and inflect damage is what they did best! Only the team from California could hope to put up numbers even remotely close to these, but Red Land wasn't playing California on Opening Night, they were playing the team from Webb City, Missouri, who had won the Midwest Region by defeating the likes of Nebraska (twice), Iowa, South Dakota, and Minnesota—the last two by virtue of the 10-run mercy rule. And they had their pitching set up to be able to throw their best hurler at the Patriots in front of an overflow crowd—but young Devrin Weathers could have no idea what type of buzz saw he was about to be subjected to.

As for the Patriots, the decision was made very early on to not throw their ace on opening night. When Coach Peifer first saw the brackets and projected how the tournament may play out, he wrote JCAC on each of the advancing bracket lines that led to the National Championship. The letters stood for his starting pitchers for each of those games so long as the Patriots stayed in the winner's bracket—a huge advantage for teams trying to line up their pitchers with the stringent limitations that Little League rightfully places on such young arms. The JCAC stood for Jaden, Cole, Adam, Cole who would progressively start each game in each round, and so long as they could "stick to the plan," there would be no need to deviate from this initial strategy.

This approach would make Cole available for two games, the most significant being the US Championship. But for that plan to work, the Patriots had to stay out of the loser's bracket where back-to-back games could wreak havoc on a manager's pitching rotation. Coach Peifer was already putting himself in the crosshairs of second guessing critics if his squad could not pull out a victory while their ace stood helplessly at first base, knowing that the hits Webb City would be getting off of one of his teammates may not have happened if he were on the hill. Without a doubt, the Patriots had to win on Opening Night! But Jaden Henline, the starting pitcher for that night, had no intention of having anyone doubt the single biggest decision that Coach Peifer had to make—who would start the first game. There was a purpose to his decision and he was confident, as all the coaches were that he knew exactly what he was doing when he named him the starting pitcher on this most significant of opening scenes of this epic five act play.

It was no secret that Red Land's coaching staff preferred to bat first and be considered the visiting team (at least on the scoreboard) every chance they could. This game was no different. Throughout the summer, when the coin flip was won, Red Land always chose to bat first. And why wouldn't they? Red Land's offensive juggernaut managed to outscore their opponents 38-4 in the first inning, and only a handful of times (5) did they not force their opponents to play from behind after they got to bat. Coming into the Webb City game, the Patriots had scored in the top of the first in seven straight games, which catapulted the Patriots to early leads that most times were insurmountable. In nine of the sixteen wins the Patriots posted on their way to Williamsport, they scored enough runs in the first inning to secure a victory.

Only one time all summer had they faced a deficit. It was at the hands of a team from Camp Hill, who went up 1-0 at the end of the first inning. Red Land went on to win 25-1 and win their District 6 Championship. This team was ready to swing their bats with reckless abandon, and they wanted to do it right away.

On this night, though, there would be no first inning explosion. After the Patriots went down rather benignly in their first chance to bat, all eyes turned to Jaden Henline and how he would handle the spotlight of being the first pitcher the Patriots would turn to on their quest for a National Championship. His first pitch, a 71 mph fastball that was taken for a strike, was a good indication that Jaden was worthy of the massive stage he was on and the blinding spotlight cast on him. Jaden threw 15 pitches that first inning, 12 of which were strikes. After setting aside Webb City, the Patriots were ready to begin their onslaught.

It started with Chayton Krauss, the Kiwi from New Zealand, and one of Red Land's most consistent hitters. Though somewhat overshadowed by the larger-than-life presence and power of Cole Wagner, Chayton's 13 home runs and .500 batting average in 16 games certainly did not require him to take a backseat to anyone. The differences were Chayton lacked the presence at the plate and on the mound that Cole commanded, but his explosiveness, was every bit as compelling. The ball erupted when Chayton hit it, and the frequency with which Chayton made contact was every bit as often as Cole. It just did not always have the same kind of trajectory that Cole Wagner's balls had when they left the yard. Chayton's were just as powerful, but they did not always leave the yard, and in a sports society that thirsts for supremacy, singles and doubles do not get nearly as much attention as home runs do. As a result, Chayton was often an unfair afterthought by outsiders. Those on the inside, however (his coaches, the players), knew his role was every bit as significant as anyone else's on the team was.

It was his line drive rocket to left that got the Patriots rolling in the 2nd inning. He went from first to second on a passed ball, and it was then that Coach Peifer strategically relieved him with Cam Walter, using the "Special Pinch Runner Rule" that Little League allows. The move would instantly pay off, as Cam utilized his speed and intellect and moved to third on a ball that was not quite caught cleanly by catcher Eli Goddard. When Jake Cubbler singled him home, it marked the first run scored and the first RBI for a Red Land player in the 2015 World Series. However, this evening, this inning, and Red Land's courtship with destiny was just getting started.

The next batter was the manager's son, Kaden, who also served as the team's catcher. Kaden's unique hitting style, with his massive leg lift before swinging, became an immediate source of attention of not only the fans at the game and spectators at home, but of the ex-major league ball players and ESPN Sportscasters who were broadcasting the games.

"Wow!" exclaimed John Kruk, who produced a .300-point batting average over his ten-year playing career that saw him don the uniforms of the Padres, Phillies, and Chicago White Sox before retiring in 1995. The three time All-Star finished in the Top Ten for Batting Average in three different seasons, peaking in 1992 when he hit .323 for the Phillies and finished 3rd overall in the National League for hitting that season. John Kruk knew a thing or two about hitting all right, and he was astounded!

Kaden's first swing at a 70 mph fastball by Devrin Weathers sent him corkscrewing across home plate and drew chuckles from the three men upstairs in the broadcast booth.

"Whoa! Easy. Easy, my man!" joked one of the three men in the booth.

"Peifer!" They were clearly enamored by the ferocity of the young man's approach at the plate.

"He's getting on a horse!" added Karl Ravech, the host of Baseball Tonight and former ABC27 local news anchor in the Harrisburg area.

"It looks like he's starting a motorcycle!" responded Kruk. (Somewhere, Kyle Wagner was hashtagging #UniqueDoesn'tMeanWrong.)

What Kaden was doing was naturally trying to generate as many ground forces as possible. The Red Land team, many of who were trained by Kyle Wagner and had been indoctrinated with the Green Light Hitting philosophy since they were eight years old, was never formally instructed to generate a leg lift prior to swinging. It was a byproduct of naturally trying to generate as much force as they could to hit the ball, and so, it was never discouraged. Contrary to popular belief, however, it was never encouraged either. It was just a part of allowing hitters to do what helped them feel comfortable in the box. Kyle, and the other Green Light Hitting instructors, simply encouraged them to be free moving athletes while they were in the batter's box. Nobody embraced the concept of this completely unfettered approach to hitting and took greater advantage of that freedom than Kaden Peifer.

The first two swings that Kaden took were wildly misguided. The force of his swings sent him flailing across the plate as he swung and missed. He was completely letting loose in the batter's box, and there was not an ounce of restraint in him. To specialized hitting instructor Kyle Wagner, those were good signs. "The swing and miss is an unexpected event, and the fall was nothing more than a reciprocal force—an athletic hop if you will. We don't tell them to swing as hard as they can *in case* you hit it. We tell them to swing as hard as they can *because it gives you a better chance to hit it*."

On the third pitch that Kaden saw, he did not swing and miss. He sent a 250 foot laser over the right field wall that didn't stop until it was in the hands of an ecstatic fan, who was both equally thankful that she was not harmed by the force and acceleration of the baseball and that she was the recipient of the first of many souvenirs the Red Land kids would propel into the crowd on the hill. As he rounded third, his teammates were all waiting to greet him with hugs, slaps on the back, high fives, and helmet slams. They rejoiced like kids who had just been given free ice cream. It was exactly what the Red Land kids needed. From that point forward, they relaxed and played the kind of dominant baseball that they had been playing all summer long.

That first night in Williamsport will rank as one of the most joyous, enchanting evenings that the people of Lewisberry will ever experience—for those who witnessed it first hand in being a part of the crowd, to those who watched from local pizza shops and restaurants back home. They came together as a community and were elated to be a part of the campaign that had just begun. Red Land had arrived; their presence was now validated. The concerns, if there ever were any, of there being too much hype, of not being able to live up to the persona that had been created, of this being some kind of a fluke, were dismissed as that ball cleared that fence. This team was not just happy to be there, this team had a chance, a legitimate chance, and now the entire baseball world knew it.

Over the course of the next two weeks, they would learn about these kids, their town and neighboring locals, and they would fall in love with every aspect of the Red Land community. Kaden Peifer kick started the process when that otherwise arbitrary home run, the 81st that had been hit by this team that summer, cleared that fence. That home run did a heck of a lot more than just give the Patriots a 4-0 lead.

As he entered the dugout on the third base side, Tom Peifer, his manager, allowed himself a moment to be just a proud dad. He waited patiently for him in the dugout and quickly and subtly grabbed his son for a hug and kiss on the top of his head as he removed his helmet. Just as quickly, he turned to the next batter and gave him the "Hit" sign.

Anyone who knew the special relationship between Tom and his son, to those who knew the countless hours they had spent preparing with the hopes that a moment such as this could occur, the beauty of that moment went far beyond just baseball. It was the beauty of an irreplaceable moment between a father and a son. It was a moment that only an organization like Little League Baseball could provide. It gave a father and son the opportunity to bond together through the playing of a game so they could forever cherish moments just like these. Moments such as these allowed fathers to teach their sons some of life's most important lessons and develop their boys into young men. It helped them demonstrate the values of persevering through adversity, and to ultimately, as on *this* night, at *this* moment, bask in the glories of a memory that will never be forgotten.

While all of the excitement unfolded, John Kruk reflected, "That's the beauty of baseball." He was referring to the fact that a batter could miss so blatantly on the first two pitches and recover to hit a home run on the third. Baseball gives hitters three chances, sometimes life only gives us one—baseball was fairer in that sense.

◆◆◆◆

Once the doors of the barn are opened, the horses will run to the fields. When Kaden Peifer kicked open the proverbial doors on the Red Land offense, there was nothing that was going to contain the stampede that was about to ensue. Clearly rattled by the dramatic turn of events, the smile that was evident on young Devrin Weathers' face had completely vanished. The next three pitches were off target, as he seemed to be aiming the ball to avoid further damage, which is much like adding water to a grease fire. Adam Cramer soon smacked a double, which brought up Braden Kolmansberger at the top of the line up. A wild pitch followed by a BK single gave Red Land a 5-0 lead but also served as an indication that Webb City was starting to lose traction on the stable ground on which stood.

When a team, in general, and a pitcher, specifically, is trying to balance its collective equilibrium, Cole Wagner is not who one would want stepping into the batter's box, but that is exactly what was about to take place. Determined to make a larger splash than the one his first inning single made, Cole dug in with the mentality and determination of a deep sea fishermen desperate for his next great catch. Possibly sensing the same thing, Webb City skipper, Eric Parker, made a pitching change.

Out was 5'9" lengthy Devrin Weathers, whose smile was as wide as his arms and legs were long, and in came Cole Gayman to take his absolute best shot at getting the first out for the Champions of the Midwest in the second inning. The five foot two inch, 126-pound pitcher fired seven pitches at his five foot nine inch, 159-pound counterpart, and Cole swung at every single one of them. From darts that were just foul down the right field line, to pitches he fought off in hopes of a better serving, neither competitor was about to give into the other.

Finally, on the last pitch of this confrontation, Cole smacked a ground ball that went flying past the second baseman like an absolute rocket. The ball that originated as a grounder in the infield had such velocity that it made it all the way to the wall 225 feet away, and when it was bobbled, Cole Wagner never lost stride in the 11.75 seconds it took him to round the bases.

During his sprint around the infield, his father, and third base coach Bret Wagner, screamed "GO!" no fewer than 14 times as his son made it to home plate without any threat at all of being thrown out. The third base coach's unbridled plea for an all out assault on home plate symbolized the uncompromising, passionate pursuit this team would evoke on their hunt for a championship, and now, that quest had more than officially begun. When the dust settled, Red Land was up 7-0, and the demolition was under way. The atmosphere in the stands, and on the hills of the outfield, quickly turned from reserved curiosity to hysterical, optimistic exuberance, not only for the moments they were currently witnessing, but for the opportunities they dreamed might be waiting in the immediate future.

◆◆◆◆

Essentially, the outcome of the game was no longer in question. Nevertheless, as the remainder of the second inning continued, there were two subtly symbolic moments that clearly captured why this team for Lewisberry, Pennsylvania, was so undeniably successful. They were just passing moments in the game that were otherwise inconsequential, but they represented the core values of this team, their coaches, the players, and their extraordinarily high level of standards, the trust they had in each other, and the uncommon modesty of their manager.

Following Cole Wagner's inside the park home run, which was ruled a double and a two base error by the official scorekeeper in Williamsport, the Patriots continued to feast on Midwest pitching. Through the seven batters that Red Land sent to the plate, three had singles, two had doubles, one batter walked, and Peifer had hit the home run. The regularity of the havoc that Red Land inflicted on Webb City was disconcerting to anyone not in red that evening.

Though a brief hiatus was given when the next batters were retired, Red Land quickly loaded the bases again and looked to impose their will even further as Kaden Peifer was set to step into the box for the second time this inning. Webb City's manager Eric Parker made his second pitching change in the inning. Only, in what was a shocking move to many, when new pitcher Cale McCallister threw his first pitch, it was not to Kaden Peifer—it was to a pinch hitter, Jarrett Wisman.

Even the guys in the ESPN booth were astonished by the decision. "Jeez!" mused John Kruk. "Guy hits a home run and you're gonna pinch hit for him. Apparently, he didn't hit it far enough."

It was a decision Tom had been making all season. Part of it was to fulfill the Little League requirements that every kid must have at least one at bat on a team that consists of 13 players, which the Red Land team strategically had. On a team of only 12 players, each player must not only get an at bat, but they must also play two innings in the field. Not wanting to deal with that extra burden of dividing playing time, the staff, even before try-outs started, decided that their team would be comprised of 13 boys. In order to ensure that the four players who did not start the game got their required at bat, Coach Peifer had to be creative.

No matter what strategy he employed, it always involved taking away an at bat from his own son. Therefore, despite the fact that it was Kaden who had gotten this rally started, and despite the .419 batting average he had accumulated over the course of the summer, Coach Tom Peifer removed his son from the line up.

"Tom earned credibility because of the way he handled Kaden," said Kyle Wagner, who had an integral part in developing Kaden, not only as a hitter, but also as a catcher. "He was asking him to serve as the foundation of the pitching staff, to handle the velocity of Cole and Jaden, the movement of Adam Cramer, to not let a ball get past him while he was behind the plate, to be able to consistently hit for average and for power, and then be unselfish enough to understand that he was going to take his second at bat away from him every game. That's a hard thing to ask of a kid, but an even harder thing for a father to ask of his son." But any father who has ever had the dilemma of having to make a tough decision about what's best for the team knows that sometimes it is easier to ask your son to sacrifice something for the team instead of somebody else—but not much easier.

"Kaden never said anything about it, but I sure heard about it from my father!" partially joked Coach Peifer months after looking back on the sacrifices he asked his son to make.

There is an old cliché in coaching that goes "A team is a reflection of the coach." That was never more evident than it was with *this* team, and *this* coach. Tom Peifer never wore a microphone throughout the entire Little League World Series. He never felt the need to validate himself as the manager, forcing himself into the spotlight. He asked his players to fill their roles and play an unselfish brand of baseball that put the team before any individual player. He asked his own son to graciously forfeit some of his own personal opportunities, and he was willing to do so himself.

The level of humility these kids exuded enamored fans from all around the community, the state, and, eventually, the country. And it all started with their manager. If Tom could ask his own son to concede some of his glory, if *he* was so willing to do so himself, then surely, *they* could do it as well. What this team showed was an uncommon display of dignity, grace, respect, and decorum—and that was clearly nothing more than an extension of their manager.

Kaden's replacement, Jarrett Wisman, drew an RBI walk, Dylan Rodenhaber scored the 9th run on a passed ball, and then Adam Cramer singled in Jake Cubbler to give Red Land what must have seemed like an overwhelming and insurmountable 10-0 lead.

◆◆◆◆

The second moment came in the bottom of the second inning, after striking out the first batter, Jaden Henline walked the second batter on four pitches. Clearly disagreeing with the umpire, Jaden outwardly showed minor frustration. That was enough to bring pitching coach Bret Wagner out to the mound for a quick conference with his pitcher. It was only a subtle display, one that stemmed more from annoyance than anything else, but it was enough for Coach Bret.

"Hey, this is a legitimate strike zone, it's not a Little League strike zone. You just gotta be a bulldog, okay, keep battling the zone." Throughout the entire discussion, Jaden looked at his coach right in the eye, and not one time was that eye contact ever broken between player and coach. Coach Bret spoke, and Jaden attentively listened and nodded as he accepted his coach's assessment. Never did Jaden attempt to project blame onto the umpire, probably knowing that Coach Bret would simply not accept that kind of rationalization. The communication was clear, direct, and fully accepted.

Before he left the mound and returned to the dugout, Bret leaned in to the right ear of his pitcher so the microphone that he was wearing would not pick up on his final piece of instruction. It did. "I don't want to see bad body language out here." With that, he returned to the dugout.

They were up 10-0. At that point, Jaden Henline had only given up one hit. This batter, Matt Woodmansee, was the first hitter he had walked, but the coaching staff saw something they did not like, and they were not going to wait to deliver their message—and Bret Wagner was the coach that was going to deliver it. There were so many factors represented in the otherwise irrelevant exchange. The first was how much trust existed in the dugout between the three men who led these boys. Early on, it was decided that manager Tom Peifer would best serve the team by staying in the dugout rather than serving as its first or third base coach.

Tom would make sure that all the playing time requirements were fulfilled and pitch counts were meticulously kept based on how many days rest one of his boys would need after surpassing a certain plateau. Consequently, he authorized his assistants, JK and Bret, to control the runners; in them he had complete confidence that they would do more than an adequate job. He also delegated the responsibilities, like pitching and hitting, catching and fielding, to those individuals who had a particular expertise in that specific category. He had no problem with being able to allow these specialists to be the loudest voice the kids would hear on those particular subjects.

Ego never played a factor in any of the countless decisions that Tom Peifer had to make. He asked his kids to be willing to swallow their pride by being willing to alternate positions (sometimes even mid-inning based on hitters), serve roles as designated runners, hitters, and even being willing to be hit or run for when a teammate could better fill the need...and he was willing to divide the authority amongst his staff. In doing so, he earned even more respect in the eyes of his players, their parents, and his assistants.

Tom never felt the need to take on more than what he could contribute expertly just because he was the manager. He never felt compelled to substantiate his role on the team by forcing himself into the public eye. He stayed in the dugout, managed his team, delegated his authority, and was admired by his players, his peers, and his coaching staff because of it. Because he would not be out on the field of play, ESPN never put a microphone on him. As often as the managers on other teams became as much a part of the game as the players (the coach from Texas would become a temporary celebrity; the coach from last year's New England team would be a guest analyst in the booth), Tom never felt the need to demand the spotlight. He, like every other coach and player on the team, had a role, and it was no bigger than anybody else's on the team. As protocol would have it, Coach Bret went out to the mound to talk to Jaden. Nobody cared who got the credit, as long as the results were beneficial.

The second tenet that was demonstrated was the fact that even the slightest variation from the task at hand would be confronted regardless of the circumstances that surrounded it. The coaching staff was equally as demanding on each player, and not only did they want their team to win a championship, they wanted their players to conduct themselves as champions. Players got honesty from their coaches. They got it often, and they were expected to accept it upon receiving it. It was a relationship that was built on trust and respect, and it was palpable.

When Jaden Henline was reminded of this, he immediately put himself back on the path of dominance. Of the next nine pitches, six were strikes, and the next two batters were struck out looking. It was Red Land's turn to bat again, and though a message had clearly been sent with their ten run second inning, an entirely different dictum would be sent not only to Missouri, but to every team that had come to Williamsport with hopes of winning a Championship—the road to a National Championship and possible World Championship, was going to have to go through Red Land.

◆◆◆◆

There are historical moments, and then, there are moments that become historical. The first are the predetermined significant events that everybody knows ahead of time are going to become a reference point for all those who witness it. The later are those spontaneous instances that resonate such an impact that they will never be forgotten.

If anyone suspected that Red Land would become complacent after scoring ten runs in the previous inning, they would have grossly miscalculated. Jaden Henline's thirteen second consultation on the mound with Coach Wagner was not only heard by him, but by the entire infield, which included his son Cole, who just happened to be the first batter of the next inning. Cole, who had not let a strike go by him without a swing all evening, unloaded on the second pitch of the inning and absolutely pummeled a ball over the hedges in center field. The ball traveled so far that it extended beyond the light towers and was never seen as it disappeared into the night. Contrary to legend, the ball did eventually make a landing just shy of the centerfield camera tower some 318 feet away.

Before reaching his father who was waiting with a fist pound in the coaching box at third base, Cole received acknowledgments from shortstop Treghan Parker and third baseman Mekhi Garrard. Before any of his teammates could slap helmet, give him five, or hug him, catcher Eli Goddard gave him his proper credit with a glove slap of his own. Even the opposition seemed to know the offensive shellacking that they were receiving was something genuinely exceptional.

The Patriots continued to hit. Three more singles, two more walks, Cam Walter got hit by a pitch, and Kaden Peifer had another RBI when a fielder's choice increased the lead to 14-0, and only exacerbating the situation for the Midwest, it brought Cole Wagner to the plate for the second time this inning, and this time with the bases loaded. All manager Eric Parker could do was keep visiting the mound, smile at his guys, and continue to pound them with optimism. To his credit, that is exactly what he did. "Head up, head up, head up. We're all right, we're all right. Chin up. They said this team could hit, and they proved it. We just have to tip our hats to them right now. Buzz saw." With each passing meeting on the mound, he became more salesman and psychologist and less baseball coach.

During one of the conferences, Devrin Weathers, who started the game, was heard saying, "This team can hit, and they've got the biggest crowd in the world."

Even the most bright-eyed idealist could not diminish the undertaking that Mekhi Garrard had in front of him. Cole hadn't swung and missed all day, his two previous resulted with him crossing home plate—the first a result of his speed, the second a product of his power.

As Cole Wagner approached the plate and stepped into the box, the crowd in Williamsport rose to its collective feet, and Cole Wagner was not about to disappoint them. Before a pitch was even thrown, former New England Little League Coach and now guest analyst for ESPN, David Belisle, who in 2014 secured his niche in the heart's of Little League fans everywhere with his inspirational pep talk that was caught on camera after his team lost a heartbreaking, one run game that ended their run in the Little League World Series, chimed in with his classic New England accent, "We got a new staaaar in Williamsport." Cole's rise to fame, glory, and Little League immortality was only beginning.

The first pitch was high and tight. Cole let this serving go by. However, when the second pitch caught just enough of the outside part of the plate, Cole unleashed every ounce of power and fury that he had in his 12-year-old body.

"OHHHHHHHHHHHHHHHHH!!!!"

"ANOTHER ONE!!!!!!!!!"

The voices of admiration that came from the adults in the booth, who had spent their professional lives watching grown men hit home runs with regularity, were clearly in awe of what they saw.

"*I* waaanna go down there and shake his hand," declared Belisle.

The colossal blast that was launched off of Cole's bat went even farther than the one that he had destroyed in the previous inning. Legend will create a memory that had the ball landing a greater distance away from home plate and higher up the second hill with each passing year.

The astonishment that the three men in the broadcast booth were bestowing upon this young superstar quickly turned to admiration, but it was not for Cole Wagner—it was for the boy who threw the pitch.

There was absolutely no doubt of the magnitude with which Cole Wagner had hit that ball. On impact, the question was not *if* the ball would be a home run, but by *how far* would it clear the fence. Fans knew it, Cole knew it, and the boy who threw the pitch, Mekhi Garrard, knew it. His reaction to giving up this "tape measure tater" captured everything that Americans love about this event. Rather than throwing his glove to the ground, or confrontationally challenging the hitter, Mekhi turned and watched the ball take flight.

As it ascended into the nighttime Pennsylvania sky, his facial expressions were those of wonder, reverence, and appreciation. It was one of the most prominent, poignant moments of sportsmanship this tournament has ever experienced. It is why people tune into this event by the hundreds of thousands every summer—the authentic reaction of a child. Imagine a major league pitcher responding to a crushing round tripper in the same capacity. For that matter, not many kids would have responded in the same good-natured manner that Mekhi did.

"Our kids would have never reacted like that," said Cole's mom when she later saw the highlight run on SportsCenter. Mekhi's reaction was played and replayed as many times as the home run itself. The sport's world, and everyone who saw the response, fully embraced the righteousness and gamesmanship displayed by Midwest players and coaches on what could have been a very difficult night to remain honorable by less virtuous individuals.

The remainder of the game was virtually uneventful. Nothing could possibly live up to the theater that had been created in the 2nd and 3rd innings. As Chayton Krauss came in for the final inning and two-thirds, allowing only one hit, and giving up no runs, the irrefutable message that was reverberating throughout Lamade Stadium and the dorms that surrounded it was that the Mid-Atlantic Champions from

Lewisberry, Pennsylvania, were a monstrous force that were going to have to be reckoned with if anyone had any aspirations of winning this tournament.

After a historic opening day that included 8 games, 1,560 pitches, 345 official plate appearances, 172 strikeouts, 68 total runs, and 19 home runs, the lights were turned off in Williamsport. And as the thirteen players, three coaches, and thousands of fans tried to ground themselves down from the hysteria that still radiated around the events from earlier in the evening, they went to bed—not dreaming of what *might* be, but *knowing* that it was very much a *realistic* possibility. There is a magical aura about a child who believes that literally anything is possible and the world truly can be conquered. As these boys laid down to sleep that night, that is exactly what they were thinking—and the community that surrounded them thought so, too.

15

4LN...AND OTHERS LIKE HER

Somewhere between becoming the Pennsylvania State Champions in Newville, Pennsylvania, and the Mid-Atlantic Regional Champions in Bristol, Connecticut, the run the boys were making became much more than just winning baseball games. Though specific details suggest that it was probably more fate than intention, the Red Land boys realized that their name now carried with it some status, and they wanted that influence to be directed toward something positive, something that was bigger than just their own benefit.

After their third and final victory in Bristol, the one that assured them that they would play in the Little League World Series, Scott Shirley, whose father was the legendary baseball coach in Mechanicsburg and who had fallen victim to cancer, contacted Assistant Coach Bret Wagner about connecting the team with the "Vs. Cancer Foundation." This organization raises money for children who are inflicted with this deadly disease, many of whom are treated at the Penn State Hershey's Children's Hospital, which is home to the Four Diamonds organization.

The Four Diamonds was established in 1972 by Charles and Irma Millard and is based on a story written by their son Chris, who at age eleven was diagnosed with cancer. In the later stages of his struggle against cancer, Chris wrote about a knight who was in search of four diamonds, which represented Courage, Wisdom, Honesty, and Strength. Chris associated these four qualities as the essential attributes not only for his knight, Sir Millard, and his quest to defeat an evil sorceress, but also in his own battle against cancer that would last three years.

In Chris' honor, Four Diamonds was created, and since its inception, hundreds of millions of dollars have been raised to combat childhood cancer. When the team learned of the story of Chris Millard and the Four Diamonds, they were more than willing to increase their influence in combating pediatric cancer and officially became associated with one of the noblest organizations in Central Pennsylvania.

The opportunity to link themselves to a charitable organization of this magnitude was an amazingly humbling experience. Here were a group of kids who were just trying to get around on a 72 mph fastball, yet by doing so, and doing it well, they would be helping other kids who were fighting for their lives. It provided a sense of balance to these boys who sometimes are exposed to a world in which adults all too commonly lose complete perspective of such a concept.

It was a perfect pairing, kids helping other kids, and the children on the receiving end of their benevolence were in desperate need of whatever support these new 12-year-old celebrities could generate. In a very brief period of time, the boys generated over $6200 for "Vs. Cancer." They believed that the longer they played, the more exposure this honorable organization would receive, and the more money it would raise, thereby being able to help and possibly save, more children.

For that to happen, they had to continue to win. The coaches and players basked in the opportunity to be associated with something so noble, so positive, and so powerful. Their sense of purpose to win became even greater. Soon the message spread, and funds began to pour in. To date, the team has raised over $25,000 for research against pediatric cancer!

More than the money that has been raised to help researchers find medical breakthroughs to discover a cure for cancer, these boys became a national flag bearer for an organization that still remains obscure to so many, even in the Central Pennsylvania area. What the team provided, what all the teams involved in the Little League World Series provide, is a positive source of energy during a time when so many families try to salvage any reason to smile, to feel good, to be able to have just a moment's respite from their all-consuming battles with this dreaded disease.

These boys administered that hiatus, that sense of relief. From that, hope had a chance to emerge, and quite possibly, even prevail. What these boys did for the spirits of those children and their families was every bit as significant as what those doctors and nurses did for their bodies.

No one will ever be able to put a dollar value on that. Sometimes, lost in the magnitude of the millions of dollars raised by these charities, are the individual stories and how even the smallest gestures can mean so much to those needing to cling to even the smallest sliver of optimism. The boys and their quest for a championship provided that minuscule ray of sunshine in their otherwise cloudy days.

◆◆◆◆

Gabe Angus was diagnosed with leukemia when he was just four and a half years old. Soon, his father's dreams of being able to play baseball, golf, or even go fishing with his little buddy were in grave jeopardy. His father, Hank, recalled just how difficult the next three years would be as Gabe waged war with this far too victorious disease. "It takes so many years away. Not just at the end, but in the middle, too. We didn't get to do the kinds of things that little boys should do with their fathers. All of that got taken away." But Gabe was a fighter.

"He was so strong. He was, and still is, my hero," said his mother, Connie, who had her own skirmish with breast cancer and knows first hand the difficulty of staying optimistic against a raging sea of despair.

For the next three and a half years, Gabe Angus would be in and out of the Penn State Hershey Medical Center, would be seen by an infinite number of oncologists, doctors, specialists, and nurses, would have a myriad of tests performed upon him, and would take more medications as a child than most people take in a lifetime.

Fighting cancer becomes an all-consuming crusade—and not just for the patient. "There were nights that I would fall asleep standing up over his bed," recalled Connie. The ebb and flow of what seemed like a never-ending encounter wrought havoc on the Angus's lives.

One afternoon, Hank watched his son playing with a neighborhood friend, and as excited as he was just to see his son playing outside as a boy should do, he cowered at the sight of Gabe trying to keep up with his playmate. "He really wasn't even running; it was more of a labored walk, one where the spirit wants the body to move faster, but the body simply can't oblige. And I knew, I just knew, that some things were always going to be difficult for my son."

"He's just got a little hitch in his giddy-up," says Connie, who shares Hank's admiration for their son and how he has endured all that he has been through. They have witnessed it first hand, as have his sisters, Ronnie and Sydney, who had their lives frozen as Gabe tried to defeat this deplorable form of sickness known as leukemia.

Remarkably, Gabe was one of the lucky ones! He was declared cancer free at the age of eight and completed his treatments in Hershey. Throughout the entire process, Connie and Hank never paid a dime for the services they received from the Medical Center—the Four Diamonds Fund provided every penny that they needed to get their son healthy again.

All of it, from meals at the hospital, gas for traveling, music therapists, co-pays, medications (some of which cost $2,000 for a week's supply) was paid for by the Four Diamonds Fund. Toward the end of Gabe's treatment, he would spend time in the intravenous immunoglobulin (IVIG) immunity chair that would have cost the family $15,000 a sitting! "That chair allowed Gabe to not only be alive, but to LIVE!" recalled Hank. "It let my son live." Again, the Four Diamonds Fund paid for every session.

In 2011, as Gabe Angus continued to show progress in his recovery, Hank wanted to do something that all dads want to do with their sons— he wanted to go to a baseball game. Never much of a player himself (Hank described himself as a pile of dust lumbering down to first base on those rare occasions when he happened to hit the ball), he still had an affinity for the game. He wanted to share those special moments, like playing catch or just sitting out in the sunshine watching a game with his son. However, cancer deprived him of the opportunities to do that.

Now, maybe the time was right. Hank's boyhood teammate in Little League, Stephen Keener, was now Director and President of Little

League Baseball and Softball and had always invited Hank to come up and enjoy an afternoon of baseball in Williamsport. In the summer of 2011, Hank's hometown team of Lock Haven had climbed the Mt. Everest of Little League and made it to the World Series.

Indeed, it was a risk, as the hills of Williamsport are not sympathetic to anyone, especially those recovering from leukemia, but Hank knew the rewards would be worth the risk. So, on this special day, Hank packed up the car and took his son to his first baseball game—the Little League World Series. "Gabe, get in the car. We're going to Williamsport!"

So were 41,846 other locals from Clinton County, a record at the time before the team from Lewisberry surpassed it twice in the summer of 2015. Hank made the journey with his family to support these new hometown heroes, and when they arrived, he was overwhelmed by what he saw.

"There are more deer than people in Clinton County, but I swear the whole town was there that day. Being a part of that environment, that crowd, the excitement, and being there with my son...I've never been happier to be sitting anywhere with my son—my healthy son. Together, in that stadium, with that crowd, on that afternoon, watching those kids just play baseball...it felt like I got some of those years back. It was the best day of my life! That's the power of the Little League World Series."

Four years later, when Red Land made it to the Little League World Series, it was Gabe who would excitedly pack up the car and declare, "Dad, we're going to Williamsport!" Instead of being a team from Hank's childhood, it was a team from Gabe's, and now years removed from his battle with cancer, years that Connie and Hank never thought they would experience, they realized just how much of an impact this "game" and the kids that play it, had on their lives. It was now a part of them, a counterbalance of positive memories to the years of horrific fear that was all too substantial for far too long. The Little League

World Series allowed them to remember the most glorious stage of Gabe's encounter with leukemia—the recovery.

◆◆◆◆

Ellen Lynn Smith loved Johnny Depp, the Beatles, the color green, and art. Her best friend, Sara Powell, loved softball, music—and Ellen. Both lived in the Red Land area. Together they endured being diagnosed with life-altering illnesses, and though Ellen's cancer of the brain severely trumped Sara's Type I Diabetes, together, they were strong for each other.

As Gabe was recovering, Ellen was being diagnosed. As glorious as the summer of 2011 was for Gabe, the spring of 2011 was equally as horrifying for Ellen. As Gabe concluded his battle, Ellen began hers.

For the next four years, Ellen inspired a support group that stood in awe of the courage and compassion of this child. She touched the lives of everyone with whom she came in contact and left them amazed at the depth of her bravery and humanity. Through treatments, surgeries, cruel moments of brief, misleading recoveries that only lead to heartbreaking relapses, Ellen kept trying to smile.

"She would tell us, 'You all are a lot more worried about this than I am,' and you know what, she was right," whispered her mother, Tracy McLain, tearfully, as she tried to explain just what the little league team from Red Land did for the spirits of the family.

As the boys from Red Land were just beginning their fight, Ellen was at the conclusion of hers. As Coach Tom Peifer was calculating pitching matchups and batting orders, Perry Smith, Ellen's father, and Tracy were preparing to make funeral arrangements for their little girl.

Their home was always open, and friends, family members, representatives from the Four Diamonds who had adopted the Smiths (known in this case as the Hershey Kisses) would stop in regularly to check in on them to see how they were doing. "Some of the most powerful moments I've ever known have been in this house because *this* house was so filled with love. That's not always the case," a torn Hank Angus struggled to recall as we sat down together and reflected on the final months of Ellen's life and the impact it still continues to have on so many that knew her. "I was once told that cancer was like leprosy," Hank said. "They put you in a village and just want you to stay there."

Thankfully, Ellen's village was filled with love, and her supporters came pouring in every chance they could.

Ellen's friend Sara Powell not only visited Ellen daily, but she refused to let their friendship change. She did not put on a façade of strength for her friend—she was genuinely strong. Their friendship did not dwindle; in fact, it solidified and become stronger than it had ever been. They ridiculed each other as much as they did before doctors became as frequent a visitor as cherished friends did.

When Ellen lost her hair, Sara lovingly teased, "At least I can still comb my hair!"

Ellen would affectionately respond to her newly diagnosed diabetic friend, "At least I can still eat cake!" And they would laugh. Often. When Sara would leave, if she left, only then would she cry, but she would never cry in front of Ellen! If her dying friend could be strong, then so, too, could Sara. And she was! She did not always want to be, but for her friend, she would be. That is the power of friendship.

"I never had a friendship with anyone like Sara and Ellen had. Nobody I know does," says Sara's older sister, Emily, as she whimpers while she speaks, trying to summon the same kind of strength her sister found while dealing with Ellen's final days.

As she tells the story of her baby sister's loyalty, the admiration she has for her younger sibling is evident. "Sara told me, 'She'll still be my maid of honor at my wedding. Nobody will ever take that title.'" In the final days of her life, both Emily and Sara struggled to find any reason to be optimistic.   Ellen was losing her battle, and it was becoming abundantly clear that the end was going to be sooner rather than later. On what was supposed to be a joyous day for Emily, the day she got her senior pictures taken, she called Tracy to ask if she could stop by.

"Of course, honey, you should. You should definitely come by. Today. Soon."

When she got there, Emily knew that something was tragically wrong. Nobody there was naïve enough to think that this end was not inevitable, but the finality of death has a way of sneaking up on even the most prepared individuals. The day Ellen died, Sara was with her, and she somehow knew she had to say good-bye to her friend forever.

Therefore, she did. She walked into her room, had her last private moment with her friend, and left. She never saw her friend alive again. "I watched my little sister have to say good-bye to her best friend," said Emily. "A middle school kid shouldn't have to do that." The void that was left in the hearts and souls of Tracy, Perry, Sara, Emily and so many others was one that would leave them aimlessly searching for some greater meaning in this life.

Many felt that exact same way. Following Ellen's death, having a reason to smile just did not exist—neither did a desire to even try to find one. Then, along came the story of the Red Land Little League boys. Soon, the community that came together to mourn found another, more uplifting reason to connect. For at least two hours on game day, people had an escape from the cruelty of Ellen's death.

Rather than dressing oneself in black, they could cover themselves in red, and surround themselves with their neighbors who were doing the same. It was as if for the first time since Ellen's death, if only for a few fleeting moments, the family and their loved ones were able to take a deep breath without feeling the restricting weight of the burden they would now have to carry forever.

Perry and Tracy developed quite an affinity for those 12-year-old boys and the mission they were on. Somehow, their mission to win the World Series became symbolic of their own mission to persevere through the exhausting and catastrophic pain they were feeling since the loss of their daughter.

They could mark their days by the days on which the team played. Days that the boys would play would now provide for those who would otherwise spend their days grieving, a chance to look forward to something, *anything*, if only just a baseball game. They took on the mentality of, "If we can get through the next two days, then the boys will play, and that day will at least have a little bit of happiness. At least that day will be better, so we can tolerate today's heartache for just a little bit longer."

Somehow, cheering for these kids, these boys who were slightly younger than Ellen was when she died, felt appropriate. It shook them from their otherwise mundane, uninspired existence. Mornings of waking up wondering, "Why bother?" could be endured for a while because at least they had something to look forward to other than more sorrow.

As the boys continued to win, Perry and Tracy's respite from sorrow became more frequent. As the boys continued to progress day by day, advancing through the tournament, so, too, did Perry Smith and Tracy McLain advance.

And so, together, with other grieving family members and friends who were equally as devastated, they waited, watched, cheered, and with the help of these 12-year-old boys from Lewisberry, PA, they endured. When the game was over, they returned to the cold reality that awaited them, knowing their daughter was no longer with them, and they would cry again and wait for the team to play again, but they had to hold on for two or three more days.

As they watched the boys continue to win and advance, it provided a glimmer of sunshine in what felt like an endless string of gloomy, cloudy days. When someone feels as if he has nothing to cling to, he will grasp for anything. These boys, this team, became a lifeline for those left abandoned by Ellen's sickness and death.

And though awkward at first, this small sense of relief from the constant agony that had become a permanent fixture in their lives was a welcome diversion from the misery that was now and would forever be all too common. They learned to hold on, one day at a time, from one moment to the next, and the boys helped them to do that.

Nobody could ever suggest that a Little League Baseball team winning a few games could provide compensation to a mother and father, and a whole army of loved ones, for losing a daughter, but when one must explore for even the slightest reason to feel not *good*, but *less miserable*, well, these boys made that exploration less debilitating.

When it was announced on a local newscast that the boys would be joining forces to raise money for the Four Diamonds organization, not a sound could be heard from the home on Oak Hill Road. In that very same room where hundreds of well wishers and strangers, who would ultimately become supporters, gathered to provide even the smallest act of kindness, first for Ellen, and now for her parents, not a sound could be heard.

The boys had just demonstrated one of the greatest gestures of compassion without ever realizing they had done so. Tracy and Emily, who happened to be together when they first heard the news, both reacted in a similar fashion. "We froze. When we first heard the news, we just froze," said Emily, speaking on behalf of Ellen's mother, who still has a hard time recalling those chilling final days of her daughter's life and the impact her death has had.

"I softly cried, but then, then, I just smiled. For the first time since my baby died, I actually *smiled*. They joined our fight. OUR fight. What those kids did and what it meant to us is beyond words." Perhaps it was knowing that another family might possibly benefit from the money that would be raised because of this team.

Tracy knew it was too late to help her own daughter, but somebody else's child could benefit from this team becoming associated with the organization that had done so much for her family. Perhaps it was because she knew that these boys, children themselves, were now showing the same tenderness that her own daughter would have shown.

Maybe it was because she knew that Ellen would be looking down from heaven and smiling, too, on what the kids from her hometown were doing—perhaps as a direct result of her death. The news of Ellen's death reverberated throughout the Red Land community, and now her spirit would continue to live on through the action of these boys.

At that moment, Tracy, Perry, and so many beyond the Central Pennsylvania area had become life-long fans of this little team from Lewisberry—and for reasons far greater than their innate ability to hit or throw a baseball. Tracy felt an amazingly strong personal connection with not only the team, but with each of its members, and she was obliged to give her full support to the team that helped her feel that connection to her daughter again.

◆◆◆◆

Following the team's final game, Perry and Tracy, along with the rest of Central Pennsylvania, knew it was time to return to reality—a *new* normal for them that would not include their daughter. In an effort to ease the financial burden created by their daughter's three-year clash with cancer, Connie Angus took the lead in setting up a fundraiser for the family called "Hope for Ellen."

Though Four Diamonds assisted them by paying every cent of their medical expenses, there were still the normal bills such as mortgage payments, credit card bills, grocery bills, heating bills, and expenses that continued to bombard the family despite their inability to conduct a normal life. Cancer certainly does not take an eight hour break so one can put in a work day, and a child with tumors certainly would not understand 'I gotta go to work.' It just is not an option.

With time missed, so are paychecks, and as understanding as bosses would like to be, there are still bottom lines that have to be met. "We had to do something for them," explained Hank, "so Connie started to plan the event. Unfortunately, she was in no condition [due to her own bout with breast cancer] to do what she was about to try to do." But she did it anyway.

She organized a 5K Run, a chicken BBQ, a chili cook-off, a silent auction, a vendor fair, a bake sale, and a HITATHON. The HITATHON was an idea that stemmed from Sara Powell, who loved softball almost as much as she loved her friend.

Sara struggled mightily to move on from the death of her best friend. So once again, a game was used to provide some comfort to those who were hurting. For Emily, it was not enough. It broke her heart to see her sister meander through her days ever since Ellen had passed. For her, that HITATHON was as much about helping her sister transition to life without her friend as it was celebrating Ellen's life. She reached out to the boys who had provided so much inspiration to so many in the Red Land area. Much to her amazement, they responded.

"The boys would love to be involved," responded Lucy Gnazzo, the team's Public Relation consultant on Facebook to a post Emily had made imploring the boys to make an appearance at the event. Under the brilliant blue skies of a late September Sunday afternoon, the boys arrived, as requested, to be a part of this celebration of Ellen's life.

As they had done at so many of these events, the boys had their pens, ready to sign autographs for their new admirers. This event, though, was much different from any other they had been to. There would be very few autographs, if any at all. Though the boys were more than willing, this event was not about autograph signing. It was about giving back—giving back to the memory of Ellen, to the life of Sara, and to the boys who captured the hearts and imagination of an entire community.

So instead of signing, the boys hit—or at least they tried to. With the help of a pitching machine that peppered fast pitch softballs at its victims, the boys confidently stood in the batter's box ready to inflict the same type of damage they had inflicted on the best twelve-year-old pitchers in the state, country, and the world all summer long. Only, they didn't. They couldn't.

Something about the angle of the pitch, the difference in velocity, the timing, *something* made these softballs almost unhittable to these otherwise dominant hitters. And their feeble attempts to impose their will on the machine delighted the crowd, their teammates (who were thankful not to be in the batter's box, at least for the moment), and the family members who couldn't help but feel just a little bit better amongst all the grief that had enveloped them for so long. It was for many, the perfect remedy.

As the day started to wind down, once again the boys prepared themselves for the line of autograph seekers that would inevitably bombard them. They were all too willing to oblige. Only, they did not have to. As they took their seats behind the red clothed table, THEY were presented with baseballs that had been signed…by the Four Diamonds families that wanted to thank the boys for all they had done for them.

With the assistance of many, the 4LN4EVER (for Ellen, forever) event planned for September 27, 2015, was a raging success for all of those who were involved. It provided laughs, comfort, and perspective. So often, the impact that one person has on another is limited or finite. Such was NOT the case with Ellen Lynn Smith!

What is undeniably irrefutable is the vast positive impact that her life had on so many. Ellen inspired with her courage, comforted with her peace of mind, and lifted the spirits of all of those around her, not by the way she died, but by the way she lived. That is why she drew so many to her…and in their own way, the same could be said about this Little League team and these 12-year-old boys from Red Land, who with the generosity of spirit and their will to use their celebrity for a greater good, helped to console and brighten the lives of those struggling to find hope—like Ellen, and others like her.

16

"DON'T GO DOWN!"

There was no way the kids from Red Land could have lived up to the disproportional frenzy that was now surrounding this team. In their first game, they not only opened the door of opportunity upon their arrival, they knocked it down and tore it off the hinges.

With that, their popularity soared. They were already beloved by those who knew them, but now their notoriety was growing. The coaches were bombarded with requests for appearances on ESPN, most of which they declined. One night when they were not playing, the crew from Baseball Tonight asked them to come down live on set after the game that was being telecasted was complete. "We'd love to come down, but it's past the boys' bedtime." When jokingly asked if it was past the coaches' bedtime, and maybe *they* could at least come down, Coach Peifer explained that *he* was not the story, the kids were. Therefore, he would have to pass.

They did arrange, however, for ESPN's Tim Kurkjian to be able to attend their batting practice the following afternoon ("Or is that during their nap time?"). When he arrived, he was fascinated with the raw power with which the boys hit the ball. "They're just phenomenal," he told the coaches. "I love them!" He then asked if he might be able to throw a session of batting practice to Cole. "Don't worry, I've done this before. I won't hit him or hurt him."

The coaches all looked at each other and started laughing. "Mr. Kurkjian," responded Coach Peifer. "We're not worried about Cole. We're worried about *you!*"

An appreciative Kurkjian understood, but was willing to take the risk and fortunately made it out of the cage unscathed.

◆◆◆◆

Earl Weaver, former Baltimore Orioles manager, once coined the baseball adage that "Momentum is the next day's starting pitcher." If that were true, then Red Land would have every bit of the momentum that they were able to build in their previous game against Missouri.

On the mound that night, Red Land had America's most recent celestial phenomenon, Cole Wagner, whose larger than life power hitting exhibition included two freakishly monstrous home runs, which caught the attention of not only ESPN and its entire viewing audience, but also Mekhi Garrard, the 12-year-old pitcher from Missouri who had had the misfortune of giving up Cole's second home run of the inning, this one being even more majestic and ceremonious than the first—and the first one was, indeed, impressive. Mekhi refused to play the role of victim, and, instead, opted to join the caravan of admirers. And America fell in love with him because of it!

However, tonight, America would get a chance to admire the skills of Cole Wagner, the pitcher, instead of Cole Wagner, the power hitting first baseman from Etters. His first inning was nothing short of brilliant—ten pitches, only one of which was actually put into play. The rest were called strikes, an occasional ball, or were desperately fouled off, more in self-defense than attempts to actually getting a hit.

It seemed like the only figure that was more intimidating and dominant than Cole Wagner, the hitter, was Cole Wagner, the pitcher, and fortunately for Red Land, they would never have to face each other. However, the hitting Cole would never really get a chance to contribute on this night. South Carolina knew they could not do much about having to deal with Cole's dominance on the mound other than just taking their hacks at him, but they were going to drastically limit the chances he had to dominate them at the plate. It speaks to another baseball adage that a team can always intentionally walk a hitter, but they can never get around a dominant pitcher. Since they were not going to be able to avoid Cole Wagner, the pitcher, they were going to do everything they could to avoid Cole Wagner, the hitter.

In the bottom of the inning, the clubbers from Etters showed that the onslaught from Friday night was not going to be an isolated event. As quickly as Cole retired South Carolina in the top of the first, Red Land managed to have the bases loaded in the bottom of the inning when

Braden Kolmansberger (BK) once again found a way to get on base with a perfectly placed dart between the shortstop and third baseman.

As he would be throughout the series, BK was the perfect harbinger for good things to come. Every single time BK was able to get on base, be it by a hit, a walk, or an error, the young man scored. EVERY time. It is a record that can never be broken—nine times on base, nine runs scored. He just had a nose for finding home plate. His single, followed by a four pitch walk to Cole Wagner (a theme that would recur throughout the night) and a five pitch walk to Jaden Henline (this one was not on purpose), filled the sacks with runners and brought cleanup hitter Ethan Phillips to the plate.

Though relatively quiet in the first game, Ethan was the perfect example of just how complete this team really was. Tom Peifer's philosophy revolved around his offense and determining who his nine best hitters were. Then, once the specialty positions were taken care of, he would find a position in the field where they would be successful.

On a team with such notable, big name hitters, Ethan was designated as their "Clean Up" guy for the first two games, and he delivered the first blow. Ethan connected on a curve ball from starting pitcher Bradley Lewis that went right over the bag at third and continued all the way to the wall in left field. By the time Ethan hobbled into second (he tweaked his ankle just a little rounding first), the bases were clear and the Patriots were up 3-0.

Not wanting to allow South Carolina to catch their breath even a little bit, Chayton Krauss drilled a pitch almost to the exact same spot, scoring pinch runner Cam Walter, and it appeared the route was on. After the first five batters, the Patriots had four runs, and with Chayton on second, there were still no outs.

South Carolina was forced to change their pitcher, and Braden Buffington was able to come in and minimize any further damage.

Only Chayton was able to score on an Adam Cramer single, but at the end of the first inning, Red Land had a comfortable lead. Only, nobody informed South Carolina that they were supposed to be playing the role of "the latest victim" on that warm August night in Northern Pennsylvania, and as a result, this game was far from over.

On their way back into the dugout, South Carolina coach Kevin Tumblin delivered a poignant message to his team telling them to "just chip away, chip away" at the Pennsylvania lead. He had no idea how telling his message truly was at the time, but it certainly would become evident as the night progressed.

They attempted to do just that, as Alex Edmondson led off the second inning with a rocket up the middle that Jaden Henline played perfectly by firing over to a stretched out Chayton Krauss. Chayton was able to throw him out by a full step, earning the approval of Karl Ravech in the ESPN booth. "Wow! Jaden Henline is flashing some leather!"

And after Cole sat down the next batter with his third strikeout of the night of the first five batters, Zack Sooy showed exactly what earned him a spot on the Red Land roster with his brilliance in the outfield. When Braden Golinski turned on a 76 mph fastball that one hopped the wall, Zack barehanded the ball and threw a perfect strike to Braden Kolmansberger, who was covering second base in anticipation of a play at the bag. His footwork around the bag was impeccable.

As the ball arrived in plenty of time, the runner from South Carolina seemed almost shocked at the fact that the ball was waiting for him when he arrived. He awkwardly tried to avoid the tag, but BK was able to slap it on him in plenty of time. Any sense of being able to "chip away" in this inning was thoroughly suppressed. The play would land on the ESPN Top 10 List later that evening, the first of two defensive plays that would earn Zack his inclusion on a list that was normally reserved for professionals.

It spoke volumes for the entirety of the team. They were more than just great hitters; they were more than simply dominant pitchers. They were a team that was fundamentally sound and well coached.

Zack Sooy was in that position to make that kind of play because Coach Peifer inserted him there after Ethan Phillips went down in the first inning. It was a move that Tom often made once hitters completed their first mandatory at bat. He would "marry" players at a position where one player would bat and one player would field. It was a perfect strategy that allowed him to utilize the strength of his players and allow them to feel valued, thus enabling them to productively contribute.

◆◆◆◆

It was "easy" to pick the top nine players who stood out because of their ability to hit, pitch, or field, but for the four remaining boys who were selected for the team, there had to be an intangible factor. They had to be a different kind of special player. They had to select kids with the right personality who would bring a positive energy to the dugout despite the fact that they were not in the starting lineup consistently, but still have the competitive hunger to want to be.

Each of them had to be able to fill a specific need—to be that guy who could come in late in the game and steal a base or move a runner over, like Cam Walter. To be the guy who could make a key defensive play in the field as Zack Sooy had just demonstrated. That player had to be the guy who could catch lightening in a bottle and go from the bench to the batter's box and change the course of the game with just one swing of the bat, like Bailey Wirt or Jarrett Wisman were capable of doing.

Each of those remaining players had to be passionate and enthusiastic about filling those roles. Tom Peifer, and the entire Red Land Coaching Staff, could not have selected four better players to meet those needs.

Therefore, though the South Carolina kids tried to adhere to their coach and "chip away" at the 5-0 that the Mid-Atlantic Champions had built, the Patriots simply would not allow them to do that.

◆◆◆◆

The game came to a competitive crawl, and unable to deliver a knockout blow like they had so many games before, Red Land found they were in as competitive a game as they had ever been in.

As the game moved to the fourth inning, Red Land tacked on another run and was still very much in control, up 6-0, and feeling at relative ease with their ace still on the mound and having plenty of pitches left to throw before he hit the 85 pitch max set by Little League. Then, the Southeast Champions from South Carolina somehow managed to unceremoniously scratch a run across the plate.

However, this run was against Cole Wagner, and he had not given up a run all season, so although it was just one run, it was anything but insignificant. To add to the intensity, South Carolina managed to put two other runners on base with nobody out and their best hitter stepping to the plate to face the larger than life left handed presence who had cast his shadow not only over South Carolina all evening, but also over the entire Williamsport area since his arrival.

For the first time ever, things were no longer going *exactly* according to plan and Cole Wagner was in somewhat of a jam. Trying to steady the ship and ease any panic, Cole fired two darts past Edmondson and seemed to settle down as he worked the count in his favor. Looking to deliver the knockout pitch, Cole reached back and threw his hardest pitch of the night—a 78-mile per hour fastball that was heading right over the middle of the plate.

BOOM!

According to the Harvard Database of Useful Biological Numbers, the blink of an eye lasts between 100 and 400 milliseconds—about the same time that hitters have to react to a 78 mph fastball delivered from 46 feet away. It seemed like it took even less time than that for Alex Edmondson to turn the baseball world upside down, and bring a 12-year-old baseball god down from Mt. Olympus.

Cole Wagner was indeed, mortal. Having turned on this blazing fastball, all Cole Wagner, and everybody else in the stadium, could do was watch the ball sail well over the centerfield wall that stood 225 feet away. South Carolina seized control of what seemed like pre-ordained destiny for Pennsylvania.

Suddenly, the crowd of over 32,672 people (32,600 of whom seemed to be there to see another Red Land blowout) sat awkwardly silent. The statement that titanic blast made and the silence that ensued was deafening.

Cole Wagner did not give up many hits, he surely did not give up runs, and the concept of giving up a tape measure home run of this magnitude was as mystical as the Loch Ness Monster or Bigfoot. The collective gasp that came from the parents and fans as that young man rounded the bases was palpable. As astonished as the players and fans were by the blow, Tom Peifer and the Red Land coaching staff knew it was a part of the game, and Alex Edmondson was one heck of a player with the capabilities to do exactly what he had just done.

"Go talk to him, Bret," Tom said to the pitcher's father, but Bret was already on his way out of the dugout. By the time Edmondson was rounding first base, verbally celebrating his euphoric, heavenly moment, Cole's father was heading to the mound to confer with his son.

◆◆◆◆

Mike Tyson is credited with saying, "Everybody's got a plan... until they get punched in the mouth." For the first time ever, Cole Wagner, specifically, and Red Land, in general, had been punched right in the mouth.

Or had they?

"It's a **body blow**. Don't go down!" That was all Bret said to his son. Nothing more. The conference was over so quickly; it was not even picked up by the television cameras. There was nothing tactical discussed, nothing strategic. "Don't Go Down!" He looked his son straight in the eye and spoke to him as any father would who knew his son was rattled. This was not a pitching coach talking to his pitcher. There was no message about finding his release point or extending his follow through for just a little bit longer.

His dad was referencing a conversation that the two had had earlier in the day, when Bret equated this tournament to a heavyweight boxing match. He told his son then that the quick knockouts were over. He informed him that all the teams remaining were champions, and that every remaining game would be a battle of will for who could endure the longest—who could resolve to be the last team standing. This was a father talking to his son, and the message was simple. The meeting out on the mound took less than six seconds. The message, however, would resonate for much longer than that. With that, Bret walked back into the dugout.

Perhaps, while he turned and walked back to the dugout, he thought about all the body blows he had endured over the course of his baseball life—the broken leg that prevented him from being a first round draft pick right out of high school (*body blow*).

The seemingly endless grind he tried to endure through the minor leagues (*body blow*) going from one no-name town to the next trying to figure out some way to figure out how to get to the big leagues (*body blow*).

The trade from the Cardinal organization to the Oakland A's that he truly believed was a death sentence for his chances to become a major league pitcher (*body blow*).

His inability to deal with failure for the first time in his life and the persistent feeling that he was not fulfilling his destiny, or reaching his potential (*body blow, body blow, body blow*).

Bret Wagner went down. He never got back up.

He could not allow that to happen to his son.

"It's a body blow. Don't Go Down!"

Every pitcher gives up home runs, but not every pitcher responds to it well. It took three pitches to see if that message had been received. Cole readied himself for his next pitch, the first pitch after giving up the first home run he had ever fallen victim to in his life.

"Don't!" Strike one, swinging at a 77 mile per hour fastball.

"Go!" Strike two, swinging at a 75 mile per hour fastball.

"DOWN!" Strike three blistered by so fast that all the boy on the other end of the pitch could do was watch it smash into Kaden's glove. "That one stung!" Kaden confessed months later.

Cole had clearly regained his equilibrium and displayed a level of poise and maturity that 12-year-old boys simply do not normally possess. After walking the next batter, and realizing that he was trying to strike out the side all at once, Cole settled in and struck out the final two batters of the destructive fourth inning.

He did his best to walk rather than stagger back to the dugout, but the damage had clearly been done. Cole knew it, his teammates knew it, and so did the 36,000 fans that had piled into Williamsport that evening. Every bit as significant, if not more so, South Carolina knew it.

In the eyes of the kids in the other visiting dugout, Cole Wagner was now a mere mortal, an equal, and just another pitcher who threw hard. He was no longer untouchable, not even unhittable. Alex Edmondson had proven that—and his teammates now believed it.

Moreover, this team, this collective group of bruisers who battered balls over fences all up and down the East Coast with ridiculous ease, was suddenly, and for the first time ever, vulnerable. Red Land still had the lead, but South Carolina had all the momentum, and had been able to cast doubts in people's minds.

The bottom of the 4th only increased the confidence for the team from South Carolina. With Terrance Gist rolling through the bottom part of the Red Land line up, he faced Braden Kolmansberger to lead off the fourth. Red Land wanted nothing more than to take back control of the game, and BK was the perfect guy to lead off the inning. However, BK went down looking on a nasty curve ball from Terrance, who had now struck out four Patriot batters in a row.

However, South Carolina seemed to be playing two games simultaneously, the one they were presently in, and the one they may have to play next if they were not able to complete the comeback vs. Red Land.

After 23 pitches, Terrance Gist was removed from the game, keeping him eligible to pitch the next day should they lose. Red Land was all too pleased to see his work that evening come to completion. Throughout the Little League World Series, and even in Bristol, Connecticut, whenever games were televised and the coaches had microphones clipped to them, Tom, Bret, and JK would pass notes to each other in the dugout when they did not want their voices to be picked up by the cameras.

They were strategic notes that they would pass to each other, such as scouting reports on hitters that were coming up, or possible scenarios that they were thinking as far as pinch hitters, possible pitching changes they were contemplating, or any other information that the three men wanted to keep among themselves. With Terrance Gist exiting the mound, a perfect note that might have been written at that moment would have been, "I'm not sorry to see him go!" or "That Helps Us!!!"

As Ryan Soug entered the game, the first batter he would face was Cole Wagner. Clearly following the strategy of his coach, one with which very few would argue, he threw his first three pitches safely off the plate trying to minimize the damage Cole Wagner could inflict upon them. The catcher was situated so far outside that he was squatting more behind the right-handed batter's box than he was behind the plate.

However, on his fourth pitch, though still very much outside and clearly a ball, Cole attempted to extend his arms and made a vicious swing on the ball, actually making contact. As the ball flew into the third base bleachers, the pitcher from South Carolina knew he had gotten away with a pitch that was far too close to Cole's smash zone. He would not make that mistake again. The final pitch of the at bat was safely thrown low and away, not catching any of the plate, and falling safely into the catcher's glove for ball four.

With a runner on first, Soug was able to strike out equally as dangerous Jaden Henline and got Ethan Phillips to ground out to short for an inning ending fielder's choice. South Carolina had quietly retired the most dangerous part of the Red Land line up and was ready to come back to the plate and "chip away" at the two run lead that Pennsylvania was desperately clinging to.

The 5th inning was relatively quiet as Cole Wagner seemed to fully regain his composure and blew away the first batter of the inning on three pitches and got the second batter to fly harmlessly to left field. However, when Ryan Chapman drilled Cole's 76th pitch of the game back up the middle for a base hit, Terrance Gist stepped to the plate representing the tying run.

In what evolved into an epic individual nine-pitch skirmish between two heavyweights, Cole Wagner eventually struck out Terrance on his 85th pitch of the night. After the third strike, Terrance jogged back to the dugout with a smile that only a boy would have after being struck out—clearly riveted and amused by the confrontation he had just had. Though Cole had won this confrontation, there was a greater significance to the at bat.

The nine pitches it took for Cole to dispose of Terrance meant that Cole Wagner's pitching night was finished, and with Alex Edmondson leading off the top of the 6th, it would be incumbent upon somebody else to get him out. That somebody was Jaden Henline.

But before Jaden would come in and attempt to secure the Red Land victory, the Patriots had the bottom of the 5th to try and pad their lead and somehow try to re-capture a little bit of the momentum that they once enjoyed.

It did not happen. Leadoff batter Chayton Krauss went down swinging, and when Bailey Wirt made it to first on an error by second baseman David Mershon, South Carolina would use that moment to solidify the very bond that had brought them back into this contest.

Clearly upset by the fact the ball had gotten under his glove, David stood at second base visibly dejected. Rather than let a moment such as that fester for a teammate, catcher Braden Golinski walked to the pitcher's mound not to speak to his pitcher, but to pick up his second baseman. He walked right past Ryan Soug and, instead, shouted encouragement to his crestfallen teammate. In another display of true camaraderie, Terrance Gist, the boy who struck out to end the previous inning, came running in all the way from centerfield to put his arm around Mershon and offer his reassurance that the team would get past his error.

The companionship and concern shown by those teammates for each other that night, from the time they had fallen behind 6-0 to their present dilemma, captured once again the essence of this venue. Children so often provide adults with spontaneous illustrations of all that could be right in this world if only more adults acted more like children and less like adults.

Imagine a world where instead of placing blame and deflecting accountability, teammates came together in our most vulnerable moments and solidified their allegiance. That was exactly what Terrance and Braden did for David Mershon.

When Cam Walter lofted one to Alex Edmondson at shortstop, it turned into a double play, as Bailey's Wirt's aggressive base running proved costly and ended the inning. For the first time all season, Red Land had gone three consecutive innings without scoring a run. The tension, the uneasiness, and the pressure was mounting for these kids. They were playing in front of 32,000 people who had come to see them not only win, but continue to dominate in the same fashion that they had all summer.

South Carolina was preparing for its last at bat, and Alex Edmondson, the young man who had single-handedly turned this game around with one swing of his bat back in the fourth inning, would be the first batter who Jaden Henline would face. Red Land was clearly facing a challenge they had not yet seen all summer.

On any other team, Jaden Henline would be considered an ace, but he clearly did not have the same velocity, ferocity, or mystique, that the boy who threw in the first five innings did—and South Carolina sensed that. The first two pitches Jaden threw to Alex were curveballs. Knowing that Edmondson would be cranked up to hit another blast, Coach Wagner tried to keep him off balance. That is exactly what Jaden did.

The second pitch was lofted dangerously high into right field, so much so, that it allowed second baseman Braden Kolmansberger the opportunity to run under it and attempt to make a play. At the same time, right fielder Jake Cubbler, playing understandably deep for Edmondson, had plenty of time to run under it. Though he was a safe distance away, centerfielder Adam Cramer was also able to be in the neighborhood when the ball began to descend. As Braden ran out, clearly intending to attempt to catch the ball, Cubbler ran to it, determined to do the exact same thing. Too many times in baseball, these types of moon shots have ended in disaster—this, too, had that potential.

However, Jake Cubbler would not be distracted. Jake, whose focus was as sharp as anyone's on the team, who was once described by one of his coaches as, "the essence of a kid who wanted to be a ballplayer and had the will and determination to become one," steadied himself under the ball, and as Braden went to the ground while back peddling on the ball, Jake maintained his footing and calmly secured the first out into his glove.

Their first out was the biggest—but not their hardest. The next batter, pitcher Ryan Soug, was peppered with fastballs, off speed pitches, and even a quick pitch to keep the South Carolina batters from finding any kind of rhythm against Jaden. It worked. Jaden was able to strike out Soug and get the second out of the inning.

As ESPN began to run their credits, the Red Land faithful rose to their collective feet in anticipation of a victory. After all, the greatest threats in the South Carolina batting order were now in the rear view mirror.

On the third pitch of what appeared to be the last batter of the game, Braden Golinski rolled a dribbler that got past an outstretched Henline. Henline deflected the ball, which was skillfully bare-handed by Kolmansberger, who then fired it across his body to first in an attempt to get the hustling Golinski, who was barreling down the first base line. In what appeared to be the last out of the game, the Red Land coaches and players began moving up the dugout steps and onto the field.

However, with the mistiming of the play and the combination of the velocity of the throw with the short distance between Cole and Braden, the ball popped out of the first baseman's glove, and South Carolina, somehow, still had life.

"They stay alive!" declared Karl Ravech. Though their heartbeat was anemic, it was a heartbeat nonetheless, and South Carolina would turn that into a new life.

That hit, ruled a single, was followed by another single, and then 92 pound David Mershon, who was last seen fighting back tears at second base when he made an error back in the 5th that he thought would cost his team a run, stepped to the plate.

What ensued was nothing short of a brilliant display of heart, grit, and determination between two competitors that refused to yield even an inch of sacred ground. Three straight perfectly placed fastballs put Henline ahead in the count at one ball and two strikes. The fifth pitch was a ball, evening the count. The sixth pitch was fouled off to left field, and when Zack Sooy, who appeared to be screened by the left field umpire, could not make the catch, David was still alive. Pitch seven was a check swing on a fastball up in the zone, that, on appeal, was confirmed a check swing—the count was full. Pitch eight found the left field bleachers, and after Henline tried a quick pitch on his ninth delivery to Mershon, which was again fouled off down the left field line, the count was still full. As he blessed himself before he stepped into the box for the tenth pitch of the at bat, David Mershon worked himself a base on ball. The bases were now loaded.

"What a great at bat by Mershon!" announced former big league pitcher Kyle Peterson, who was now doing play by play.

All of the tension, all of the pressure that was so palpable in the 4th and 5th inning had returned to the stadium, and along with it, it brought urgency and crisis. As the crowd roared for both sides with a ferocity and desperation—one side for one more out, the other for some kind of a hit—it was hard to keep in perspective that these were 12-year-old boys.

The boys' younger siblings sitting up in the stands felt that same tension. Landon Henline, who was only ten and was watching his brother on the mound do whatever he could to preserve this game for what not only seemed like his team, but his entire hometown, began to cry. "My brother can't concentrate! They need to be quiet! Everybody needs to be quiet!"

That request was futile. The crowd had worked itself up to a fury that was part excitement, part panic, and there was no quick relief to be found.

The next at bat for Brock Myers was not nearly as long and dramatic as the previous at bat. Brock, who came in as a pinch hitter in the 5th and was immediately struck out on three pitches, sent the very first pitch from Henline down the right field line and over the head of Jake Cubbler. With that swing, Brock was able to not only clear the bases and expunge the lead that Red Land had once comfortably possessed, but he also eradicate the chokehold that this team from Etters had had on every other competitor in Williamsport.

When the dust settled, Brock Myers was standing on third and the scoreboard in left center read 7-6 in favor of South Carolina! With the air of invincibility shattered, the next batter, Gage Landon, knocked Brock in for what seemed like an insurance run, and the entire stadium, with the exception of maybe 100 South Carolinians who were donned in gold along and behind the third base dugout, stood silently aghast. It appeared that Rome had indeed fallen.

Jaden's mother, feeling helpless while sitting in the stands watching her son struggle to get the final out and having to endure the agony on an entirely different level, felt completely helpless. "I wanted to go grab him off the mound and take him home with me and just comfort him. I was preparing my 'mom speech' in my head and going over it and thinking, 'What can I possibly SAY to him to make this all better when it's over?' I couldn't imagine how I would leave him there in Williamsport and go home for the night after a game like that—after a loss like that."

With a runner on first, and still two outs, Jaden Henline had to figure out a way to get the next batter out, as behind him, Terrance Gist and Alex Edmondson loomed. Somehow, Jaden found the composure and strength to stagger to his feet and strike the next man out. The inning was *finally* over...but the game was not.

As the South Carolina kids sprinted to their dugout, the Red Land kids quivered to theirs. Clearly shaken by the unfolding of events, the boys could not hide their disappointment. They could not even find the strength to fake it.

They cried. It was not one or two kids; it was the overwhelming majority of them. Despite the hype, their physical maturity, their talent, and their strength, inside each and every one of them, they were still young boys—and at that moment their hearts were breaking, their dream was being shattered.

And not only did they feel like they were letting down their teammates and their coaches, who for three of them were also their fathers, they felt like they were letting down their community, who had grown to love them and had come to support them. So, as boys do when their hearts break, they cried.

"STOP CRYING!" Manager Tom Peifer met them in the dugout, and there was not an ounce of consolation in his voice. "I said... STOP CRYING! Do you hear me? All of you, right now, stop crying! We still have to hit! WE STILL GET TO HIT!!! This game is NOT over. It's not! They still have to get us out—three times!!! You want to be champions—then start acting like champions! Stop feeling sorry for yourselves! Stop looking defeated, like we've already lost! We still get to hit!!!" His voice was raised to a feverish level that the boys had never heard before. Its intensity and sense of urgency was not one of panic, but of purpose.

And then he turned to his son. "AND IT STARTS WITH YOU!"

Kaden, who also was guilty of crying and was the youngest player on the team and knew how much his dad had invested in the team to make this season possible, was the lead off hitter for the bottom of the 6th inning. He knew how much he had invested to become the catcher that he now was, and the magnitude of the moment as he walked off the field into the dugout was more than he could take. Now, his father was confronting him in front of all of his teammates, in front of all of Williamsport, in front of what seemed like the world.

"...IT STARTS WITH YOU! DON'T GO DOWN!!!"

"I've never seen Tom like that," said assistant coach Bret Wagner. "Never. But it's exactly what the team needed at the exact moment that they needed it."

Coach JK confirmed that it was a different Tom Peifer than the one that was usually a bit calmer. "Tom's speech in the 6th inning was one of the most inspiring things I've ever witnessed. It was not what he said, cause I'm not sure what the words were. It was the way he said it—the *passion* that he had when he said it. I know it had an impact on the kids."

Kaden gathered himself. He defiantly removed his catching gear, grabbed his bat, and prepared to go hit. "Don't Go Down, Kaden. Don't Go Down!" He muttered the words to himself as he went to the plate.

In the stands, Amy Peifer prepared for her son's monumental at bat. "Karsyn [Kaden's little sister] turned to me and said, 'Don't worry Mom, Cole's up.' I told her, 'Not yet honey, Kaden's batting!' She just turned away and went, 'Ohhhhhhhh!'"

Americans adore their heroic figures from a safe, disengaged distance, but more than their heroes, America admires and loves the underdog. The great American story is not about a boy born into prosperity; it is the tale of the man who overcomes hardships in his life to ultimately, and finally, experience success.

The greatest heroic characters ever created in literature are those with the grit and resolve of Tom Joad from *The Grapes of Wrath* or Atticus Finch from *To Kill A Mockingbird*, not the wealth and entitlement of Jay Gatsby. Though none of these boys had ever heard of any of these characters, they were quickly, and much to their chagrin, thrown into the role of underdog.

It had taken three pitches for Cole to show his father he had heard every word he had said out on that mound. It took Kaden Peifer, the boy who dazzled the big-leaguers everywhere with his exaggerated leg kick, the boy who symbolized the brashness of this team with his boisterous whacks and "consequences and failure be darned" mentality at the plate, the exact same number of pitches to send *his* father the exact same message that Cole had.

"Don't Go Down," thought Kaden. "Don't Go Down!"

Strike one, looking. ("Don't").
Perhaps there were still a few tears in Kaden's eyes.

Pitch two was a ball. ("Go"). His composure was returning.

Pitch three. Fastball, right down the middle. ("DOWN!!!").

Kaden kicked a little higher, swung a little harder (if that was even possible), and he hit that ball as hard as he could. As the ball cleared the wall in right field and settled into the *Red Sea*, Kaden let out a scream as intense as his father's speech was only moments earlier.

As fast as Kaden Peifer rounded those bases, his teammates were equally as quick to get out of that dugout and greet him at home. Dylan Rodenhaber could not even wait until he touched home plate, he greeted him almost halfway down the third base line.

It was the first hit that Pennsylvania had had since the second inning, and it reminded everybody in the stadium just how dangerous this team was. Kaden was their eighth batter—he would be a cleanup hitter on just about any other team. Here, from the eighth spot, he served as the catalyst for the greatest comeback this team would ever have, if they could keep it going.

As the collective crowd took a huge breath for the very first time since the Edmondson home run in the 4th inning, Red Land reminded every one of those 32,672 fans who filled the bleachers, and occupied every piece of land on the lower and upper hills, who wedged themselves behind the concession tents and walls so they could see at least part of the field, just how good this team was.

Kaden's home run kick started (pun clearly intended) the comeback that everyone now knew was going to happen. Red Land still trailed 8-7, but essentially, the game was over—only the details needed to be filled in. As that ball sailed over the right field wall and into the Williamsport night, the swagger that had been hijacked from this team returned. Now that they got it back, it would not be taken for granted ever again.

"It was awesome!" said Kaden, who swung so hard his back foot was actually off the ground when he made contact with the ball. "I don't know how else to describe it. It was one of the best feelings I've ever had in my life."

Adam Cramer, who served as the team leadoff hitter for part of the season but was moved to the bottom of the line up, not as a demotion, but as a means of being able to have a second high percentage batter hit in front of Cole because of his propensity to turn over the batting order, stepped to the plate. It was another brilliant move by Tom and the coaching staff, as it would pay dividends throughout their time in Williamsport. Adam did what so many leadoff batters do so well; he drew a walk, which was followed by a double to left-center from Braden Kolmansberger.

Though normally stoic, Adam could not contain his emotion as he stood on second representing the winning run. The next batter was

Cole Wagner, but South Carolina, unlike his previous at bats, was not going to disguise their intent to avoid Cole's prowess in the batter's box. In came David Clark, the fifth pitcher that South Carolina would use that day, and he immediately followed his coach's directive.

"Listen to me," the Coach told his new pitcher, "we're throwing him four balls, okay!"

Kevin Tumblin brought his infield in to give them the best chance to throw down a runner at the plate and prepared his team for a showdown not with Cole Wagner, but with the next batter, Jaden Henline.

The intentional walk complete, Jaden came to the plate with the bases loaded. Just a half an inning earlier, Jaden had felt the burden of failed expectations lowered upon his shoulders. However, baseball, more often than life, usually provides opportunities for redemption. Jaden Henline intended to take full advantage of this opportunity.

Coach Peifer's message still ringing in his ears, Jaden prepared himself for atonement. "Don't Go Down, Jaden!"

"Don't." Ball one, way outside. So much so, it took a great stop by Golinski to save a run from scoring.

"Go." Ball two. Another pitch outside.

"DOWN!" Jaden Henline turned on a pitch and ripped it down the left field line. It one-hopped the wall and allowed the tying and winning runs to cross the plate.

As the boys ran chaotically onto the field, they were torn as to which direction they should go. Some ran toward Adam Cramer and BK, who had scored the tying and winning runs. Others attempted to catch Jaden, who was still rounding the bases. Finally, the boys converged in a dog pile at third base and took turns hugging, jumping, and carrying on in complete euphoric jubilation.

As they peeled away the layers of teammates from the mass of happy, victorious boys, they began shaking the hands of their rivals from South Carolina, for whom they all had a newly formed and well-earned respect. As they walked through the line shaking hands with one another, David Mershon and Jaden Henline embraced as competitors do after battle, so, too, did Terrance Gist and Cole Wagner. It was the only time all night that Terrance could be seen without a smile on his face.

"I learned a lot about myself, my son, and his teammates that night," explained Stephanie Henline. "I learned how much of a fighter he really was and just how special it was for him being able to play on a team like this with the type of teammates that he had. I knew all that already, but somehow I had forgotten. All those boys were just so together when they got down. They picked each other up. They never gave up, not on the game, and not on each other."

Though she was referring to Red Land, she could have just as easily been referring to South Carolina as well. Facing a seemingly insurmountable deficit, down 6-0 to the impermeable ace of the Red Land staff, they, too, never gave up, not on the game, not on each other.

"When I saw them in that pile, and Jaden at the bottom of it, I just thought to myself how lucky Jaden was to be a part of such a special group of kids. It made me so proud to be a parent—and I know every other mom and dad in the stands that night felt the exact same way."

Again, the lines began to blur as to which sets of parents she could have been referring to. If there was ever a time for a moral victory, for honor in defeat, the kids from South Carolina certainly had earned that distinction. They could walk off that field with their heads held just as high as the kids from Red Land; they were every bit as valiant, every bit as resolute—they just didn't score as many runs.

That night, the boys went back to the dorms, unsure which was their more dominant emotion: exhilaration or exhaustion. Eventually, exhaustion was victorious. As Coach JK came in to read the next day's agenda, he revised the one he originally created. This one was a little simpler. It read:

Monday, Aug. 24th

Eat When You Are Hungry,
Drink When You Are Thirsty,
Sleep When You Are Tired.
           —Well Done Boys.

Of all the lines that have been written about the legendary competition that took place in Williamsport that evening, all the articles, all the Facebook posts, no better words could have been written than the last three by Coach Kolmansberger. Once again, the ambiguity as to which boys he was referring to became evident, except this time, it was intentional.

17

"LUNCH WITH MY SON... AND AN ICE CREAM CONE"

Lisa Cubbler had been away from her son far too long. Not only had the boys been away from their homes for over twenty days (22 to be exact), but also the quality time that families were able to spend with each other was limited and pretty much non-existent. As the pressure continued to build, and possibly even mount, on the Mid-Atlantic Champions to become National Champions, Lisa decided to have lunch with her 13-year-old son. She wanted to so much that she took a day off from work and headed to Williamsport.

It was an off day for the boys, meaning they did not have a game, but they did have practice and time in the cages. Pitchers had their bullpen sessions, and coaches had their daily meetings—with each other, with the media, and with the officials from Williamsport.

Despite the increasing demands on the members of the team for appearances, Lisa would not be denied.

"It's not like it was hard on Jake, he loved it. It was like having twelve brothers to live with for three weeks! But I missed my son, and I wanted to spend some time with him—just him and me, the way we normally did every summer." Lisa is a schoolteacher in the Mechanicsburg School District and looked forward to the extra time she was able to spend with her son while the two of them enjoyed summer vacation together. Now, with Jake serving as the team's starting right fielder (or left, depending on who was pitching), the time that mother and son were able to spend together was very limited.

Much to her dismay, upon arrival she realized that taking him off the premises was not as simple as she had hoped. Their lunch plans, therefore, were adjusted to the concession stands. As they started to walk from one end of the complex (where Jake's dorm was located) to the other, a crowd gathered around the two. Lisa could feel the eyes staring at them and heard the whisperings of a few asking, "Which one is that?" or "That's Jake, that's Jake!"

Some of the more daring children even approached him. It wasn't that Jake was wearing his jersey. In fact, the only form of identification he had on was his LLWS Lanyard that players were required to wear to ensure their entrance into the more secured locations around the complex. However, that was enough, and at this point, every member of the Mid-Atlantic team was identifiable and sought after. "Jake, Jake, can I get your autograph?"

His head turned toward his mom, awaiting her approval, and she immediately gave it. "Go ahead, honey, I'll wait." Little did she realize she would be waiting such a long time. As the crowd grew, Jake graciously signed for everybody who asked. Only then did the two begin their walk again. Only this time, Jake took off his lanyard and put it in his pocket, hoping for just a hint of anonymity. He put his arm out, Mom locked hers in his, and mother and son continued their walk through the pathways around Lamade Stadium.

"I would have never guessed, would have never suspected, that my son would get that kind of attention. I mean, he was an outfielder! He wasn't a pitcher. He wasn't a home run hitter. But they *knew* him. It was unbelievable," she said. As they continued their walk, they stopped for ice cream and sat on the hill to watch the game that was being played at the time. When Lisa turned, she saw Dylan Rodenhaber surrounded by approximately fifteen adoring fans, mostly middle school girls, laughing and basking in the spotlight that was shining down on him at the moment. Again, her son looked at his mom and just kind of smiled.

"We're not having lunch today are we, Jake?" she rhetorically asked. "Go ahead, be with your friend." And off he went. Before he reached the group, Jake turned around and gave his mom a kiss and hug.

"Thanks for the ice cream, Mom, and thanks for coming up. I really enjoyed this," he told her as he turned back around, put his lanyard back on, and headed toward his teammate.

"So did I, Jake. So did I." She was not even sure that he had heard her.

As she watched him walk away, a little tear formed in her eye. Her little boy was growing up, not only in front of the entire nation on ESPN, but also right in front of her. And she was not quite sure which was tougher to watch.

◆◆◆◆

Stephanie Henline had a similar experience with her son when she was able to "steal" him away from the spotlight—if only for a little while on a rare off day for the team from Red Land. After providing the heroics in the South Carolina games, Jaden Henline was becoming the face of the Mid-Atlantic team. His smile was fit for the cover of any magazine, and his boyish good looks were breaking young girls' hearts all over the country. Wanting to spend time with her son, Mrs. Henline packed her youngest son, Landon, in the car and decided to take a trip to Williamsport in hopes of some quiet time with two of her boys.

After meeting Jaden outside his dorm, his mom greeted him with the kind of hug that only a mother could give, and it was warmly received.

"Ice Cream!" said his mom, "Let's go get some ice cream!" There is nothing more American or traditional than an ice cream cone at a baseball game on a hot summer afternoon. That was the exact kind of afternoon Stephanie Henline wanted to have with her boys.

As the three walked down the sidewalks of the stadium, Mom stood arm and arm with her two escorts, twelve-year old Jaden, and ten-year old Landon. No mom could have been prouder or more excited to spend the day with her boys. Soon into the walk, she felt a thousand eyes upon her. The whispers turned to screams, the screams to giggles, and soon it was no longer just the three of them walking to go get ice cream. She could feel the crowd slowly starting to close in on them, letting their desire to get closer overtake their inclination to be polite.

"I'll go get the ice cream, you guys stay here," she told her sons, trying to deny what was really going on around her. With that, she turned and went to the concession stand to order one chocolate and two vanilla cones (with sprinkles, of course).

When she returned, her son was surrounded by teenage girls who wanted their pictures taken with #12, their programs signed, or a "selfie" with Jaden. Jaden politely excused himself after signing, posing, and speaking with everybody who was around him.

As the first wave dismissed, word must have traveled fast that Jaden Henline was behind the grandstand giving autographs and taking pictures. As the three walked, talked, laughed, and shared their perspectives of all the events that had happened already, a second mob began to form around the 12-year-old heartthrob.

"Oh, my God!!! It's Jaden!!! It's JADEN!!!!" They would yell in a pitch that is only possible to be reached by a young teenage girl.

"Jaden, can we have your autograph?"
"Jaden, can we take a picture with you?"
"Jaden, can you sign my shirt, my ball, my program, my hand?"
"Oh, my God!!! It's Jaden!!!"

Each time, Jaden would smile, hand his ice cream cone to his mother, and graciously meet their request. He would smile for their cell phones, he would sign their items, and he would thank them for their support. "Thanks for being a fan." Having heard that, they would jump up and down, unable to contain their excitement.

In between the requests, Jaden would turn to his mom and try to take a bite of his ice cream cone, but really, it was a futile battle—the hot August sun, and the fans, were winning. Stephanie Henline stood back almost in awe of her son the entire time, marveling at just how accommodating, cordial, and courteous he genuinely was. He never seemed annoyed, never seemed rattled, never seemed unappreciative of everything that was happening around him.

When the flock had finally moved on, Jaden turned to his mom, who now stood with an empty cone in her hand and a melted piled of ice cream on the ground beneath her.

"Sorry, Mom," Jaden said with the same glorious smile that was making him fans all over the country.

"Sorry? You do not have to be sorry, Jaden. I'm proud of you." She looked at her son. He seemed so grown up. She wondered when that had happened. She also wondered if she would ever have him back all to herself ever again—to just be able to have an ice cream cone. She smiled. She took his arm, she took her youngest son's arm as well, and together the three of them walked back to the dorm—two of them full of ice cream, and one not so much so, but all three of them smiling like only a Henline can smile.

18

THE ARTIST

As much as the Little League World Series relies on having stars, the baseball virtuosos like Cole Wagner, Alex Edmondson and Terrence Gist from South Carolina, and Jarrett Tadlock from Pearland, Texas, whose testosterone has kicked in at an earlier age than their competition, the beauty and allure of this tournament flourishes on the emergence of the unsung heroes from around the world who stand barely over five feet tall and just about 100 pounds. The little guys, the common boys—those children that remind us of who we were when we were twelve are the kids who sometimes become the most memorable. For most of us, it is hard to relate to a kid like Cole who grows seven inches in a year and stands taller than some adults may ever stand and is stronger than many can imagine.

Instead, we are drawn to the kids like Mekhi Garrard, who at 5'1" and 85 pounds had one of the most symbolic moments of the tournament with his priceless reaction to the mammoth grand slam he gave up to Cole Wagner on Opening Night. By the end of the two weeks, that replay would be shown as often (if not more) than any highlight that was made, as it captured everything that the world embraced about these kids. Of all the highlights that emerged from the 2015 Little League World Series, this may prove to be the most enduring.

But there were others: Kids like five-foot, 92-pound David Mershon whose ten-pitch at bat for South Carolina just three days earlier contained all the drama and grit from which legends are made. So, too, was the at bat that followed by five-foot two-inch, 98 pound Brock Myers, whose bases-clearing triple gave South Carolina a lead, which at the time they believed they would never surrender. Additionally, the world was just three days away from meeting Ryan Farmer who would make his own contribution to Little League lore with his performance in the United States Championship Game.

But *this* night, in the third game Red Land would be playing in the Little League World Series, would belong to Red Land pitcher Adam Cramer.

Adam stood at a very average height of 5 foot 4 and weighed a very ordinary 122 pounds. However, on *this* night, Adam Cramer would be anything but ordinary.

On *this* night, Adam Cramer would become an *artist*. His canvas of choice would be a series of curve balls and change ups, mixed in with just enough fastballs that would defy the prognosticators and awe the baseball world as he painted the corners and led the Patriots, not in a traditional slugfest, but in a pitcher's duel that would not only dazzle the more than 35,000 fans that had come to watch these boys on this night, but baseball purists everywhere.

If Cole Wagner had the dominance, power, and intimidation of Nolan Ryan, then Adam Cramer had the grace, poise, and precision of Greg Maddux. Cole had the intimidating intensity and exuded a rare kind of ferocity on the mound, at the plate, and in his daily activities that only enhanced the first impression one correctly conjured when bearing witness to this athletic anomaly. As for Adam, he did everything with a smile, not a scowl.

When fans watched Adam hit, field, run, or pitch, they confirmed that they were indeed watching a boy *play* a game rather than an adversary trying to win one. He—It was nearly impossible not to like a kid who went by the alias of "Ace McSizzle," a nickname given to him by teammate Cam Walter because the #11 (a family favorite) that Adam wore looked like two strips of bacon. However, behind that marvelous little boy smile that revealed a pair of heart-warming dimples and an affectionate nickname, there existed the heart of a champion and the spirit of a bona fide warrior.

Pitching Coach Bret Wagner still marvels at the accuracy that Adam possessed at such a young age, "I used to go down to the bullpen to keep him sharp when he wasn't pitching in games, and the more I did, the more I noticed that no matter what I called and where I told him to throw it, I never moved my glove. It was like a video game. Bang. Bang. Bang. Strike. Strike. Strike. I've never seen anything like it, but as I've said before, 'I never really learned how to be able to pitch like that.' Adam did..."

But this setting was different. This was not a bullpen session; this was Williamsport, Pennsylvania, and the crowd that he would be pitching in front of would be exponentially larger than any crowd that Adam had ever pitched in front of before.

Adam embraced that kind of spotlight. He relished the chance to show what he could do in front of a crowd like this, with lights this bright, and stakes this high. "Sometimes the stage gets bigger than the talent level," said assistant coach JK Kolmansberger, "but with Adam, we never worried that that would be the case."

Adam once told Coach Kolmansberger that he only wanted to pitch in the really *big* games. He craved them. There certainly was no grander setting than now: prime time television on a Wednesday night on ESPN for the right to play for a National Championship. But for that to happen, Adam's absolute best would be needed as they faced a Pearland, Texas, team that was flying high off their major victory over heavily favored California just three days earlier.

Since the teams had arrived, the biggest discussion had been the power hitters from Bonita, California. If there was any team that could match the brute force of Pennsylvania, it was California, but Texas had stifled their hitters, and they had not used their best pitcher to do it. With that pitcher available for this contest, Texas believed they had the ability to stifle the sluggers from Pennsylvania as well.

When the question was asked as to whom was the best pitcher the Red Land boys faced in Williamsport, their response was consistent:

"Tadlock."
"Jarrett Tadlock."
"Oh yeah, Tadlock without a doubt."
"It was definitely Jarrett Tadlock."

Tadlock threw hard; he had a great breaking ball; he varied his speeds; and he knew when to do it. He was for Texas what Cole Wagner was for Pennsylvania, and he would be pitching on this night against Adam.

Adam, unlike the two previous Red Land starting pitchers, Jaden and Cole, did not use velocity as his means to pitching success. Adam's fastball maxed out at about 63 miles per hour (no comparison to Cole Wagner, who was clocked as high as 78 mph, or even Jaden's at 72). Adam's 63 miles per hour equated to a modest 82 miles per hour from a big league mound and was very much considered average speed for pitchers at this elite level.

Adam was a composer, a craftsman, a true maestro in every sense of the word, rather than just a kid who threw hard. His change up would come in a full ten mph slower than his fastball, and he rarely, if ever, left a curve ball hanging over the middle of the plate, and he could place the ball wherever he wanted it. "They were always at the bottom of the zone. His pitches, when he's really on, are simply unhittable!" said Coach Bret.

"His arm slot was always the same, so batters had no idea what pitch was coming," added his manager, Tom Peifer, who was equally as generous with his praise of Adam and his propensity for being brilliant on the mound.

There was still somewhat of an unknown factor with Adam and how he would perform in Williamsport though. Many wondered exactly who would get the nod to pitch in a game of this magnitude, but to Coach Peifer it was never a question. As he did before Game One, when the single biggest decision he would make throughout this entire tournament was made (to pitch their #2 pitcher instead of their #1), Coach Peifer consulted his bracket. It was Game three, the «A» in the JCAC format that he created. That meant Adam was his pitcher.

It was the right strategy for Game One, paid huge dividends in Game Two, and there was no reason to believe that it would not be the right approach in Game Three. However, with each passing day, each victory, the crowds grew larger, the spotlight shined a little brighter, the stakes were raised, and the stage got bigger.

Therefore, as adamant as Coach Peifer was with his initial JCAC (Jaden, Cole, Adam, Cole) pitching rotation, there was a small curiosity, since Adam really had not been overly used to this point in their post season run. Truthfully, Adam had not thrown a pitch yet in Williamsport, and he had only pitched 2.2 innings in the three games in Bristol.

And though his performance in the Regional Playoffs resulted in a solid 13-2 win over Jackson, New Jersey, the four hits and two runs he allowed, along with having no strikeouts, was far from what one would call "dominating." Throughout the entire summer and sixteen games that Red Land played leading up to Williamsport, Adam was only called upon to pitch 11 2/3 innings.

Regardless of all of this, Tom Peifer, and the rest of the Red Land coaching staff, would not deviate from the faith that they had in this team, or their players. Adam Cramer would start this game, and they were confident that he would be brilliant.

As much faith as they had in Adam, so, too, did the coaching staff for Texas have in their starter, Jarrett Tadlock. He was a fire-balling right-hander who blazed fastballs by hitters with great regularity. Jarrett was every bit as fearsome, if not more so, than any pitcher the Patriots had faced all year.

In his opening day performance, Tadlock put together a 53-pitch gem over 4.1 electrifying innings, striking out eight along the way and surrendering only one hit en route to a 1-0 win over Oregon. In addition to having their ace on the mound, Pearland, Texas, had a long-standing history at the Little League World Series that they could surely garner.

This 2015 version of the Southwest Regional Champions was the third in five years to reach Williamsport, and they embraced the success their organization had established throughout their existence. Each practice began with the team from Pearland running down one of the outfield lines to get a close-up view of all the State Championship banners that had been accumulated through the years. Preliminary research puts that number at thirteen.

Practices would end with the team running down the opposite line to see the banners that had been earned by the 2010 and 2014 teams who had reached Williamsport. In addition to being able to add yet another banner down that line, this year's team hoped they would be able to add the word "CHAMPIONS" to those Williamsport banners.

Pearland, Texas, is a southern suburb of Houston near the Gulf of Mexico with a population of over 100,000, making them the second largest region of the eight remaining teams. The largest team was Portland, Oregon, population 609,456, whom Texas had defeated in their first game.

Compare that to the population of 356 from Lewisberry, and the equally as small surrounding areas, in addition to the fact that every step that Red Land continued to take forward was the first down this illustrious trail, and this matchup had all the characteristics of David and Goliath. Except, the combatants in this conflict would not be using slings and rocks on one another—their weapons of choice were Easton bats and fastballs, or, in the case of Adam Cramer, curveballs and change ups.

His demeanor made what he was doing look so effortless, and he radiated what seemed to be a true sense of joy with every passing moment. Whatever it was, there was no doubt he had the entire Red Land community behind him as the Patriots took on what appeared to be a heavily favored Southwest team from Pearland, Texas.

As the crowd of over 35,000 settled in, there was an anxiety that did not exist in either of their previous two contests. Red Land was shown to be susceptible in their game three days earlier, and that, as well as the uncertainty of the pitching matchup of the evening, increased both the apprehension and the energy. If Red Land was ever going to be considered an "underdog," this would have certainly been one of those times when that label would actually fit, rather than be forced.

With word spreading among the other coaches in Williamsport that Red Land preferred to hit first, Texas elected to be the visiting team, when they won the pre-game coin flip. This meant that Adam would start on the mound rather than be able to pitch his first inning with some kind of a lead.

As the dangerous Isaac Garcia stepped into the box, Adam braced himself for what would become the most memorable night of his life thus far. Garcia, in Texas's opening victory over Oregon, had the team's only hit—solo home run. He entered the game batting a lofty .428 and was looking to send a statement in the top of the first, which Pennsylvania was used to giving rather than receiving.

The only message that would be sent, however, was one by Adam Cramer. On his third pitch of the game, Adam threw a curve ball that started on the outside half of the plate at eye-level and ended up at the ankles of a frozen Isaac Garcia. Though he made an attempt, he was clearly perplexed by the movement of the ball thrown by Cramer. It was a look that many of the Texas hitters would continue to make throughout the night.

He swung, looked down at where the Patriot's catcher, Kaden Peifer, actually caught the ball, looked at his bat, stepped out of the box, shook his head, and looked down to his coach at third base for some kind of an answer. One would not be provided.

On the fourth pitch of the at bat, Kaden called for a fastball on the outside edge of the plate. He set up slightly off the plate, looking to expand the zone. As Adam reached back to deliver his pitch, Kaden never moved his catcher's glove, and though it properly was not called a strike, the coaching staff loved what they saw.

"He's hitting his spots! That's a really good sign!" The notes were passed from one coach to the next. They could hardly contain their excitement. If Adam was going to be overwhelmed by the crowd, by the noise, by the moment, there were absolutely no signs of it!

"Pinpoint!"

The next three pitches were a snapshot into the precision that Adam Cramer would put on display for the rest of the evening. Kaden Peifer set up inside (again, slightly off the plate), and again Adam Cramer placed the ball into the center of his glove. Peifer sprang to his feet for the second time, wanting to throw the ball down to Chayton at third— as the team does after a strike out with no one on—but once again, the umpire would not oblige.

"Don't change a thing!" hollered the team's pitching coach, Bret Wagner. "Keep locating!"

He was thrilled with what he was seeing. Finally, on the seventh pitch of the at bat, Adam threw a curve ball that buckled young Garcia's back leg and catatonically froze the leadoff batter, leaving him motionless as the ball went past him.

"Strike 3!" bellowed the home plate umpire, and finally, Kaden could begin the toss around the horn. As he did, 35,000 loyal Pennsylvanians sprang to their feet with him and let out a roar that they had been holding in for what seemed like an eternity.

But Texas had a dangerous line up of hitters that do not provide a pitcher with much of an opportunity to rest. So despite the fact that their first batter was retired; there was plenty of work left to be done. As the next two batters (Ben Gottfried and Jarrett Tadlock) reached base, suddenly the initial enthusiasm that was shared by everybody in the Mid-Atlantic dugout and all of their followers was a bit suppressed as power-hitting Zack Mack stepped into the box. Adam was in the midst of his first (and biggest) test of the night.

Watching a pitcher wield his craft is truly a thing of beauty. Equally as elegant was watching Kaden Peifer skillfully receive every pitch that Adam delivered. No fewer than 16 of the 28 pitches that Adam threw in the first inning were at or in the dirt—but not one of those pitches ever reached the backstop. He slid, he blocked, he scampered, he dodged, he did whatever he had to do, but for every one of the breaking balls that Adam exquisitely flung past the hitters, Kaden Peifer was equally as polished to catch them.

Mack was a contact hitter. He had only struck out one time in sixteen at-bats in the Southwest Regional tournament, but he was no match for Cramer. Adam continued to weave his pitches inside and out, changing his speeds as elegantly as a conductor did. He disposed of young Mack on five pitches.

"Ahhhhh, he pulled the string on that!" said the guys up in the booth.

"Oh, baby, I liked that!" agreed ex-major league pitcher Kyle Peterson, who pitched multiple season for the Milwaukee Brewers. "Adam Cramer's showing you don't have to throw hard to be able to strike guys out; you just have to throw them in the right spots."

It was not only his coaches that Cramer was impressing. As the final batter of the inning flied weakly to dead centerfield, Dylan Rodenhaber squeezed the third out, and the Patriots were finally able to hit.

The Red Land hitters knew exactly what they were up against in Jarrett Tadlock. In the opening game against Oregon, he was nearly perfect as he struck out and mowed down eight batters without walking anyone, and the only hit he gave up was a meaningless single. No batter reached second base at any point vs. Tadlock, and the dominance he showed in the Southwest Regional, where he struck out 22 batters without walking any, was just as impressive, and dominant, as the numbers Cole Wagner was putting up. The Texas pitching staff, in general, had a vice-grip control over their opponents, as teams were only batting .156 against them, and so the Patriots knew that they had a tremendous amount of work ahead of them on this night.

The inning started auspiciously for the Patriots. Braden worked a walk and set up an epic confrontation of power vs. power as Tadlock stood on the mound and Cole Wagner came to the plate. A walk to lead off a game is not exactly earth-shattering news, but in this particular case, it did catch the attention of Tom Peifer in the Red Land dugout. It was the first walk Jarrett Tadlock had given up in nearly a month. Coach Peifer knew that Tadlock was dealing with an awful lot in his mind: the crowd, the daunting Patriot line up, and now, he had to deal with Cole Wagner. He liked what he was seeing.

On first base, BK went through his normal progression. He checked the signs from third base coach Bret Wagner, he verbally got the game situation from his father in the first base coach's box, and he tried to figure out a way that he could get to third base with less than two outs.

In the batter's box, Cole Wagner hovered. He physically sent a message to pitchers that he owned the prized piece of real estate that was known as home plate, and he was going to dare them to pitch inside to him. He stood so close to the plate that pitchers had the natural inclination to throw the ball outside, not wanting to hit Cole and give him a free pass to first base. He could easily reach those pitches and launch them in any direction over the fence. That philosophy of crowding the plate, being quick enough to turn on the inside pitch, and being able to reach the outside part of the plate came directly from the Red Land Coaching staff and the instructors at GoWags.

"You've got to be able to turn on an elite fastball and adjust on a really good breaking ball," explained Tom Peifer. "If you can do that, you can be a really good hitter on this level." Then he paused and thought. "Really, if you can do that, you can be a really good hitter on *any* level."

Jarrett Tadlock was not the type of kid that was going to be intimidated—not by Cole Wagner or anybody else. He was every bit the intimidator that Cole was. He stared through batters from 46 feet away, showing only his eyes from behind his glove, and he caked on eye black, despite the fact that this game was played at night. This was a classic confrontation of power vs. power.

His first offering to Cole was a 73 mph fastball at the young hitter's ankles. It clearly was a purpose pitch to back him off the plate. Cole instinctively lunged away from the pitch. He glared out at Tadlock, who met his glare with an equally defiant gaze in his eye. As the catcher, Ryan Farmer, hustled to retrieve the ball that dribbled away from him, Tadlock's momentum brought him toward the plate. By the time he angrily snatched the ball out of the air, he was no more than ten steps from Wagner.

With the message sent, received, and confirmed that it was indeed a message, Tadlock prepared to make his second statement. This time, it was a 74 mph fastball right down the middle. A challenge.

"Hit this if you can…"

Cole tried. He swung. He missed.

Tadlock took five steps toward the plate to get the ball from his catcher. He stared at Cole the entire time he approached his catcher.

"Whewwwwww!" came from Peterson in the booth. "Jarrett Tadlock just challenging Wagner on that one, and he was *late* on it."

"There is no doubt this is power on power," confirmed Karl Ravech. The adults in the booth, who were used to covering college and major league ballplayers, were clearly engaged in this showdown.

Tadlock's third pitch, quite possibly, was his nastiest—a 75 mph cutting fastball that broke across the plate and toward the knees of Cole Wagner. Cole had no choice but to watch it into the glove of Ryan Farmer.

"Strike Two!" bellowed the volunteer home plate umpire as the ball flew across home plate.

"Ahhh…good pitch!" said Ravech.

"Yes!" echoed Peterson.

"Maybe a little breaking ball in the dirt here?" suggested Ravech, trying to get into the mindset of the Texas pitcher, who was masterfully trying to dispose of the Patriots' most dangerous hitter.

However, finesse was not really a part of either one of these combatants make up. They were baseball warriors. Competitors. They lived for confrontations like this.

Tadlock stepped back onto the rubber. Daggers shot from his eyes as he got the sign from Ryan Farmer and nodded acknowledgement. While he did, Cole rebelliously inched even closer to the plate, waggled his bat as he anticipated the pitch, and almost dared Jarrett Tadlock to throw that pitch again.

He did. At least he tried to, but this 75-mph fastball did not have the same control that the last one did, and it sailed to the backstop. As it did, Braden Kolmansberger was able to move to second base—he was halfway to where he needed to be.

It also marked the fourth pitch of the inning that had gotten past the catcher. It reflected many things :

1. The ferocity with which Jarrett Tadlock was throwing.
2. The fact that Tadlock did not have the normal control that he was used to having because he was trying to throw just a little harder than he normally did.
3. Just how difficult it was for the catchers to keep pitches like these in front of them—and how masterful Kaden Peifer had become at doing just that.

On the final pitch of the at bat, Jarrett Tadlock reached back even farther. He found an extra mile an hour, blazed a fastball up in the zone at 76 (which equates to 99 for a major league ball player), and got Cole Wagner to swing and miss for strike three.

Round One to Tadlock.

As he turned and walked to the dugout, Cole altered his path by only two steps so he could give a high five to his teammate Jaden Henline who was up next. He did not slam his helmet to the ground upon entering the dugout, he did not throw his bat, and he did not scream at the umpire for the pitch he called a strike. He walked out of the batter's box, encouraged his teammate, and went into the dugout to watch the end of the inning.

Striking out is, and has always been, a part of baseball. Players strike out nearly ten times as often as they hit a home run. In 2015, there were 37,446 strikeouts in the big leagues. There were 42,106 hits. There were only 4,909 home runs. Cole Wagner was well aware of these statistics. He knew, acknowledged, and accepted that Jarrett Tadlock won this battle, but he also knew that he would get another chance in another inning or two. When he did, he knew it would be the same fierce confrontation that this one had been. At least he hoped it would be—and he knew that Tadlock hoped for the exact same thing.

With one out and BK on second, Henline was the next to take his shot at the slinger from Texas. Though Cole was a vital clog in the Patriots' hitting machine, it is not as if he were their only weapon. With hitters like Jaden, Chayton, Dylan, and Ethan following Cole, there was not a whole lot of relief for pitchers if they were able to get him out. Jaden Henline certainly did not intend to give the Texas pitcher any reprieve.

Clearly amped up after his small triumph, Tadlock continued to punish the radar gun with his deliveries. After just missing the strike zone on his first offering, his second pitch to Henline short-hopped the plate and caught Ryan Farmer's bare hand before ricocheting to the backstop, allowing Kolmansberger to accomplish his goal of getting to third. More concerning for Texas was the physical condition of their catcher, who now appeared to be injured, and the mental state of their ace.

Assistant Coach Jeremy Tadlock (Jarrett's father) first went out to check on Ryan Farmer behind the plate. The young man tried to hide the obvious pain that he was in. When the coach first reached for the 12-year-old's hand, Ryan actually put his hand behind his back as if he were trying to hide any evidence of injury.

It was clear that despite any significant pain this young man may have been feeling, Ryan Farmer was not about to come out of this game. Feeling assured of the physical health of their catcher, Jeremy Tadlock walked to the mound to have a brief conference with his son.

Though it was not as concise as the conference Bret Wagner had had with his son during the South Carolina game, the message was every bit as direct. "Relax!" It was easy to read the lips and body language of the young pitcher's father. It was a good time to deliver that message. His son seemed to be trying to throw the ball not only past the hitter, but through the catcher, through the umpire, and through the backstop as well.

With his increase in velocity, there was a decrease in his accuracy, something that was quite uncharacteristic of Jarrett. Of his first thirteen pitches, four of them were wild—not a good sign for a pitcher normally as precise as Tadlock. And as a result of his somewhat erratic beginning, whether it was due to nerves from the raucous crowd, or the magnitude of the game, Braden Kolmansberger was standing on third base with the potential of giving Red Land a 1-0 lead that they may have never relinquished. Head Coach Andrew Solomon, a professor of law back home, was very much aware of that.

As the Red Land faithful began their signature chant of "We Are" / "Red Land" Jarrett Tadlock tried to collect his composure and go back to work on Jaden Henline. His next pitch was another 75 mph dart that went straight into the glove of Ryan Farmer and set the count at two balls and one strike. For the moment, the ship seemed to have settled.

On the fourth pitch of the at bat, Tadlock perfectly located yet another 75 mph fastball. This one was riding in on the hands of Henline, who fought off the pitch and lifted the ball awkwardly over the head of the second baseman, the manager's son, Alex Solomon. Racing backwards on the ball, Alex tried to make an over the head catch to preserve BK from scoring from third. However, he was unable to secure the catch and as the ball fell to ground, BK was able to cross home plate and score the first run of the ballgame.

It was now Jarrett Tadlock's turn to serve as the calming influence in this turbulent sea of red.

He walked off the mound and moved toward his second baseman, who was obviously dejected that he could not complete this difficult catch.

"Alex!" he screamed. "Alex!" He got his attention. Then without saying another word, he waved his hand and shook his head to let his teammate know that everything was all right. It was yet another poignant moment of the bond that teammates share from the Little League World Series. Here, amongst the mayhem and excitement that was unleashed from the 35,000 Red Land fanatics, a 12-year-old boy, who was battling to control his own emotions and nerves, served as the consoling figure because his teammate needed that.

There was no further damage inflicted by the Patriots that inning. Jarrett Tadlock struck out the next batter and got a ground out to end the first, but Red Land had given Cramer the lead they had hoped to provide, and now it was his turn to preserve that lead.

If the longer first inning provided Adam Cramer with anything, it gave him an opportunity to really settle in to the evening, and once Adam got into a groove, it was hard to shake him. What the capacity crowd was about to witness on this night in Pennsylvania was nothing short of brilliant.

After Tristan Schwehr rolled a dribbler back to Adam on the mound, the next fourteen outs would all come via the strikeout. There were hits along the way, a few minor rallies that were started but never completed, but ultimately, the rest of this game and the outset of the next game were dominated by the pitchers, rather than the hitters, for this Mid-Atlantic ball club.

One of those hits was by Carter Ostrom, who followed the advice of his coach who told the team between innings to "Scoot up in the box, scoot up on the plate, and go to right field." He also asked them, almost rhetorically, "What did we see, boys? Nothing we can't handle." He was a master at keeping his team positive and calm, a quality that was very much needed amongst the havoc that the *Red Sea* and the Red Land hitters tried to create.

However, the only commotion that would be created on this night was the kind that followed yet another strikeout recorded by Cramer. His mastery of changing his speeds, his location, whether it is up or down in the zone, or inside or outside, completely kept the hitters from Texas perplexed. The only batter who did not strike out against Cramer was the aforementioned Schwehr, who grounded out in his only appearance against "Ace McSizzle." As Adam raced off the mound having struck out Raffi Gross to end the top half of the 2nd, he clearly felt his confidence building.

So, too, was Jarrett Tadlock's, who was able to retire the Patriots in 1-2-3 fashion in the bottom half of the second inning. But his outs were not coming as easily as Cramer's. In the top half of the inning, Cramer was able to retire the hitters from Texas using only thirteen pitches. In the final at-bat vs. Tadlock in the second, Kaden Peifer forced the pitcher to throw nine just to get him out. Kaden fouled off difficult breaking balls, fought off inside fastballs, and let anything outside of the strike zone go by without an offer. As powerful as the Pennsylvania hitters were, they were equally as disciplined with their approaches at the plate. One could call them *brazen*, but *reckless* was not a word that anyone with knowledge of baseball would ever use to describe their philosophy in the batter's box.

As the two sides moved to the third, it was clear that as great as some of the individual pitcher-hitter matchups were going to be on this night, the greatest duel would take place between the two starting pitchers trying to keep up with one another and the blanks they were putting up on the scoreboard. So far, Adam Cramer had an early lead in that category, as there was nothing but blanks coming from the Texas offense.

◆◆◆◆

There is something magical about watching a player get into a "zone." Daniel Murphy got into a zone during the 2015 National League playoffs when he launched six home runs in six straight games. "I can't explain why the balls keep going out of the ballpark, but they do," he told Adam Rubin of ESPN after the Mets defeated the Chicago Cubs four games to none to clinch their spot in the 2015 Fall Classic.

As Adam Cramer continued to baffle the Texas hitters with his curve balls, fastballs, and change ups, he, too, was entering "a zone." The first batter he would face in the third was leadoff batter Isaac Garcia. Garcia, who had struck out in his first at bat, was determined not to let that happen again. He jumped on the first pitch he saw from Cramer but was only able to foul it back to the screen. As the two battled through the at bat, Isaac saw the full arsenal of pitches that Adam had in his bag of tricks. Curve balls, sliders, change ups, fastballs, it was an onslaught of pitches trying to gain the upper hand. He fouled some off and let some go by, but when Adam dropped the speed of his final pitch to Garcia, the Texas shortstop was too far out in front of the pitch and went down swinging. One out.

The next batter, Ben Gottfried, would not last quite that long. His at bat lasted three pitches. Curve ball. Change up. Fastball. Strike one.

Strike two. Strike three. Next up was Jarrett Tadlock. Though this match up should have had all the drama of the one that Jarrett and Cole had against each other in the first inning, that theater never came to fruition. After the first pitch, Tadlock was behind 0-1. After the second, he was behind 0-2. On the third pitch, Cramer attempted to extended the zone just a little bit by throwing a fastball a little farther off the plate than the home plate umpire would allow to be called a strike. Refusing to deviate from his game plan, Cramer threw the fourth pitch to that exact same location with a slightly different outcome.

"Strike 3!"

Adam sprinted off the mound toward the dugout. The first one to greet him was Cam Walter. Adam screamed at the top of his lungs. He was halfway through the game, had a 1-0 lead, and was virtually unhittable. He was not just pitching well, he was pitching *majestically*. This was not just a good night, it was becoming historic—and Adam Cramer knew it.

As he stormed into the dugout, being mobbed by his teammates, there was another showdown brewing. Due up third for the Patriots in the bottom of the 3rd was none other than Cole Wagner, and he couldn't wait to redeem himself vs. Tadlock and try to give Adam a little bit of breathing room that he wouldn't necessarily need, but he certainly would like to have. Round Two of the heavyweight matchup between Cole and Tadlock would provide all of the tension and drama that the first round did.

The first batter of the bottom half of the 3rd inning was Adam Cramer himself. The funny thing about being in a zone is, it is contagious. It is a state of mind that does not limit itself to a particular area. As Adam Cramer launched a 73 mph fastball over the head of left fielder Ben Gottfried, he pulled into second with a double and could hardly contain his excitement. It was an emotion that he really had not shown all night. The only thing bigger than his smile were the dimples that appeared when he revealed it, and both were fully displayed as he stood on second applauding and encouraging his teammate, Braden Kolmansberger, to hit him in.

On the very first pitch to BK, Tadlock drilled a chopper to third baseman Caleb Low, who properly looked the runner back to second before firing across the diamond to Zack Mack at first. As Low released the ball, Adam immediately broke for third. It was the same instinct that BK had whenever he was on base. In fact, Adam served as the leadoff hitter for the first portion of the team's season and was every bit as capable of running the bases aggressively as Braden was.

Batting him ninth allowed Coach Peifer to have a second leadoff batter, another high percentage hitter to get on base for Cole, who always batted second. He, too, fully bought into the concept of getting to third with less than two outs by any means necessary, and for the time being, it appeared that was exactly what he had done.

But instant replay showed that Mack's throw back across the diamond to Isaac Garcia, who was properly covering third when Low's momentum pulled him away from the bag, had beaten Adam to third base and the initial call of "Safe" was overturned. Instead of having Cole Wagner step to the plate with one out and a runner at third, he came up with two outs and nobody on.

Tadlock collected himself behind the mound. He knew he had won round one. He also knew that winning round two would be a lot harder. Unlike the first at bat, Tadlock started Cole off with a breaking ball. Cole took a hack but was unsuccessful. He had not made contact on any pitch that Tadlock had thrown him all night. The next pitch was a perfectly placed inside fastball at 74 mph. Strike two. Jarrett took his usual five steps to receive the ball back from his catcher. Cole stepped out of the box. He clearly was not used to being on the wrong end of a competition, but here he was again, facing defeat.

The third pitch from Tadlock missed its intended target. Catcher Ryan Farmer was again set up inside looking to jam Cole Wagner with another fastball to end the inning. However, this pitch never broke inside. Instead, it stayed up and away. Cole took it the other way, and in a matter of seconds, it cleared the left field wall and doubled the Patriots' lead.

It was a brilliant piece of hitting. Had he tried to pull it, he most likely would have grounded out weakly to the shortstop or third baseman. By taking the pitch to the opposite field, Cole was able to allow his power to carry the ball over the fence. He went with the pitch rather than fighting it, and the result was a missile over the left field wall. What Adam Cramer was on the mound, Cole Wagner was at the plate. He was not just a powerful fanatic who hit home runs; he was a hitter who understood the nuances of how to hit, not just for power, which he could do exceptionally well, but for production as well. Though he evened up the individual battle with Tadlock at 1-1, the more important score was 2-0, and by the way, Adam Cramer was orchestrating on the mound, that appeared to be more than enough.

As Cole rounded third and headed for the reception awaiting him at home plate, Jarrett extended his hand and acknowledged that Cole had won that round. They were two competitors with mutual respect for one another, and one another's ability, and they genuinely appreciated that each was pushing the other to be at their absolute best—less than that, and defeat was certain. That type of rival respect is rare, and there was nowhere else in the world where this was more visible than at the Little League World Series.

Outwardly, Jarrett Tadlock showed no signs of being rattled by Cole's line drive to left-center field. The ball had gotten over the fence in what seemed like record time. So hard was Cole's ball hit, that had it not cleared the fence, the young powerhouse might have been held to a single, his ball reached the wall so fast. Had it been fielded cleanly, and relayed properly, it could have just gone down as one of the hardest hit singles ever. That is a discussion that would never be however, as it *did* clear the fence, and it doubled the lead that Adam Cramer and the Red Land Patriots now had.

Coach Jeremy Tadlock went to the mound to speak to his son, and the young pitcher settled himself in for his next challenge, Jaden Henline. As his father left the mound, the younger Tadlock smirked ever so slightly, indicating that he was unnerved by the preceding events.

"Look at him, he's smiling!" admired ESPN Commentator Kyle Peterson. "I think he's okay." The other two in the booth chuckled with approval.

Tadlock blazed a 73-mph fastball past Jaden Henline, showing that he still had his composure and plenty of energy left in his tank. After quickly jumping ahead in the count and putting Jaden in a two strike hole, he induced a lazy fly ball in foul territory down the right field line that probably should have been caught but was mishandled by the Texas right fielder.

Having new life, Henline took the very next pitch and almost deposited it over the right field fence, but instead, it short hopped the wall and put another runner in scoring position for the Patriots. When Tadlock hit Chayton Krauss on the first pitch of the very next at bat, perhaps it showed that the young Texas pitcher was a little more unnerved than he originally let on.

As Chayton limped at first base as a result of being hit and was then removed momentarily for pinch runner Cam Walter, Jarrett strolled to first base and checked on his rival. He shook his hand and obviously wanted him to know there was no intent behind the fastball that rode in on the Mid-Atlantic clean up hitter and caught him just below the back knee. It was the second time Tadlock would shake hands with one of his counterparts, and both were an indication of what kind of sportsman this young man was. He loved the game, cherished the opportunity to compete, and respected his opponents.

Presently, however, he was in somewhat of a dilemma with runners at first and second and yet another batter, Dylan Rodenhaber, with the capability of launching one into the warm Pennsylvania sky and putting this game completely out of reach—if it wasn't already—the way Adam Cramer was pitching. Hoping to pounce on the jolted pitcher, Roddy swung on the very first pitch and just missed making solid contact with a ball that was caught by shortstop Isaac Garcia. The inning was over.

The team from Pearland, Texas, was able to wiggle off the hook without any further damage being inflicted, but there was, indeed, damage done. The team from Pennsylvania was able to double their lead and was showing signs of being able to consistently make contact vs. Texas' top pitcher. At the halfway point of the game that would determine who would play in Saturday's National Championship, Red Land was holding a 2-0 lead, and the young man they had on the mound wasn't showing any signs of allowing that lead to slip away. But after South Carolina mounted an unlikely comeback in the previous game, Red Land was taking that lead for granted.

Coming off a three up, three down on three strikeouts third inning, Adam Cramer looked to build on the momentum that his left arm and Cole Wagner's bat had built. Although Zack Mack drilled an offering from Cramer down the left field line for a stand up double, Texas was never able to really put together any kind of threat in the fourth, as Cramer continued to baffle hitters and keep them completely off balance with his mixture of fastballs, curve balls, and the ultimate of all equalizers, his change up.

Cramer started the next batter with a ball on the outmost edge of the plate for a swing and miss. Trying to get Marco Gutierrez to extend his strike zone, Adam threw the next pitch just a little farther outside, but Marco wasn't biting, so the next pitch came inside for a ball pulled foul for strike two.

The fourth pitch of the at bat was over the middle of the plate, but at eye level, again trying to get the hitter to swing a ball outside of the strike zone. No two pitches ever landed in the same location twice in a row, and Adam masterfully used every inch of the strike zone to keep the Texas hitters flailing at his pitches. Just before his fifth and final pitch of Gutierrez's at bat, Karl Ravech made the comment, "A lot of times, a hitter, the second time they come up to bat against a pitcher, has the ability to figure him out a little bit."

Nomar Garciaparra, former All Star shortstop for the Boston Red Sox and Los Angeles Dodgers, agreed. "Yeah, you see his release point, you know how he's been trying to pitch you with the off speed stuff." But on *this* night, there was no figuring out the brilliance of Adam Cramer. Pitch five was a pitch down and away on the lower left corner of the strike zone that Gutierrez couldn't catch up with, and Cramer had his eighth strikeout of the night, and his sixth of the last seven batters.

"Cramer continues to mow them down!" declared Ravech.

Notes continued to be passed between the coaches. "That was big."

"Clutch."

As the nation continued to marvel at the performance that Adam was putting together, coaches Peifer, Wagner, and Kolmansberger were not. Each knew that he had a performance like this in him. "Some guys melt in that kind of spotlight," said Coach Peifer. "Adam lived for it."

His demeanor while on the mound never changed. After each strike-out, Adam never celebrated, stared down the hitter, or theatrically responded in any way. As Gutierrez left the batter's box, Adam got the ball back from his catcher, checked the runner at second, and prepared for the next batter.

The curve ball that he started Ryan Farmer with in the next at bat was almost unfair. The 12 to 6 drop on the ball and difference in speed from what he had shown to the previous batter buckled the knees of the hitter and made him temporarily catatonic.

"Strike!" bellowed the home plate umpire. It was an indication he had grown accustomed to making most of the evening, as 44 of

Cramer's 65 pitches had been strikes. Pitch two was another teaser up and away, testing the plate discipline of the Texas hitter, trying to get him to chase a pitch outside of the zone. Always aware of the importance of conserving pitches, Cramer honed in on finishing off Farmer.

After a foul ball gave the Texas catcher a two-strike count, Cramer threw a curve ball that bounced right in front of the plate. It was skillfully blocked by Kaden Peifer, who threw down to Cole Wagner on first base to secure the second out of the inning. The fact that Coach Bret Wagner would call for a pitch like that with a runner at second marked the level of confidence the coaching staff had in their catcher to not allow a pitch like this, one they knew would have to be blocked rather than caught.

After smothering the ball with his chest, Kaden took a few steps toward second to show the runner on second he had not forgotten about him and yelled repeatedly, "INSIDE! INSIDE!" indicating to his first baseman which side of the baseline he would be throwing to. "INSIDE!" and he threw down to first. Cole cleanly caught the ball from his catcher, and jumped off the bag to ensure that the runner on second base wasn't going to go anywhere. There were now two outs in the inning.

The final batter of the fourth never really had a chance. On three pitches, Cramer disposed of Lloyd Richards III. Adam had the young hitter looking to his third base coach, into the dugout, and then finally up to the sky above in search of the answer to the riddle that was Adam Cramer. The headshake that he gave to himself indicated that there was no answer to be found.

After a swing and a miss on the third pitch (another 45 foot curve ball; home plate is 46 feet away), Kaden Peifer once again smothered the pitch, yelled, "OUTSIDE! OUTSIDE!" stepped to the dugout side of the first base line, and completed the put out for the final out of the Texas half of the fourth inning. As he did, Cramer allowed himself to burst off the mound and enjoy another triumphant inning while being greeted by his teammates who continued to support him on every pitch.

The quartet in the dugout that included Bailey Wirt, Cam Walter, Ethan Phillips and Jarrett Wisman were every bit as into the game as any of the players in the field, maybe even more so, because they could celebrate every swing and miss, every called strike, and every punch out from the confines of the dugout without worrying about being seen by the crowd or risking "showing up" their opponents. Their enthusiasm for their teammate could be completely unrestrained, and his unforgettable display of excellence only fueled his passion to finish the mission and lead his team into the 2015 National Championship. Now, with Texas set aside in the top of the 4th, that reality was only six outs away!

The bottom of the 4th brought a pitching change. Jarrett Tadlock surpassed the 65 pitch mark, meaning he would have to have three full days rest, a significant point as these two teams would meet only three days later, and Tadlock would be ineligible, after striking out Zack Soy and walking Cam Walter. Resistant to being pulled, Jarrett realized that his day of work was done—at least on the mound. He saw his coach appear from the dugout, exhaled deeply, and attempted to release the tension that had been germinating in his neck for the previous 3 1/3 innings.

"Hey, hey, good pitching," said Coach Solomon. "You hold that team to two runs over four innings. Very good pitching." As he called Marco Gutierrez in from centerfield to take the hill, he added, "Now, we just have to get our sticks working." As difficult a task that he knew it was to stifle the hitters from Red Land, he also knew that "getting the sticks working" for the remainder of the night against Adam Cramer was going to be equally as problematic.

The first batter that Gutierrez faced was Jarrett Wisman, who came in as he normally did to bat for Kaden Peifer the second time through the batting order. After striking out Jarrett, Marco hit the second batter he faced, none other than Adam Cramer, who limped down to first after being struck in the leg by a pitch. As Coach JK encouraged him to "walk it off", Adam looked up and scanned the crowd. It was the first time he really had the opportunity to notice the hysteria that he helped create with his magical performance. In the midst of the frenzy, Adam heard the voice of his older brother, Alex, and the two made eye contact.

"Adam, you all right?" screamed his brother, who had run down the first base side of the bleachers to check on his little brother.

Adam just smiled. His dimples appeared, he shook his left leg, and he gave a subtle nod and pointed in the direction of his big brother. It was the perfect moment between two brothers at a time when the younger one absolutely needed it. It was the ideal way to help him stay focused, grounded, and to remind himself that amongst the tens of thousands that were there to support him, the ones that meant the most to him were there, too.

"It was the best moment of the series for me as a mom," said Mrs. Cramer. "Alex and Adam bonded during the Bristol / Williamsport run like they hadn't ever bonded before. They are eight years apart, so sometimes it is tough for them to relate to each other. But they came together during this bond in a way that I had never seen before. It made it all the more special for me."

As Alex went back to sit with his parents, he told them, "Adam's fine," and the entire Red Land contingency breathed a little easier. By the time he sat back in his seat, Bailey Wirt had stepped to the plate with runners at first and second, and just as quickly, he found himself facing an 0-2 count. Looking to get out of the inning, catcher Ryan Farmer called for a pitch up in the zone at eye level of the hitter, but Marco drastically missed his target. As the ball went down and out, it shot back toward the backstop and up the first base line, and both runners were able to advance. But the Patriots were unable to get them any further. As the game moved to the 5th, the score was still a very tense 2-0.

Entering the fifth inning, Adam Cramer had thrown 70 pitches. The maximum number of pitches a Little League pitcher can throw in a game is 85. As well as he was pitching, as unhittable as he had been, the chances of Adam being able to finish this game were minuscule.

Coach Peifer had already sent Jaden Henline down to the bullpen to warm up while the Patriots were batting in the fourth. Adam had fifteen pitches left to use for the evening. He had already struck out ten batters and scattered three hits with his previous seventy. As the inning started, the crowd had worked itself into a frenzy as the fans in the outfield would call, "We Are…" and the fans in the bleachers would return with an equally deafening, "Red Land!"

Adam calmly toed the rubber and fired his 71st pitch of the night, a strike on the outside edge of the plate. There would be no "teasers" this inning. He couldn't afford any, as pitch two and three were fired past a helpless Conner DeLeon, first with a slider that fell off the table toward the back ankle of the hitter, and then a fastball that painted the back of the plate for strike three.

The next batter, Alex Solomon, suffered the same outcome, as it only took three perfectly placed pitches to record the second out of the inning. Now leadoff batter Isaac Garcia fell behind 0-2, and it seemed as if his fate would be sealed in the same manner as his previous two teammates. But Garcia managed a walk after seven pitches, and as Adam's total stood at 83 pitches, he prepared to face his final batter. Ben Gottfried was the one batter who already had a hit against Cramer, and certainly he had the capability of tying the game at two with just one swing of his mighty bat.

The first pitch skimmed over the outermost part of the plate and was generously called a strike. It was a pitch that Adam had used all night to get ahead of the hitters. Possibly thinking that Adam would come inside with a curve ball, Gottfried dug in for the next pitch. However, Peifer would set up outside again, and the fastball that stayed away seemed to catch Ben off-guard, as he was late on his swing.

Adam was quickly ahead of yet another batter, 0-2. At this point, Adam had struck out twelve batters, six of those took only three pitches, and the last ten outs, extending back to the 2nd inning, were all recorded via the strikeout. Sprinkled in between those ten strikeouts was one walk and two hits, but despite all of that, Adam still had to get this final out to be able to securely pass along a lead so that teammate Jaden Henline could finalize the evening and secure Red Land's spot in the 2015 Little League National Championship.

The crowd became euphoric as over 35,000 people came to their feet. 35,000 voices wailed their support, desperate to cheer this young hero back into the dugout. Only a small group of parents and siblings in purple along the third base side of the diamond wanted something, anything, besides a third strike. They rose to their feet as well.

Adam glanced at the dugout. Ben Gottfried stepped out of the box and took a practice swing. Somehow, amongst the delirium, tension, emotion, and pressure of the moment, Ben was able to hold back from the next pitch that Adam delivered—a curve ball that broke ever so slightly outside of the strike zone.

Ball One. It revealed a plate discipline that is acquired through years of practice. 35,000 other amateur umpires thought it was an incorrect call. Replays showed that it was not.

Adam walked to the back of the mound. He checked the runner at first. He got the sign from his catcher, took a deep breath, and fired his final pitch of the night. As Gottfried swung through yet another fastball that painted the outside edge of the plate, Adam Cramer sprinted off the mound having struck out his 13th batter of the night.

His teammates and coaches, well aware of the fact that Adam's night on the mound was complete, and fully appreciating the magnitude of the moment, greeted him as a conquering hero. When he finally got past the swarm of teammates relishing in the chance to congratulate him, Cramer slapped the wall above the entry into the dugout. His night of pitching was over. His work was done, and he could finally let out all of the emotion that he had contained all evening. Red Land had to bat in the bottom of the 5th, but that was a far distant thought from just needing three more outs.

Three. More. Outs.

Unlike the previous fifteen, somebody other than Adam Cramer would be responsible for getting them. That responsibility would fall upon the shoulders of Jaden Henline, who had failed in the same role just three nights earlier when he blew the save against South Carolina. Despite the fact that he was able to redeem himself at the plate, he had not had the opportunity to redeem himself on the mound. That chance would no longer have to wait.

In the Red Land portion of the 5th, the Patriots were able to add yet another insurance run. After Cole Wagner struck out to start the inning, and Jaden Henline grounded out to short, Chayton Krauss got aboard with a single, Dylan Rodenhaber and Ethan Phillips walked, and when Jake Cubbler was hit by a pitch, earning a RBI the hard way (and he had the mark to prove it), Red Land was up 3-0. As Tadlock, now playing third base, made a nice play on an anything but routine ground ball that had some difficult spin on it, the Patriots handed the proverbial keys to the car to Jaden Henline and hoped that he could drive them the rest of the way to the promised land.

The men gathered their teams. Tom Peifer for Pennsylvania and Assistant coach Joe DeLeon for Texas. Coach Peifer's message was simple. "One out at a time boys, just get one out at a time." It was vintage Coach Peifer. Cool. Calm. Calculated. Very rarely did he get emotional with these boys. It was not his style—that's why when he did, it got their attention, as it had prior to the bottom of the 6th inning vs. South Carolina.

Tom Peifer knew that the boys did not need any emotional speeches while in Williamsport. The emotion would come from the crowd. Their palpable passion could be felt all the way back to Lewisberry, 97 miles away. No, Coach Peifer knew what these boys needed was stability, and that was exactly what he provided. "One out at a time boys, just make three routine plays. Jaden, you just throw strike one." In addition, with that, he handed the ball over to his game one starter, now game three closer, Jaden Henline.

The emotion came outside of the Texas dugout from Assistant Coach Joe DeLeon. "Fight. Show me your heart. Fight to the end, every pitch. Give me your heart. Show them what you got! We're Pearland. Fight to the end. Right here. Fight to the end!" He passionately implored his team to continue to pound away. Maybe now, without Adam Cramer on the mound, they could scratch a run across—or three. There was nobody better to send to the plate to start that rally than Jarrett Tadlock.

Jaden Henline had other results on his mind. Wanting to erase any trace of memories that still may have been lingering in his mind, he attacked the first hitter. The first two pitches that he threw were nothing more than straight gas as they blazed across the plate at 70+ miles per hour—pitches that probably looked even faster than that since the hitters from Texas had not seen that type of velocity while Cramer was on the mound. As Tadlock lunged to foul off the third pitch from Henline, it was quite evident that Jaden was not trying to fool anybody. He was giving him his best pitch, and he would live with the results regret free. His fourth pitch froze the young Tadlock as it broke right across the outer portion of the plate, and as thirteen previous batters had done, he returned to the dugout without hitting the ball.

Out in centerfield, Adam Cramer nodded his head wildly with approval.

"Attack the hitters" read the note in the dugout. Bret Wagner, who called the pitches, wanted to keep Jaden's pitches simple. "Don't think, just throw." He also would on occasion call for a "*Quick Pitch*" where Jaden would not come to a complete stop at his waist before he released the ball. When nobody was on base, this tactic, also used in the big leagues, is perfectly legal. However, with a runner on base, it would be considered a balk in Major League Baseball, as a pitcher must come to a momentary stop before releasing the ball. But in Little League, runners were not allowed lead off bases, so this tactic was legal all the time. The coaching staff found that Jaden greatly benefitted from being able to use this quick pitch strategy.

As Zack Mack, who had previously hit a double for Pearland, stepped into the box, Jaden threw his first off speed pitch to start the at bat. It short hopped the plate and skipped to the backstop. Ball one. Bret Wagner immediately called for the fastball. As it tailed away from the young hitter, it caught just enough of the plate to be called a strike. So did the next one, and suddenly, Jaden was ahead of his second hitter 1-2. The next pitch caught the exact same location, and when Kaden Peifer received it, he fired it down to third, assuming it, too, would be called a strike—but it wasn't.

He immediately turned and apologized to the umpire, but he still wanted that call. So did the three men in the dugout, the young man on the mound, and 35,000 other frantic Red Landers. Instead, they got an even count at 2-2. After fouling off another tough pitch, and letting a high fastball go by, Zack Mack stood in the box staring down a full count. When Jaden's next pitch caught too much of the middle part of the plate, Zack Mack was able to muscle the ball right back up the middle of the field, and Texas had their first base runner of the 6th inning.

"Show me your heart boys; show me your heart!" As Marco Gutierrez stepped into the box, his Coach DeLeon's words continued to rain down the first base line as he stood in the coach's box.

Before anything that could resemble a crisis occurred, pitching coach Bret Wagner went to the mound. Though the meeting was disguised as tactical, "Look, when I call for it up, I don't want it eye level, I want it above the belt. We're trying to get a swing and miss. They're not going to swing if it's at their eyes." There was a greater purpose to the meeting than just the words he was saying. He wanted to look into his pitcher's eyes and know he could conquer the moment.

He left the mound confident. The note he passed to Coaches Peifer and Kolmansberger confirmed what he wanted to see. "He's all right."

Nevertheless, the Texas hitters were prepared for a battle. Marco Guitierrez endured a nine pitch at bat that included fouling off three put-away pitches, just like the one Coach Bret had called for when he visited the mound, but Marco would not be put away.

As Cramer watched from right field, he motioned a couple of times on what he thought was strike three, but the home plate umpire saw it differently. It was a form of emotion that he had to stifle all evening. Now, off the mound and out of the spotlight, he could allow some of the emotion to bubble over. On the ninth pitch of the at bat, Marco was able to take a free pass down to first base.

As Tristan Schwehr stepped into the box, the *Sea of Red* that surrounded Lamade Stadium drew in a collective breath. Only after the first pitch was called a strike did they momentarily exhale. The relief did not last long, as the second pitch was drilled out to Cramer in centerfield, and now, the bases were loaded, and there was still only one out.

"I wish I could go out there NOW!" Another note passed in the dugout. But Coach Bret could not go to the mound again, if he did, he would have to remove his pitcher. The staff had no intention of doing that. They believed in Jaden and knew he could finish the job.

The resolve this team had shown all year was equaled only by their composure. As the fans on both hills gasped in anticipation, and once again collectively became emotionally paralyzed, Jaden Henline collected his thoughts and prepared for Caleb Low. "Just get Strike One!" he thought to himself. "Just get Strike One."

He did. He got the benefit of a low strike that Kaden was able to pull up before it hit the ground. Didn't matter. It was called a strike, and Jaden was ahead of the hitter. Strike two was right down the middle and blown right past the swinger.

The next two pitches were fouled off, but the batter thought the fifth pitch was outside, and he let it go by. That was a mistake, as it caught the outer edge of the plate as Cramer had done all night. A roar came up from the crowd as the second out of the inning came via yet another strikeout.

Out in centerfield, Adam Cramer could hardly contain himself. He howled unlike anything he had done for himself all evening. The beauty of team sports is that individuals are able to share moments of glory with others—and Adam Cramer could not wait to officially celebrate with his teammates.

Painfully though, there was still work left to be done.

"Just get Strike One." It was how he could sustain his mental and emotional balance amongst the growing chaos. The crowd. Its energy. The pressure. The noise. One out away from the National Championship. An entire community hanging on every pitch. Jaden Henline and most of the other boys in both dugouts were 12-years-old. Such composure! "Just throw Strike One."

As Carter Ostrom stepped into the box, he was probably trying to keep his mental approach equally as simplistic. Perhaps his mantra was, "Just make contact." Whatever it was, he jumped on the first pitch, a 70 mph fastball, and just missed it as it sailed up into the crowd behind him.

"Didn't miss it by much," declared Karl Ravech.

"Once again, a first pitch strike by Henline," observed Kyle Peterson. In fact, it was the tenth straight strike that Jaden had thrown. He had not missed the strike zone since he walked Marco to allow the tying run to come to the plate. As dialed in as the Texas hitters were trying to be, so, too, was Jaden Henline.

When his breaking ball crossed the plate, the entire stadium once again came to its feet. Stephanie Henline, however, stayed seated. She remembered the epiphany of emotions she had gone through the last time her son was in this situation. She could not look away as some moms do, but she also could not fully immerse herself into the anticipated joy of the crowd. For her, the stakes were too high—and too personal.

The cameras caught a glimpse of the *Red Sea*. Cell phones were everywhere trying to capture this moment. The roar of the crowd echoed throughout the entire region, and the world for one brief moment seemed to freeze…

"Quick pitch!" observed Karl Ravech. "STRIKE 3!!!"

"Pennsylvania goes to the title game!!!" bellowed the Pennsylvania native from the booth. He could hardly remain neutral in the face of all this joy. Gloves flew into the air, players ran from every position, coaches emerged from the dugout, smiling…as elated as the players. And no one was more ecstatic than Adam Cramer. He laughed and screamed every single step of the way from centerfield to the first base line as the boys lined up in single file to shake the hands of their counterparts from Pearland, Texas.

The final sixteen outs were all recorded by way of the strikeout. The only two other outs recorded were a fly ball to centerfield in the first, and a comebacker to the pitcher by the first batter in the second. Every other out was a strikeout—thirteen by Cramer (who was told he should change the spelling of his name to KKKKKKKKKKKKramer), and the final three by Henline.

As the crowd dispersed, Adam Cramer tried to explain his performance to the media afterwards. In typical fashion, the young man deflected the attention he received. "I didn't really have any nerves because I knew I'd get run support." He did not get much. He did not need much.

In three days, this team of boys would have a rematch with the team from Texas for a US National Championship. The roles would be completely different on Saturday, though. Red Land anticipated having their ace pitcher on the hill in the form of Cole Wagner. Texas' ace would be unavailable. So, too, would their second and third pitchers. Red Land would be a predominant favorite. However, they knew how dangerous the unsung heroes were—they were proof of that. So too was the boy who was sitting behind a microphone with a smile as wide and as bright as the dimples that were revealed when he flashed it.

Adam Cramer, Ace McSizzle, had captured the hearts of America in a prime time showdown against a team from a town of over 100,000 people. Those numbers were now microscopic compared to the number of people who were falling in love with these boys from Lewisberry, PA. Yet another chapter was written, another story told, and now these young valiant baseball knights were one step closer to their fairy tale ending.

19

"HE'S STILL MY LITTLE BROTHER..."

S ometimes it is more nerve-wracking being up in the stands than it is to be down on the field. At least down on the field, as a player, you have influence on the outcome of the game. You can *will* yourself through a tough at bat, take comfort in the fundamentals you have been taught to make the right play on the field, trust the discipline that has been instilled in you to not give into this hitter, not give him too much of the plate on this next pitch, to trust that your change up will keep him off balance. Up in the stands, there is none of that.

Sure, as a fan you can cheer, and you can lead an entire section in a chant or two to make sure the kids on the field know that they have an entire *Red Nation* behind them, but sometimes, that's too insignificant—too indirect. And when the boy on the mound, or at the plate, is your little brother, the one you were left in charge with to babysit while Mom and Dad went out for a little while, the agony is somewhat overwhelming.

"I know I got a lot more nervous than he did," said older sister Hollis Kolmansberger, a grader at Red Land when discussing how gut-wrenching it was to watch her brother continuously come up to the plate at crucial times during the series. "But he was always so calm, he seemed so relaxed. I gained a lot of respect for the way he handled himself throughout that entire summer!"

"Oh, my gosh, I had no idea my little brother could pitch like that! He was amazing!" an enthusiastic Lindsay Cramer exclaimed as she looked back on the journey she was able to make with her brother throughout the summer of 2015 from Pennsylvania, to Connecticut, back to Pennsylvania. "I loved every minute of it until..."

Until it was over.

"I remember crying at the end, not because they lost, but because we didn't have anything to look forward to anymore with baseball. All summer it was, "Okay, if we win, we have the district championship, or the state championship, or regionals. It was just all so exhilarating!

Then, just like that, it was over. I just remember hugging Hollis and Molly, and just crying. We all were. As great as it all was, it was just as sad when it ended."

"It was tough on all of us," remembered Cheyenne Phillips, who watched her brother battle a case of pneumonia and homesickness as much as he was battling the pitchers from Texas, South Carolina, and Japan. "Ethan got really sick, and I felt so bad for him. It was really hard for me to watch him struggling. He was just a kid, who was sick, and he wanted to be at home with his mom. What kid doesn't want to be comforted by his mom when he gets sick?"

One night, he had taken some medication and fell asleep before the rest of the boys. When he woke up, he was in a state of delirium wondering where his phone was. He was crying, screaming, in a complete panic, "Where's my phone?!"

The coaches ran into the room.

"Ethan! What's wrong?"

"My phone. I can't find my phone." The coaches had allowed him to have it so he could call his mom whenever he felt the need to.

"Okay," consoled Coach Peifer. "Give me your number. I'll call it and we'll be able to find it. What's your number?"

"Number 19. Ethan Phillips. Left Field," answered Ethan as if he was doing his own introduction on ESPN.

It was a comical moment in a situation that was not really funny. However, it was able to calm him down. When the coaches finally got his *phone* number from Ethan and discovered his phone was actually right under his pillow, the entire room was able to have a light laugh. It was then decided that a night at home would be best for Ethan.

Ethan was able to go home, spend a night in his own bed and with his family, and the next day, he woke up his dad and said, "Let's go back up to Williamsport." Rob Gildea made record time getting Ethan back up with his team. The only problem was the doctor at Williamsport was not so quick to let him back around his teammates just yet.

"Twenty-four hours," explained Rob, thinking about his encounter with the doctor. "He wanted him to be away from the team for twenty-four hours to prove he wasn't contagious. And he wasn't budging. I tried to explain to him that the doctor back home had cleared him, but that didn't convince him. I knew physically Ethan was all right—the medication had taken care of that. But in order for him to be better mentally and emotionally, all he needed was to be back around his teammates, his brothers."

After the allotted time, Ethan was able to rejoin the team. What the medication had done for his illness, the camaraderie amongst his teammates did for his well-being. It was a peace of mind that only friends, family, and teammates could provide.

"My brother and I fight about everything," said Cheyenne, Ethan's sister, who was going to be a freshman at Red Land. "Being so close in age doesn't help. We fight about what to watch on TV, where we want to sit while we watch it. Just everything. But he's still my little brother and after they won in Connecticut and knew they were going to Williamsport, my brother came up and gave me the biggest hug ever! I think that's the first time he's ever really done that! It was a really neat moment for us. Maybe that's what made watching him struggle once he got there so tough on me."

20

LOOKING FOR AN ADVENTURE...
AND A CHAMPIONSHIP

In 2007, Paul Krauss brought his family to America "looking for an adventure." In 2015, Tom Peifer brought his team to Williamsport looking for a championship. Both would find what it was they were seeking, but neither road was easy.

Paul and his wife, Pip, bought a one-way ticket from Christchurch, New Zealand, to America. They had three suitcases and two children. Their first stop was Los Angeles, California, where two significant events occurred: the first was the family attended an Anaheim Angels baseball game because as Paul tells it, "it was something to do," and Pip bought her youngest son, Liam, a Mickey Mouse baseball uniform that he fell in love with and wanted to wear every day. Both helped big brother, Chayton, fall in love with the game of baseball. Each day, Liam would get in his Mickey Mouse uniform and beg his big brother to play catch with him. Each time he asked, Big Chayt was more than willing to oblige. He dreamed of playing in a stadium like the one he had seen in Anaheim, in front of a crowd that big, on grass that green.

Chayton was the more quiet and reserved of the two Krauss children. He never swam with a shark, he never dove off a cliff, and he never bungee jumped from a bridge that extends over a river. Those types of risks were reserved for his younger brother, who had already done all three by the age of ten. No, Chayton was much more reticent and never felt the need to take such treacherous risks and draw attention to himself. To a certain extent, in some ways, nothing much has changed. On the team that was playing for National Championship, he stayed in the shadows, content to contribute when he could, able to flourish when called upon.

◆◆◆◆

"…but be not afraid of greatness. Some are born great, some achieve greatness, and some have greatness thrust upon 'em."
William Shakespeare

Through the 2015 season, Chayton was as reliable and subtle as a morning paper. One never knew when it was going to be delivered; you just knew you could depend on it to be there when you needed it. That is exactly the type of player Chayton Krauss was for the Red Land Patriots. His .486 batting average, 13 home runs, and 35 RBIs were all good enough to be 2nd or 3rd on the team, but in terms of star appeal, Chayton was far more comfortable being a stagehand instead of playing the lead role.

Chayton never had the need or burning desire to have to be front and center in the spotlight, but sometimes athletes do not always get to make those choices.

When Chayton Krauss found himself thrust into the spotlight for an opportunity at greatness, he delivered with calmness as if he were born for that moment. And when he performed in the moment that demanded greatness, young Chayton delivered for his father and his coach that which both men were seeking.

◆◆◆◆

"We came here to win a championship, and that's exactly what we intend to do." The almost defiant words of manager Tom Peifer showed the deep seeded resolve he, and the entire coaching staff, had to stick to the controversial decision to pitch their ace in the US Championship Game rather than even consider saving him for what could possibly be a Sunday showdown vs. Japan or Mexico for the World Championship.

"They don't write books about teams that finish second," affirmed Coach JK. "If we don't win the National Championship, we would just be known as the team that got there, but couldn't get it done. We weren't about to let that happen.

Before this rematch with Texas could even take place, the Southwest team burned through their top three pitchers just trying to get into this game. After having their ace throw 67 pitches in the Wednesday night game vs. Red Land, Jarrett Tadlock was not eligible to pitch again until Sunday. And in their extra inning affair vs. California in the loser's bracket the next day, Texas used both Ben Gottfried for 86 pitches, and Isaac Garcia for 41, making both of those boys ineligible for this game. With their pitching staff significantly depleted, the only options Texas skipper, Andrew Solomon, had were Marco Gutierrez, who had pitched well for an inning and a 1/3 against the Patriots the first time around, and a relatively unknown by the name of Ryan Farmer, who normally served as the team's catcher.

Red Land, on the other hand, had every one of their top pitchers eligible except for Adam Cramer, who was nothing short of brilliant in a 3-0 victory three nights earlier when the two teams previously met. With the odds theoretically heavily in the Patriots' favor, popular logic leaned toward starting a fresh Jaden Henline in the US Championship and saving Cole for the World Championship, which for the moment, seemed inevitable. Tom Peifer would hear nothing of it.

"Our goal," said Peifer, "from the moment we arrived in Williamsport was to win the US Championship. Pitching Cole in that game gave us the best chance to do that. As adamant as I was that he was not going to pitch that first game against Missouri, is as determined as we were that Cole was going to pitch for the US Championship. I didn't care who they were throwing. We were throwing Cole. We had to close the deal. Cole gave us the best chance to do that. Cole was pitching in the National Championship."

It was that kind of determination that willed his team through not only the entire summer and previous ten days, but through their most unlikely come from behind victory over South Carolina six days prior, and it would continue to carry them through the next chapter of this two-week saga in Williamsport.

As direct and focused as Tom Peifer was, so, too, was his team. If they were successful, Tom Peifer, the coach, would no longer lurk in the shadows—he would validate what he always knew, that he was indeed Head Coach material, all he needed was a team, and a chance.

◆◆◆◆

Thursday and Friday for the boys were quiet. Their worlds had been spinning at Mach 5 speed, so it was the coaches' jobs to keep the boys grounded any time they were away from the diamond. Their practices had become public events. Their time in the cages was every bit as energetic as the games themselves.

One of the greatest experiences the boys had while up in Williamsport was walking from the dorms to the batting cages, from the cages to the baseball field. "They were like Rock Stars!" remembered Scott Cubbler. "It was like Mike Tyson walking into the ring before a heavyweight fight. Security would have to clear a path amongst the thousands of fans that were swarming just to get a glimpse of them.

"As I looked at my son, smiling and soaking up every moment, every step he was taking, I thought, 'Is there any better experience these men [Coach Peifer, Coach Bret, and Coach JK] could provide for my son?'" The answer was probably "No," but it was their guidance, their support, and their emotional and mental security that would prove to be even more valuable.

Their practices in Williamsport took on a similar pattern. They were upbeat, light, and abbreviated. "We knew we really weren't going to get any better, we were already as good as we needed to be," said Coach Peifer. "We just had to stay sharp, stay focused, and most of all, stay fresh." Practices would consist of light bullpen sessions, limited infield and outfield drills, emphasis on fundamental tactical strategies, and review of common game situations. Each one of those areas would be covered, emphasized, and reviewed.

At this stage of their season, their main objective was to allow the kids to continue to have fun and keep their interest level high. "After all," said Peifer, "we were still just playing a game—we were playing it on the grandest stage in the country, but it was still just a game. We didn't want the boys to forget that."

Except when it came to batting practice.

"Oh yeah, that was intense." The most important factor of BP was being able to simulate the same velocity and movement that the kids were going to see from the most elite 12-year-old pitchers in the country—kids like Jarrett Tadlock and Alex Edmondson. That is where Coach Bret and Coach Aaron would come in and put in their yeoman's type work. "Faster. Harder." It was then that the men knew exactly how young Kaden Peifer must have felt all those months ago. The preparation before the biggest game in any of these boys' or men's lives was not any different than any other game that they had played all summer. That is exactly how Tom Peifer and the boys on his team wanted it.

But back home, things were different. Signs that had been donated by Dick's Sporting Goods appeared everywhere. In yards, in windows, on businesses—everyone wanted to associate themselves with this team. #WhyNotUs and GOOD LUCK RED LAND signs were more common than all of the STOP signs and Speed Limit signs combined in the Central Pennsylvania area. Homemade signs from bed sheets covered fences and hung from roofs throughout the entire Etters, Lewisberry, Goldsboro, New Cumberland, and every other small town that made up "Red Land." This team had truly made their impact.

The day before the game, at a pep rally at Red Land High School, Assistant Coach Aaron Walter, a Guidance Counselor at the school, spoke before the crowd of about 2000 students, family members, and community members who had crammed into the gym.

"I am swelled with pride to see that these boys have united our area and brought national attention to the home I love so much. I am proud of the long tradition of success that Red Land baseball has achieved. This is yet another exciting chapter to add to the foundation that countless others have laid out for our boys to aspire to. People in Williamsport ask, 'Where is Red Land?'"

He paused. He had maintained his composure for the overwhelming majority of the rally, but when he spoke of his hometown, he could not help but be overcome with emotion. He tried to collect himself. The crowd roared.

"People in Williamsport ask me, 'Where is Red Land?' 'Where are you guys from?' Red Land to me is home. It is this school that has enabled me to build lifelong relationships with people I am honored to call my friends, and neighbors. This is where I grew up. This is where I still live. I believed in this community so much that I wanted to raise my family here and want my children to enjoy the same upbringing that I have come to cherish.

"Red Land has given me the education and foundation to be the man I am today. Each of you here today has now contributed to this legacy, and that is why I am so proud to call myself a Patriot. Our team, our families, thank you, the high school students, the *Red Sea*, for embracing our mission and supporting our sons, and for making this wild ride all the more enjoyable. On behalf of all the boys, I cannot thank you enough."

Always the showman, Walt stepped slightly away from the podium and then turned right around and screamed into the microphone, "We Are!!!"

And on perfect cue, the fans in bleachers all responded with a resounding, "RED LAND!!!"

But once was not nearly enough to release the overwhelming swelling of school pride that so many of them were feeling for the very first time in their academic lives.

"RED LAND!!! RED LAND!!! RED LAND!!!"

It became their tribal chant. Those who were not crying were screaming. Those who were crying wiped their tears so they could join the frenzy that Coach Walt's speech created.

Then, Kyle Wagner, a math teacher and founder of the Green Light Hitting Academy stepped to the microphone. Always the logical, rationale thinker, Kyle spoke of the founding philosophies of Green Light Hitting and GoWags Baseball:

"Dream Big. Work Hard. Stay Humble.

"Dream Big. Nobody has bigger dreams than these boys. They have chased this dream since the day they first hit a baseball and became enamored by the feel of the bat on the ball.

"Work Hard. As one who has worked with each of these boys in the privacy of a reformed warehouse when nobody was watching, I can personally speak of the work ethic that drives these boys to reach the level that they have. Their success is no coincidence. It is the result of countless hours of precise preparation so when the moment arrived in the form of an opportunity, they would be ready. And they are.

"Stay Humble."

It was here that Kyle had to pause as he reflected on all the work his nephew, Cole, had put in behind the scenes to become what many considered to be an "overnight, natural sensation." Kyle continued, "I don't know what's going to happen this weekend, but what I do know is this...those thirteen boys who are going to play for a National Championship tomorrow will be the same boys on Monday as they were when they left school last June. We are so proud of those boys above and beyond just what the results have been on the field." Then, he walked off and invited them all to be a part of the atmosphere that would be created in Williamsport that weekend.

◆◆◆◆

The morning of the National Championship was as beautiful as any that have ever come over the hills that surround the Williamsport area. Coach Kolmansberger went about his normal routine of waking up early and walking the perimeter of Lamade and Volunteer Stadiums. He sat in the first base dugout that his team would occupy in eight hours or so. He looked up at the empty grandstands and out on the hills that surrounded the outfields and knew they would be filled to record capacity this afternoon. A record crowd of over 45,000 people was expected that afternoon, and he knew his hometown fans would not disappoint him. He basked in the calmness of the morning.

As he walked up to Montgomery Pike, he saw the swell of fans already forming outside of the main gates. "Good Morning Everyone!"

"Good morning, Coach!"

"How's everybody doing today?" JK asked the morning faithful.

"Wonderful. Great day for baseball. Great day for a Championship."

"Well, I hope we don't disappoint you."

"Coach, regardless of the outcome of today's game, you couldn't possibly disappoint any of us."

It was the perfect reminder of why Coach Kolmansberger loved his hometown so much. Loyalty. Commitment. Friendship. They still existed in small towns all across America, and JK was proud of the fact that his family was very much a part of a very special one.

When the gates opened up, the crowd quickly ran to their spots on the lower outfield hill. Blankets were spread, chairs were aligned, spots were secured, and small patches of land on the hill were claimed. The early arrivals, many of who arrived in Williamsport before the sun did, were rewarded for their efforts with locations they hoped would be peppered by home run balls hit by their adolescent heroes. Now, with the business of the day complete, the long wait began until the 3:30 start time. A few slept, some ate, some read, and others just passed the time with whatever it was that caught their attention.

Like a man on a tractor mowing the outfield grass.

It was nothing special. Just a man on his tractor, but at 6:00 am in the morning, one does not need too much glamour to attract the attention of others—he just needs an attentive audience—this volunteer groundskeeper certainly had that. As he moved across the field, more and more people started to notice. They would cheer when he came their way. A few actually attempted to start the wave, but it was to no avail, as most were too tired to stand and cheer in unison with the Toro tractor that was making its way back and forth from left field to right, and right field to left. He noticed he was noticed, so he waved.

He smiled. The Pennsylvania faithful smiled back. It became a sort of dance—a game, if you will. Both parties were all too willing to play along. When he was done, he stepped off his tractor and took a bow. The crowd cheered. "That man just cut the grass in front of about 2000 people!" a fan said to his wife.

"I know," she responded, "And he savored every minute of it."

"So did I, sweetheart. So did I." There would not be much the Red

Land contingency would not savor on a day like today. The field was immaculate. The sky was blue, and the atmosphere surrounding the stadium was optimistic. The only problem was, it was still eight hours until game time.

◆◆◆◆

Just before the airing of the National Championship, ESPN ran a video that they filmed in Lewisberry, Pennsylvania. In it, they described the town of Lewisberry, a place with 356 residents, one pizza shop, one ice cream parlor, one barbershop, and one red light—that blinks. It was like going back fifty years in time. The highway that runs through Lewisberry isn't called by a number, it's referred to as "Space Highway," though nobody knows where it got its name because it's only two lanes, and sometimes it seems that tractors use it as often as cars.

In the video, Aaron Walter and Kyle Wagner serve as the main narrators of the piece (coaches Tom Peifer, Bret Wagner, and JK Kolmansberger were limited due to their game preparations), and they emotionally described growing up in this small town, leaving it to extend their education, and then being drawn back to it to raise their own family.

When it played prior to the game, the fans that filled the local taverns, specifically in The Mountaineer Lounge, watched almost breathlessly—not a word was spoken. As grown men watched, they wept, and they were not ashamed to have done so. Nate Ebbert, Red Land's Varsity Baseball Coach recalls watching that video from his table. "There were a lot of hard men in that place that day, working men who just loved baseball. When that video was over, it was amazing to see everybody in that place trying to wipe their eyes before anyone saw a tear fall. I was doing the same thing. But then we all realized everybody was doing it, so it wasn't as big of a deal." But it was a big deal. What those kids were doing, what they were accomplishing was a big deal. Moreover, the impact they were having on their community was an even bigger deal.

"Sports have made me cry only three times in my life," said Richard Lucera, a fraternity brother of Aaron Walter and one time resident of this small town before he moved away to pursue his professional goals on the West Coast. "The 1980 Olympic Hockey team, when the Phillies won the World Series in 2008, and when I saw that video."

◆◆◆◆

After what seemed like endless hours of anticipation, and politely watching the game between Mexico and Japan, the moment arrived for the record number of fans that totaled over 45,000 people. It could not have come soon enough.

Wilting in the hot, humid Pennsylvania heat, the throng of Patriot supporters had endured hours upon hours of anticipation. Nevertheless, it did not take long for the energy from the game to revive those in attendance. It probably started after the beautiful rendition of the National Anthem.

As Coach Tom Peifer looked out into the sea of red that had formed on almost every inch of earth that was available on the two hills of Williamsport's stadium, he stood in awe of all that his team had created. The music, the beauty of the day, the community members who had come to be a part of this experience, many of whom were making their fourth trip up to Williamsport, his players standing beside him along the first base line, the flag fully unfurled across the outfield, the Goodyear Blimp flying overhead, it was one of his proudest moments as a coach.

The fact that his son was standing beside him as his wife and daughter were in the stands right behind him provided one of his proudest moments as a man. He allowed himself just a moment to enjoy it.

It was not as if he had not enjoyed his time in Williamsport, he had. He had just not enjoyed it outwardly as much as some of the other coaches. He did not go out of his way to draw attention to himself; he did not do interviews daily with ESPN and sit on the set of Baseball

Tonight. He had not allowed ESPN to shadow him for a day or do a biographical piece on just him. "Do it on the kids, do it on our hometown," Tom told them.

And they did—and it captured the essence of the spirit of the community he was a part of. Tom Peifer was satisfied with just being the manager—but he wanted to be the manager of the National Champions, so he only allowed himself this one moment to appreciate the day, but then he had to go back to work.

Before they went out to the field, his final words to the team were simple, "No regrets, boys. Look what you've created. Now, let's finish the job!" To the joy and approval of an estimated 45,716, a Williamsport record, the boys sprinted out to their positions, except for Cole Wagner. Cole trotted at his usual pace, trying to keep himself on as even a keel as possible, knowing the whole world would be watching his performance both on the mound and at the plate today—at least that's what it felt like.

Cole had the precision, concentration, and calculated anticipation of a matador. He also possessed the intensity, the rage, and the ferocity of the bull. He was as tenacious a competitor as ever existed, a spirit that had been fueled by his desire at a very young age to just be as good as his cousin.

Throughout the tournament, ESPN continued to emphasize a quote Cole had given them explaining that of the 365 days in a year, Cole was probably working on his hitting or his pitching 360 of those days—Cole was just being modest. He was the product of not only a father with a background in baseball, but a family who cherished their baseball tradition, and here he was pitching on the grandest stage any of them, and all of them, had dreamed of being on.

That inferno that was burning inside of him had to stay contained, lest he lose his greatest asset on the mound—his control—but make no mistake, Cole Wagner fully embraced and was completely prepared for this exact moment.

At 3:44 pm on August 29, 2015, Cole reached back and fired a 75-mile per hour fastball that blazed right by Isaac Garcia, who watched it right into the glove of Kaden Peifer for strike number one of the 2015 United States Little League Championship Game.

"There is a college football type atmosphere here today with fans all over the hill in places you probably can't even see the game from," said ESPN play-by-play analyst, Karl Ravech. There was not one in attendance who dared to complain—to be there was to be a part of one of the most electric atmospheres in all of sports. To cram that many people in that confined a space, when the stakes were that high, was what competitive sports were all about. It brought out the best in the most elite athletes on all levels, and today would be no different.

Cole's second pitch had to send a message to not only leadoff batter Isaac Garcia, but to the rest of the Texas batting order as well. The fall off the table curve ball that broke right across the plate and flashed through the strike zone put Garcia in an 0-2 hole and showed just how good Wagner was feeling on the mound and how much control he had over the torpedoes he was firing into his catcher. After another 75 mph dart that easily could have been called strike three but didn't catch enough of the outside of the plate for the home plate umpire's liking, Cole discarded the batter with a fastball up in the zone.

"THAT'S the exact pitch we want!"
"THAT'S our GO-TO PITCH for a strikeout!"
"THAT'S the perfect location!"

The Red Land coaches furiously scribbled their notes to each other, and the day had officially begun—auspiciously.

The ball was fired around the horn—from Kaden behind the plate, to Dylan at third, to BK at second, to Jaden at short, who then gave it back to Cole. While the ball circled the diamond, Cole stood almost impatiently on the third base side of the mound as if to say, "Just give me the ball. I'm ready to do this again."

He did. Though the next at bat would last a little longer, Ben Gottfried had at least fouled off a few balls, but the result was exactly the same. Cole Wagner's left arm was loose, his location was exact, and his velocity was overbearing. To make contact with the ball when a pitcher was operating at this high of a level was a moral victory in itself, but there was not a player or coach in uniform today that was interested in moral victories.

As newly formed rival Jarrett Tadlock stepped into the batter's box for a reversal in roles from the confrontations these two put on display three nights earlier, Wagner quickly alleviated much of the drama. After trying to jump on Wagner's first pitch (he fouled it back to the screen), Tadlock would not swing the bat again, as Cole held him frozen in the box with his mixture of a nasty 71 mph curve and yet another unhittable fastball. The towering young lefty threw sixteen pitches in the first inning, eleven for strikes, and every single one of them was over 70 miles per hour. The last time Texas faced Pennsylvania, they saw Adam Cramer throw 87 pitches—not one of them touched 70—today, they would be hard pressed to see one that did not.

They were facing a beast with an entirely different arsenal. What the coaching staff, his teammates, and what had become the "Red Land Nation" hoped, was that he would be every bit as effective. The early signs gave all indications that they would not leave Williamsport disappointed today.

"Okay, Braden, start us off!" Tom Peifer had said it repeatedly all summer long. Most times, that was exactly what happened. Braden would get on, somebody would hit him over, and then somebody would hit him in. Sometimes, Red Land would skip the "hit him over part" and simply just hit him in. Braden just had a natural propensity for reaching home plate. After the way Cole was throwing in the first, he may only have had to do it one time to secure the National Championship.

On the hill for Texas was their regular catcher, now emergency starter, Ryan Farmer. Up to this point in the Little League World Series, Ryan Farmer had yet to throw a pitch. Throughout the Southwest Regional Tournament, that included games against Mississippi, Arkansas, and two against Colorado, Ryan Farmer was credited with pitching in one game, though he never actually faced a batter, never threw a pitch, and never recorded an out.

Yet, here he was facing what was quite possibly the most lethal offensively talented 12-year-old team in the country. It was assured that not one of the pitches Ryan Farmer would throw on the day, and his head coach had no way of knowing ahead of time just how many that would be, would come anywhere near 70 mph. As he stood on the mound staring into the catcher, Tristan Schwehr, who was occupying the position that young Mr. Farmer usually fulfilled, a world of thoughts must have run through his head.

Before those thoughts settled, BK was ready to pounce. He jumped on the very first pitch and pulled it down the third base line right into the glove of Jarrett Tadlock, who threw a perfect strike over to first baseman Zack Mack, and after one pitch, there was one out. His teammates all came to the mound to congratulate him and he could not help but flash a smile and glance at his coach in the dugout and somewhat shrug his shoulders as if to say, "Hey? Not bad. I got the first guy out! That was pretty neat."

The moment of glory quickly ended as the powerful Cole Wagner bullied his way into the left side batter's box.

"All right, so this is a big, big test," an understatement that was made by Karl Ravech.

The difference between the boy on the hill and the young man at the plate was as telling as sharks and minnows. Though Ryan Farmer was already 13, and Cole was still 12, Cole stood a full 4.5 inches taller than Ryan and weighed nearly fifty more pounds. The manner in which they conducted themselves was equally as contrasting, as Ryan exuded the persona of a child playing a game for the very first time, and Cole had the gritty look of an experienced steel worker about to put in yet another full day's shift.

As Cole waggled the bat while standing in the box, he stared out at Farmer, almost daring the boy to throw a pitch within his reach. Ryan did not. The first pitch grazed over the middle of the other batter's box. Any pitch left anywhere near the plate, or even near Cole's extended reach, would be a mistake. Ryan Farmer knew it, his coach Andrew Solomon knew it, and Cole knew it as well. However, Coach Solomon did not believe in intentionally walking other batters in Little League, and his team believed in his philosophies and strategies. There was a genuine affection between these boys from Texas and their manager. The second pitch glanced over the outside perimeter of the plate and was justifiably called a strike by the home plate umpire.

Farmer smirked. Wagner scowled. He would not let another pitch like that go by again—and he did not.

The next pitch that Farmer threw was a hanging breaking ball that caught far too much of the outside part of the plate, and with the same velocity that a Cole Wagner fastball comes in, this Cole Wagner line drive went out. His second straight home run over the left field wall showed that Cole could easily adjust his swing to however a pitcher would choose to pitch to him. Pitches on the inside portion of the plate could be turned on and drilled to right field. Pitches that tailed away or stayed away could be deposited to the opposite field. If a pitcher made a mistake and left one over the plate, well, he ran the risk of having that pitch put permanently into orbit.

As he rounded the bases, his teammates prepared to mob him at home plate as Cole Wagner the batter had given Cole Wagner the pitcher possibly all that he needed—a lead. His father had a fist waiting for him as he rounded third base, and his battery mate (his catcher) had a head butt waiting for him as he crossed home plate. Looking back on it now, perhaps it would have been wiser for Kaden to keep his batting helmet, or catcher's mask, on—but in the excitement, a lack of headgear was not about to dampen the celebration.

1-0 Red Land.

As the boys from the Mid-Atlantic continued their celebration, the boys from Texas huddled around their pitcher. Jarrett Tadlock brushed off his pitcher's shoulder as if to tell him to "brush that one off." Isaac Garcia, the team's shortstop, put his glove right into his chest to say, "You're all right!" The coach's son, Alex Solomon, who played second base, and first baseman Zack Mack, all came in to show Ryan that they had his back, and he was not alone. They were not laughing, they were not smiling, but *he* was—Ryan was okay. He would be able to continue.

With their help, with his humility, they would recover as he got the next two batters, Jaden Henline and Chayton Krauss, to pop up to second and ground out to third. After all the hype of pregame, the dominance of Cole's first inning pitching performance, which parlayed into an explosive home run off his bat, the score was only 1-0. This team from Texas had grown accustomed to coming back, as evidenced by the way they overcame the predominant favorites from California two days earlier.

After losing to Pennsylvania the first time, to even get a second shot at this team from Pennsylvania after facing deficits of 3-0, 6-4, and then 7-6 in extra innings to ultimately prevail 9-7, a 1-0 deficit was insignificant if somehow, someway, they could manage to put together a couple of good at bats vs. Cole—but that in itself was a monumental undertaking.

Nevertheless, these boys from Texas invited that kind of a challenge. As Ryan Farmer and the rest of the Southwest Regional Champions came off the field, they were met by an energetic and fist pumping manager. The high five he saved for his pitcher let them know that despite the home run that they allowed, his confidence in them was unwavering. That kind of certainty, that kind of poise, certainly can go a long way with children. Andrew Solomon hoped it would take them to the winner's circle.

There was a kind of confidence in the way Zack Mack conducted himself, and that confidence was at an all time high after hitting a grand slam in the first inning vs. California on Thursday. After seeing two pitches from Wagner similar to the lasers he had thrown in the first inning, that confidence may have been shaken—but he never showed it.

As he stood in the box with his bat on his shoulder and let the first two go by, he was timing the pitcher, getting a feel for his live fire, and waiting to make his move. When another ball entered the strike zone, Mack unleashed a violent swing and turned on yet another fastball over 70 mph, and sent it all the way to the wall in left field. With nobody out, Texas had a runner on second, and the mystique of Cole Wagner being unhittable was fading.

If there was any of that unhittable aura left, it completely vanished when 5 foot 2 inch / 82 pound Tristan Schwehr sent a 73 mph fastball right back up through the middle. As fans were still settling into their seats after the excitement of the first inning, suddenly Texas had runners at the corners with nobody out.

Perhaps, Cole was experiencing a letdown of adrenaline after the initial rush of the day. Back-to-back hits will certainly get the attention of a pitcher who was unaccustomed to experiencing any form, regardless how minor, of a setback. He honed in.

On three pitches, he struck out the next batter. He was on his way to doing it to the next batter as well, when a miscommunication allowed the runner from third to score as Kaden Peifer and Cole were confused as to how to defend the runner on first breaking for second. Wanting to go after the runner attempting to steal, Kaden threw hard towards Jaden Henline, who was covering second base.

Thinking they were going to let the runner advance and simply get the hitter's out, Cole attempted to catch Kaden's throw. It ricocheted off his glove and dribbled toward second base. When it did, Raffi Gross broke home from third and made it easily without a throw.

The small gathering of fans in purple, who were certainly not to the capacity of the *Red Sea*, were ecstatic as not only had Texas put together a string of hits, they scored a run, and now the game was tied 1-1; and they still had a runner at second with one out.

On the very next pitch, Cole slipped and went to the ground as he tried to plant his right foot. He dug his heel into the mound and attempted to do some quick manicuring. However, his next pitch sailed wildly to the backstop, and when it did, Tristan Schwehr hustled to third. When he got there, Coach Solomon was waiting with an emphatic five and a boastful, "YEAH!" He knew momentum was shifting and he was ready to invade the hallowed ground of home plate—an area that seemed simply impenetrable whenever Cole Wagner was pitching.

"Maybe this Pennsylvania team is a little rattled right now," pondered Ravech.

They were. The pressure of the moment, the air of expectation had never been a burden for these boys, but today, they were *supposed* to win. They had their ace on the hill. Texas did not, and with the *Sea of Red* at an all time high. With all of that came the onus of having to fulfill their forgone conclusions that this game was meant to be won by Red Land. Apparently, Texas never got that information. Texas was playing loose, confident; Red Land looked as if they were playing not to lose rather than to win.

The pressure eased up a bit when Cole finished by striking out Ostrom at the plate, his fifth of the game, but his father (and pitching coach) just wanted to make sure. He made a quick visit to the mound. When he arrived, Cole was digging again with his spikes in front of the rubber.

"It's pathetic!" declared Cole. They both made futile attempts to loosen the dirt on the hill, but all efforts went for not.

"Well, look, I don't think we're gonna be able to do anything with it. We got two outs. We gotta go after this guy hard. Okay."

"Yeah."

"Okay?"

"YES!"

He went to work. He was not about to let a misplayed throw down to second, or a harder than normal pitching mound derail a dream that he and his teammates were so close to fulfilling. He reached back three times, overpowered the #8 hitter in the Texas lineup and struck out his sixth man of the day. When he did that, he, along with Jaden Henline, and Adam Cramer, combined to record twenty straight outs via the strikeout. As dominant as their offensive numbers were, their pitching statistics were every bit as daunting.

However, these boys were still born to hit. After what seemed like an eternity, it was finally their turn to do it again. In the other dugout, the kids in purple were starting to believe that they could compete with these hometown heroes. They saw the evidence—two hits, a run, and the game was tied. This game had all the makings of an epic battle, but Pearland still had to keep the Patriots off the scoreboard, and every time they came up to bat, they were reminded of just how powerful a lineup they were facing.

If Texas wanted to hold onto the momentum that they had built in the top of the 2nd, Ryan Farmer gave them exactly what they needed in the bottom half of the inning. It took only twelve pitches to cast aside Phillips, Cramer, and Walter; and with each out, the impromptu starter was gaining more and more confidence.

After a somewhat nasty curve ball to Cam Walter, Farmer snuck a look into the dugout and grinned. He was not used to the attention, to being out in the open in front of everybody, and he seemed almost embarrassed by the notoriety. His teammates, on the field and in the dugout, loved him for it. "FARMERRRRRRR!!!" they would clamor, and the frequency began to increase. He smirked. He hid under the lid of his cap, a much more difficult task than usually being able to play in anonymity behind the mask and equipment of a catcher.

There was no hiding from what was becoming a potentially historic day for young Ryan Farmer. When Cam swung and missed at a third strike and the inning was over, Ryan bounced off the mound and pumped his fist. Every one of his infielders went out of his way to give him a pat on the back as they ran into the dugout. Maybe, just maybe, they thought, we can actually slay Goliath.

In what could certainly have not been predicted, the game quickly turned into the most unlikely of all pitching duels—for Red Land, the behemoth Cole Wagner, all 159 pounds of him, slinging fastball after fastball by the batters from Pearland, Texas. For the team from the Lone Star state, it was 112 pound Ryan Farmer.

Each in his own way was every bit as effective as the other. The longer the duel went on, the more in favor it seemed to sway toward Texas. The strikeouts continued to mount for Cole, but more frequently, there were balls that were put into play. Through three innings, Ryan Farmer had only given up one hit—the home run ball to Cole Wagner way back in the first that had given the Patriots their short-lived lead, and he had only thrown 29 pitches. Cole, on the other hand, had thrown 46.

As the game moved to the fourth, both teams had their best hitters leading off the inning. Tadlock was retired by a nice backhanded grab from Chayton Krauss. He was one of the most versatile players on the team, moving from first when Cole pitched, to short when Jaden did, to third base when Adam did. Whatever the team needed, Chayton Krauss was willing to fill that role. That was an attitude that was contagious throughout the dugout.

After Tadlock grounded out, Zack Mack was able to work out a walk and give Pearland their third base runner of the day. But he seemed destined to be stranded, as the strikeout of Caleb Low provided the 2nd out of the inning—that is, until Marco Gutierrez, who was only 2 for 10 at that point in the Little League World Series, drilled a first pitch change up to the wall and allowed Mack to score all the way from first without a throw to the plate.

For only the third time all season, Red Land found themselves losing in a ball game. The damage could have been even worse had Jake Cubbler not perfectly played a line drive hit to right by Coach DeLeon's son, Conner. As Jake reeled in the third out of the inning, the crowd sat silent, somewhat drained from the sun, somewhat stunned by the score. But they soon came back to life when they realized Cole Wagner would be leading off the bottom of the 4th.

Before he came to the plate, Cole called a "players only" meeting right outside the dugout as he marched off the field. "Right here! Everybody! Right! HERE!!!" What was said was confidential, but the point was certainly public. "This is OUR game. Our Championship! And no team from Texas, is going home with that Championship Trophy! It's going home with US! We get that lead back RIGHT NOW!" As any good leader does, it was going to start with him.

He stomped to the plate. He stared out at Ryan Farmer. There was a rage in the young man's eye—the kind that breeds in the heart of a competitor scorned. The tenacity, defiance, and resolve made him appear as if he were a lion on the verge of breaking free from his cage and ravaging destruction on all that he could.

Cole's victim was going to be any pitch that dared to enter into his smash zone. He waggled the bat. He gritted his teeth. He rocked his weight from front to back before settling it on his back foot.

Then he watched ball one go out of the strike zone.

It was the perfect example of contradictory forces—the fury of a storm, the calmness of a breeze. His forces were power and discipline, and he had equal quantities of both. Cole readied himself again. However, the second pitch was not any closer than the first. The thought entered more than a few minds that there would not be any ball thrown anywhere near the plate.

Those thoughts were wrong. Ryan Farmer's third pitch was a ball up in the zone, right across the letters of Cole's Mid-Atlantic jersey. He had been waiting for this pitch. It was the vision he saw when he rallied his team outside the dugout only moments before. His vision ended with that ball landing somewhere far, far away. The reality was that as hard as he had swung, he simply missed the ball.

"Whooooo! He got a big one there, but he swung and missed," said Ravech.

He stepped out of the box. He shook his head. His facial expressions were easy to read—when balls outside of the zone were called strikes; Cole's displeasure could be seen. When he missed a pitch he thought he should hit, that could be seen just as easily. This was a pitch that perplexed him.

When the next pitch short-hopped the plate, and the count went to 3-1, again, baseball logic may have suggested the best strategy would be to simply allow him to walk to first base with another pitch nowhere near the strike zone.

"They're pitching to him; doesn't mean you can't be careful," said Nomar. He too was thinking there was no way another strike would be thrown.

Farmer's next pitch was not quite careful enough. Cole unloaded on a curve ball that lingered in the air just a moment too long. He uncoiled like a python attempting to inject life into this crowd and into his team, and to deflate hopes and beliefs that were cultivating in the opposing dugout.

But his timing was off and he missed the pitch, and instead, he fouled it into the crowd down the third base line.

He kicked in the air, obviously frustrated. He put his bat on top of his helmet as if he were going to break it in half. He screamed at himself and verbally chastised his inability to tie this ballgame on that mistake that had been thrown. "AHHHHHHHHHHHH!"

"Wagner wanted that one," said Ravech.
Peterson added, "It was a similar pitch to the one he hit out earlier. He just missed it. He knows it, too."

"Do you think he's intense?" asked Ravech rhetorically.

By the time ESPN stopped showing the replay of Wagner's self-inflicted tirade, Farmer was already hurling one of his fastballs (that wasn't able to reach 70 mph) up and away, which Cole once again tried to damage.

There is a moment for performers, be it at the crescendo of their performance or at the conclusion, when they know what they have done has been successful. It is that moment when they recognize that what they just accomplished is precisely what they intended, and they allow themselves just a moment to enjoy their success. When singers hit the high notes, or a painter steps back from a canvas—they look upon their work and smile. It is in those moments where pride in oneself is truly born.

As Cole swung and missed at the third strike, Ryan Farmer allowed himself to have one of those moments.

His catcher did not throw the ball back; he walked it to him so he could share the small victory with him. His infielders all came together at the mound and congratulated him. "FARMERRRRRRRR!!!!" rang in from the dugout and the stands. His eyes got as big as his smile, as if to say, "Wow, I can't believe I just struck out Cole Wagner! Cool!" He did. He earned that moment. He had a 2-1 lead, had only thrown

35 pitches, and was seven outs away from becoming a part of Pearland folklore forever.

Meanwhile, Cole became irate. He slammed his bat to the ground, stormed into the dugout, and looked as if he were ready to explode. His coach worried it was more of an implosion rather than an explosion.

"Pull yourself together. You gotta pitch. Don't you dare take your at-bat with you onto the mound!" Those words came from his coach. They sounded more like they came from his father, but there was certainly elements of both. When your star player refers to you as Uncle Tom, well, there is a higher level of trust between coach and player than what usually exists.

Farmer was cruising. He had a one hitter, had not walked anybody, and it was entirely possible that Cole Wagner would not get another at bat. He took a deep breath—perhaps that was a mistake.

"CLINK!"

The sound that a composite bat produces when it makes solid contact makes every hit feel like a homer. This one did not just feel like one, it looked like one from the moment it left the bat. Maybe Farmer had let his guard down just enough, just a little, but Jaden Henline took advantage of it and catapulted a ball over the right field fence right into the group of high school kids who had been at that pep rally the day before.

What Cole could not make happen, Jaden did. Once again, this team picked each other up and showed what made them who and what they were. "Next Man Up" is a common phrase used in sports for those that pick up when someone else goes down. It described these boys from Red Land perfectly. It was not selfishness that infuriated Cole; it was the fact that he wanted to deliver not for his own glory, but for his teammates and the glory that they would share with each other.

It was the same reason Jaden was so pleased—not for himself, but for them, for Cole. This was not just a team that was carried by a few; it was many that carried the team. It was Jaden's turn. He produced, and as he rounded third and headed for home, the guys that he so desperately wanted to come through for, were waiting for him at home plate.

Once again, this game was tied.

The beauty of Little League Baseball is there is no specialization. The moment Jaden Henline crossed the plate and was mobbed by his teammates, he ran into the dugout, grabbed his glove, and headed out to the bullpen to warm up. Since Cole was at 64 pitches, and for the moment, having difficulty dealing with his last strikeout, and it would later be learned that a migraine started to develop (when the weight of the entire world feels like it is resting on your 12-year-old shoulders, there are bound to be side effects), Coach Peifer had to think ahead and consider his next move.

He knew Cole was most likely not going to be able to finish the game, but now he wondered if he would even be able to send him back out there for the fifth, so he sent Jaden to the pen. The catcher who was assigned to warm him up? Kaden Peifer. After all, he was five batters away, and chances were Jarrett Wisman was going to bat for him anyway.

◆◆◆◆

Imagine that in the major leagues! There are absolutely no circumstances where that would occur. Picture Albert Pujols jacking an opposite field dinger only to grab starting catcher Mike Piazza to warm him up in the pen so he could come in and pitch two innings later. Whoever the short tenured manager would be would have his phone blowing up with agents calling the moment the concept was even conceived! "My guy only pitches in save situations." "My client is entitled to a five minute respite in the clubhouse after a home run so he can watch his highlight, tweet about it, and be able to film a six second video for his private fans on Facebook."

◆◆◆◆

After the initial celebration, Coach Peifer slapped Jaden on the top of his helmet, told him, "Nice Job!" and then added, "Go throw 15 in the pen to loosen up." He did not even have to tell Kaden to go, Kaden knew. Jaden ran to the pen as quickly as he rounded the bases. He had a job to do. His previous task was over. There were six outs left in the National Championship, and he knew at some point, he was going to be responsible for getting some of them—so he obliged. It is just what he did. It is what they ALL did. They had roles. They filled them. There were no questions asked.

Cinderella recovered. After the blast, Ryan Farmer got Chayton Krauss to ground out, no easy task, as all that kid seemed to do was hit baseballs. Then, he struck out Zack Sooy on three pitches. He had only thrown 45 pitches through four innings on the day, and had 40 left over the last two innings to try to somehow lead Texas to victory. He showed no signs of wearing down and no signs of being negatively affected by Jaden's blast—there was still a spring in his step and a smile on his face.

Ryan Farmer was going to be fine—it was his counterpart that had the air of uncertainty about him as he was still showing signs of frustration. Coach Peifer never even asked Cole about going out for the fifth, he just looked at him. Cole stared back. Their eyes never broke away from each other.

"Conserve pitches," was the only thing the coach said to the player. With those words resonating in his mind, Cole lumbered out onto the field for the 5th inning.

For Red Land, the game became a contest of numbers as much as anything else. To this point, both teams had two runs. Texas had three hits, Red Land had two. However, the most important number was

Cole had thrown 64 pitches. That meant he had 21 left. Farmer had only thrown 19 fewer pitches, which indicated that he probably had plenty left to be able to finish the game. That was crucial for Texas, who had already exhausted most of their pitching in their eight inning qualifying game vs. California two days earlier. What Ryan Farmer was giving them was exactly what they needed, and if they could somehow scratch out another run and win this game, well, they would be in a very good position for tomorrow's World Championship, but nobody was thinking about tomorrow.

Cole did everything he possibly could to follow his coach's instructions. "Conserve pitches." He tried. He zeroed in on the strike zone. Although strikeouts were impressive, they still required a minimum of three pitches. At this point in the game, Tom Peifer would have gladly taken a one or two pitch out as opposed to yet another strikeout, but Cole knew the best way for him to get outs was to simply overpower his opponents.

The first batter he faced in the top of the 5th was none other than his counterpart on the mound, Ryan Farmer. Though the *Red Sea* had become somewhat silent from the tension that permeated throughout the stadium, a faint sound of "Let's Go Farmer!" began from the convoy of Texas parents who were sitting behind the third base dugout. As Farmer's parents, Susan and Mike, looked down from the stands, they admired the way their son was battling at the plate in the exact same capacity that he was battling on the mound.

He watched the first pitch go by—a called strike, though it appeared outside of the strike zone. Ryan did not show any sign of disagreement. He let the second pitch fall low and inside and evened up the count at 1-1. The third pitch of the at bat jammed him and sent a stinger up his left arm. He half-heartedly ran down to first, heard that the ball went foul, and walked his way back to the batter's box.

Thinking it was time to finish the deal, Cole Wagner tried to hurl a 71 mph fastball right by him. Farmer fouled this one off into the screen that protects the fans down the first base line. On the next pitch of the at bat, Farmer seemed to make solid contact on a 70 mph fastball. Left fielder Jake Cubbler ran under the ball, turned the play into something that was somewhat routine, and after five pitches, Farmer was retired.

The next hitter, Raffi Garcia, saw only three pitches before he jumped on a change up and made solid contact on a ball that was pulled to left field and into the waiting glove of Zack Sooy, who secured the line drive, and ended the inning.

Texas had three outs left in regulation, and Red Land had Adam Cramer leading off the bottom of the 5th. The hope was that maybe he could build on the magic that he had conjured up the other night, and as he stepped into the box, that is exactly what he was thinking, too. Unfortunately, Adam saw only two pitches before he grounded out to second. After Jake Cubbler walked on five pitches, Farmer struck out Jarrett Wisman and Bailey Wirt on a total of eight pitches. The game was moving to the 6th inning, and it was as intensely competitive a ball game that had ever been played in Williamsport.

The numbers on the scoreboard were eerily close, but a closer look indicated that, perhaps, Texas had a bit of an advantage. If Red Land could not somehow hold down the Texas hitters for one more inning and then somehow muster a run across in the bottom of the 6th, their chances of fulfilling their boyhood dream would shatter before 45,000 of their most ardent supporters. As Ryan Farmer crossed over the third base line, being careful not to step on it, he was greeted with a hug from his coach.

Cole Wagner had nine pitches left to throw. As he walked out to the mound for the 6th inning, in the back of his mind, he hoped that would be all he would need to retire the side.

If he were going to be able to do it, he had to go through the heart of the Texas lineup. Due up for Pearland were Gottfried, Tadlock, and Mack (who had not been retired all day). The first pitch Cole threw to Ben was low and inside—not exactly how he wanted to start. Cole made sure his next pitch was in the zone, and Ben made solid contact, blasting it into foul territory down the right field line.

"Ohhhh…" remarked Ravech.

"Showed a little flash there," added Peterson.

Cole hopped up a little at the end of his delivery, sensing that he may have gotten away with a pitch that caught a little bit too much of the plate. Feeling confident, Ben tried to tear into the next pitch as well but was a little late on the trigger, and instead, he found himself in a hole, 1-2. Cole wanted to end it. If he could get to the third batter before he reached 85 pitches, Little League rules permitted him to complete the at bat. That is what he wanted—to finish the game, finish the mission, and then hope to get a chance to win it in the bottom of the 6th.

He honed in. Kaden looked into the dugout to their pitching coach-Uncle Bret to him, Dad to Cole—and he called for a fastball up in the zone. "Go get him, Cole," encouraged Coach Peifer. But he had too much juice on the pitch. He was still running on pure adrenaline, and as he reached back to put just a little bit extra into the pitch, the ball went sailing to the backstop. Ordinarily, it was not that big of a deal. Under other circumstances, it would be a good thing—a bit of unpredictability and controlled wildness prevents the hitter from becoming too comfortable in the batter's box, after all, nobody wants to be hit by a 75 mph fastball.

Cole did not have the luxury of throwing "set up" pitches or sending messages. He needed outs; and he needed to get those outs efficiently. He slammed his fist into his glove—he knew he had missed his target, and he was not pleased. He glanced into the dugout at his father; he muttered to himself under his breath. He took a little extra time to stare into his catcher. He knew the sign was going to be for a fastball, but he waited anyway.

Strike three. He blew it right by Gottfried and got the first out of the inning. The problem was it took over half the pitches he still had left to do it. If he wanted a chance to finish the game, he had to get Tadlock in fewer than four pitches.

Both kids knew it. Tadlock had two jobs—somehow get on base, and make sure he saw at least four pitches. Cole reached back and fired the first pitch. Ball one. Good for Texas, bad for Pennsylvania. Even if Jarrett struck out in this at bat, Red Land would have to go to another pitcher for Mack. He stepped out of the box, looked down to his coach at third, got the signs, and prepared for the next pitch. "Strike!" He was taking all the way. There was no way Tadlock was swinging until Cole threw a strike, his 83rd pitch of the day. Now he just could not make an out on this next pitch. Most people thought he would be taking again. So did Cole. He grooved one across the outside part of the plate, making sure if this was going to be his last batter, he was going to put him in a two-strike hole. "Strike 2!"

When the pitch crossed the plate, everybody in the stadium, including the guys from ESPN, knew what that meant. "Firing them in there again, but this is going to be the last batter we see Cole Wagner face as his next pitch will be his 85th," explained Ravech.

Cole stewed. He knew it, too. He understood the Texas strategy, but was disappointed in the confrontation that was not happening between him and Tadlock. He wanted Tadlock to engage, not just because of the pitch count, but because he thrived on these types of encounters. Now it was reduced to one pitch—so Cole was going to win it.

The look on his face, almost disappointment when he saw Tadlock keep his bat on his shoulder for the second strike, said, "Come on, Jarrett, give me your best." He got the ball back, the count was 1-2. Cole Wagner had one pitch left to throw. "Here is mine."

He blazed a fastball right down the middle of the plate. He almost dared the boy to hit it. It wasn't up, wasn't out, wasn't in. Here it is…hit it if you can. He could not. As the 71 mph fastball flew by his swinging bat, the crowd came to its feet. It was over for Cole, the pitcher.

Cole, the batter, could still have the opportunity to have an impact on the outcome of the game since he was due up second in the bottom of the 6th, but as far as ever throwing another pitch in the Little League World Series, his job was done. It was an amazing job that he did—85 pitches, 11 strikeouts, 3 hits, 2 runs, 1 walk, but that was little consolation to him. He wanted to be happy, he wanted to feel good, he wanted to accept the love and admiration that was being showered down upon him by the fans in red—but he could not. He had not completed the mission. He shrugged his shoulders, he curled his lip, his head went down ever so slightly—even in his brilliance, and he was disappointed. He wanted to keep going, he burned to keep going, his arm still felt good, his heart and soul were screaming for one more batter.

Coach Peifer jogged to the mound. He took the ball from the young man, told him, "Great job, Cole." Those words were hollow. Cole stomped off the mound, not pouting, more enraged. The warrior spirit in him wanted to keep fighting. He was not ready to lay down his weapon, which happened to be a 70+ mph fastball. As he went into the dugout, he retrieved his first baseman's glove, and with him went Chayton Krauss, who would move to shortstop, and Jaden Henline who would assume the pitching responsibilities.

For Jaden, this was his fourth straight game in which he was making an appearance on the mound. He started the first game, in which he was the winning pitcher in the 18-0 blowout. He also backed into a win in the second game vs. South Carolina after he blew the save but was able to redeem himself when he came up to bat to walk off with a victory. Three days earlier, he earned and preserved a victory for Adam Cramer who was brilliant for the first five innings before Jaden came in and slammed the door in the 6th.

Now, he would be trying for his third victory in the World Series. Teams had shown the ability to get to Jaden. In 4 1/3 innings, he had given up 7 hits, 4 runs, and walked 3 batters. His ERA was an unimpressive 5.54, but he had also struck out ten and showed signs of dominance on more than one occasion. Coach Peifer was hoping this was going to be one of those occasions. On many teams, Jaden certainly would have been considered the ace, but though he may not have been Red Land's best pitcher, he was their most important—at least he was right now.

Getting his first batter of the day was no easy task. Zack Mack had already been on base twice today, once with a hard hit double to the wall. He was batting .545 for the entire LLWS with 7 RBI's and a grand slam. Surely part of Coach Solomon's strategy was to give Zack a crack at somebody else—someone other than Cole Wagner. This first at bat for Jaden, getting that third out in the inning, was crucial. As Zack stepped into the box, Kaden Peifer called time and went out to talk to his pitcher one last time.

"Time blue!" called Kaden, as he jumped up and started moving toward the mound.

"Hurry up! Make it quick," responded the home plate umpire, attempting to keep the game moving. The two boys spoke briefly and the confrontation was about to take place.

His first three pitches were all away, each one a little more outside than the previous one. The first caught the edge of the plate, but the next two were left alone, and soon Jaden found himself behind the hitter, 2-1. On the fourth pitch, he came inside and jammed Zack to the point where he lifted a harmless pop fly in foul territory, which Cole—now playing first—got himself under, quickly called for it, and secured the third out.

The Patriots would be bringing the top of the order to the plate with the hopes of being able to score a run and walk off with the 2015 National Championship. It started with the ultimate of all leadoff hitters, Braden Kolmansberger.

"Just get on base, kid. Somehow, someway, scratch your way down to first. We'll do the rest," were the instructions given to BK by all of his coaches and teammates. The words may have been different, but the message was exactly the same. "Just get on base."

Different guys had different "things." BK's "thing" was scoring runs. Nobody had ever done it better. Entering the 6th inning of the National Championship, BK wanted to continue his trend of scoring a run every time he got on base; somehow, he had to get on down there.

Ryan Farmer, possibly showing his very first sign of fatigue, made it easy for him. He threw four pitches, none of which was particularly close to the strike zone. On the last two, he looked down at the mound and indicated that he was losing his footing when he tried to plant. It was the same problem Cole had experienced back in the 2nd inning. After ball four, the Patriots' leadoff hitter ran down to first base and stared into the dugout. When Cole Wagner emerged as the next batter, the crowd once again came to its feet.

So did Coach Andrew Solomon. Perhaps he did not like the body language that he saw out on the mound. Perhaps he thought he saw signs that Ryan Farmer, who had been absolutely stunning with his grit and composure all afternoon, was finally starting to wear down. Whatever his reasons, he tried to explain them to his pitcher.

"What a great job," he said to the boy. He looked as if he were in deep thought, almost reluctant to break the news to his starting pitcher who had performed so admirably all day. "I think I'm going to go to Marco. All right?" Ryan Farmer nodded his head. Then, the boy's head went straight down. His coach tried to console him. "Hey? You did an unbelievable job today. An unbelievable job. I figure we'll give Cole a little different look; he's seen you twice already."

Then Solomon's attention turned to his next pitcher, who had a monumental task ahead of him. Getting Cole out any time is a mighty feat—but an angry Cole—a focused Cole—a more determined Cole —a Cole who was trying to overcompensate for himself, who felt inadequate for not being able to go the distance—that's asking an awful lot! "Marco, you ready? You got a good hitter here. You got him the other night, remember? You ready? All right, do your thing." Then he gave the ball to his pitcher and walked back into the dugout.

As he did, young Ryan Farmer walked out to his new position in centerfield. His step was brisk, but his head was still down. The Red Land fans in the outfield, however, recognized just how valiantly this young man's performance had been. He had befuddled one of the most dominant offensive teams in the nation and held them to only two hits for the entire day. They stood, they applauded, and they showed their appreciation and their respect. When he finally looked up and realized what they were doing, Ryan Farmer tipped his hat to his new fans in Pennsylvania. He flashed his shy, boyish grin, put his head back down, and completed the walk to his position. I would like to think that at some point he allowed himself to feel good about what he had done.

As Marco warmed up, the *Red Sea* rose. They pulled out their phones; they wanted to record this moment forever. It seemed inevitable. As the fans in the Sea prepared for their celebration, the question was not if Cole would hit a walk off home run in this situation, it was more of how far would it travel? By the look in Cole's eye, he had visions of hitting this one all the way back to Lewisberry.

He rocked in his usual motion, hovered over the inside part of the plate. He taunted the pitcher to throw one within his reach. Forty-six feet away, the 5'5" / 108 pound twelve year old pitcher stared into his catcher as they tried to figure out a way to not become the next part of Cole's heroic moments.

After throwing the first one high and outside, Marco challenged him on the second pitch. Cole discharged all of his fury into his mighty swing. He missed. His next attempt was a curve ball that did not break;

instead, it stayed way outside, and catcher Tristan Schwehr lunged for the ball to make sure BK was unable to move to second. Vowing to pitch to everybody, Coach Solomon called for another fastball, and Marco delivered one dangerously over the heart of the plate. Cole again burst into his swing, but was unable to make contact yet again. If he did not get a hit, he certainly was not going to be cheated on his attempts. When the next pitch stayed away again, the count was full at 3-2.

"I don't see him shortening up his swing at all with two strikes," predicted Peterson.

"No. He'll swing if it's close," responded Ravech.

But he didn't. As Marco Gutierrez threw a curve ball that broke softly over the inside part of the plate, Cole stood motionless in the box.

"WOW!!! Inside corner. Wagner strikes out. He couldn't pull the trigger," said Ravech.

Cole looked down at his dad at third base, then turned and walked back to the dugout. He knew it was a strike. He knew he should have swung. He was not sure why he had not.

As the fans stood stunned (and somewhat silent), Coach Jeremy Tadlock remembered that after the last time Cole struck out, Jaden Henline hit a home run in the very next at bat. He wanted to make sure that did not happen again. He called for time and went out to the mound.

Whatever he said, it was not enough. Henline ripped the first pitch he saw past the second baseman, and by doing so, it allowed Braden Kolmansberger to reach third base with only one out. All Pennsylvania had to do was hit a pop fly deep enough to let BK tag up from third. They did not even need a hit. The strategies for both managers raced through their heads as Chayton Krauss walked to the plate.

"Just make contact," Chayton told himself. "Don't try to do too much." It was advice he had given himself his entire life. Phrases like that were what Chayton lived by. He had always been happy with just filling his role. He did not need the attention, the accolades, or the notoriety. At home, he was the quiet one, the logical one. Chayton was the one who played it safe. On this team, he was the kid who did whatever the team needed. Shortstop. First base. Pitcher. Starter. Relief. Whatever would help the team. As Coach Peifer stood in the dugout, he knew the team needed him to score that run from third right now.

Karl Ravech set the scene. "The winning run is 60 feet away." The Red Land faithful were launched back into delirium.

Coach Solomon went to the mound. He explained the strategy and urgency of not letting that runner on third score. "If it's hit soft to the middle, we gotta go home. If it's hit hard to the middle, we're gonna turn them over [meaning turn a double play]." He yelled out to his outfielders, "You gotta come in a little bit. You gotta come in! On a fly ball, you gotta throw home!"

Chayton Krauss just wanted to bat. He stepped into the box. Coach Solomon turned to shout something else. Chayton stepped back out. He was batting .455 in the Little League World Series, but because none of those hits had been monster home runs, nobody really knew it. Coach Peifer knew it—he was the exact kid he wanted up in that situation. "He was the perfect guy because of how calm he was. He was always so level. So composed. His demeanor fit that situation because I knew he wouldn't try to do too much."

Some guys would want the historic walk off home run. Some would wilt under the pressure and magnitude of the moment. Chayton just wanted to make contact with the ball. He did not need glory, he just needed positive results. His first swing resulted in a foul ball dribbler down the third base line. A hit like that might be enough to get the run across, and that would be fine with Chayton, but he had to keep it fair. The second pitch produced a similar result, a foul ball down the third base line. Chayton found himself in an 0-2 hole.

The third pitch was straight from the Bret Wagner pitching school of strikeouts—a fastball up in the zone. Chayton was not biting. It was why Coach Peifer had so much faith in him. A less disciplined player, a more anxious hitter, would have chased that pitch in a heartbeat. Chayton never even flinched. "Ball." 1-2.

Catcher Tristan Schwehr looked into the dugout for the sign. It was for a curve ball. When Marco threw it, Chayton, once again, fouled it off down the third base line. He had not really made solid contact with any of Marco's pitches. He stepped out of the box to take a deep breath. The crowd joined him. Then, he stepped back in. He manicured the dirt just a little while the ball was retrieved and put back into play. There was one out with runners on first and third in the bottom of the 6th inning of the Little League World Series.

At the plate was the son of the man who had risked everything by picking up his family and moving them to the United States of America from New Zealand because there were more opportunities, and because he had a sense of adventure. Now, here his older son stood in the eye of the hurricane of emotions that consisted of anticipation, horror, excitement, and stress. His son, who had never gone out of his way to be in a situation like this, had fouled off three pitches and was one strike away from having to turn back into that dugout and stand in the shadow of his teammates once again. Part of him liked the comfort that those shadows provided. It gave him anonymity, but part of him wanted to break out from those shadows, from behind the curtain and scream as loud as he could...

"CHAMPION!!!!"

The next pitch Marco threw was a fastball low and outside, and Chayton did not miss it. He ripped it in the hole between first and second, and the ball went all the way to the fence. It got past Carter Ostrom in right field, but none of that mattered once Chayton touched first and, more importantly, BK touched home.

"THAT'S IT!!! PENNSYLVANIA IS THE LITTLE LEAGUE WORLD SERIES CHAMPIONS OF THE UNITED STATES!!!" screamed Karl Ravech from the booth, no doubt taking a tremendous amount of pride in the fact that this team was from his native Harrisburg area.

As BK came across home plate, he turned and ran toward Chayton, who was being mobbed by the rest of his teammates and coaches. Paul and Pip Krauss looked down from the stands and saw a mob of teammates hugging each other, jumping, and swarming in a circle of joy. In the center of all of it was their son. He would never feel as if he were in anyone's shadow again—and neither would his coach.

21

PAPPY, POP-POP, MEMAW, AND GRANDMA BAM!!!

They came together before each regional and district playoff game and gathered in left-center field. That area quickly became known as "Grandparent Hill." While they were there, a camaraderie developed that would last them throughout the entire summer. As they watched the games, they would share stories with one another about the boys in the field as they had watched them grow up. "I just can't believe how grown up he is" was a phrase that was repeated over and over again. "It was just yesterday I was holding him in my arms, or changing his diaper," would say one grandfather.

"You never changed any of his diapers!" a grandmother would quickly correct. The resounding laughter that echoed from the hill down to the field expressed a kind of peace and happiness that only a grandparent would understand.

Then, they would watch their grandsons play and their sons coach, and that combination made for twice the responsibility, twice the anxiety, but also, twice the joy. After the game, win or lose, they would provide an atmosphere of solitude that was free of judgment or critique. Fred Sanders, better known as Pap to Kaden, was known as the snack guy on the team. Kaden knew he could always count on Pap for the good stuff—the double stuff.

"Kaden used to come up to me after the game and we'd talk for about 30 seconds about baseball, and then he'd say, 'Hey, Pap, did you bring the Oreos?' And then I'd always hand him over a little baggie of them. It became our routine, our 'thing.'"

After the first game in Williamsport, everybody wanted a piece of Kaden. A hug, an interview, a high five. Something, anything. Fans just wanted to be around the kids.

Kaden continued to wave and appease as many people as he could. He basked in the attention that he was getting, but he had a purpose to his movements. He was looking for his Pap.

Of course! Now that the game was over, Kaden just wanted his Pap and his Oreos. So he slapped fives to everyone who wanted one, took pictures, gave hugs, signed autographs, and finally …FINALLY … he reached Pap!

Fred Sanders was so excited to see his grandson. He hugged him. "Great job, Kaden, that was amazing! I'm so proud of you!" He glowed as he talked to his grandson.

Kaden smiled, said "Thanks!" and then, just waited.

There was somewhat of a prolonged pause after that. Kaden stood patiently. Finally, he could wait no longer and broke the silence. In almost a side conversation Kaden asked, "Hey, Pap, did you bring the Oreos?"

"Oh, yeah. The Oreos. I did. Here. Take the whole package. You earned them." The smile Kaden had from all the glory, all the attention, all the euphoria of the moment, suddenly became even brighter.

"Oh, my goodness! Thanks, PAP!" Then he immediately turned to his teammates. "Guys! I got the whole pack! He gave me the whole pack!" As heroic as Kaden had been in the game, Fred Sanders, Pap, quickly surpassed even his grandson's heroic feat …and all it took was a package of Oreo cookies.

All the boys' grandparents had their own tales of how their grandchildren, and their sons, had matured through the game of baseball.

His first word was, "Ball!"
"Honey, he would say 'Ba' I don't know if that was for ball!"
"Well, what else would he have been saying?"

The memories of their children and grandchildren would weave together and create a quilt that would wrap around their lives and provide a kind of comfort and satisfaction that could only come from a life enriched by children.

As the grandchildren formed their friendships with one another now, so, too, had their fathers before them developed lasting friendships. As the story goes: After they had won the State Championship in High School, four of the friends got a matching tattoo of a Four-Leaf Clover to represent the friendship they had with each other. The same four—Tom, Bret, Kyle, and Mitch Kauffman, coach of the 2014 Patriot team that finished 3rd in the state of Pennsylvania—were married within a year of each other. When it came time to settle down, choose a career, and start a family, there was no doubt, they all would live in the Red Land area. Each had a first-born son, followed by a baby girl, and their friendship just continued to grow stronger.

The grandparents continued to reminisce about their children and grandchildren, smiling, laughing and joking through it all...

"BK's first toy was a stuffed dog named Rufus... and a baseball. By age two, he could actually catch it and throw it back. He wouldn't always throw it back to me, but he would throw it!" Jim Kolmansberger Sr. stated with a hearty chuckle. He would know, as he and son JK would coach BK in the earliest stages of baseball. "I was his first coach in tee-ball, and back then we would just throw the ball toward his glove and just hope that it somehow got stuck in there. We did that with all the kids."

As fathers and grandfathers have done with their children and grandchildren generation after generation, the adults threw themselves unabashedly into the interests of their offspring. For these kids, their earliest interests revolved around sports in general—baseball specifically. "Those kids would play baseball from the time they got off the bus until it was time to go to bed. We used to go down to the park with picnic dinners and just watch them play because we knew they weren't coming home to eat!"

As Amy Peifer was there for Kaden, all these moms were there to comfort their sons and grandsons—and, on occasion, sometimes the grandfathers as well! "I remember the time Jim came running in the house because Braden had broken his nose," recalls Carol Kolmansberger, BK's "Nana."

"Oh…he whacked me!" says "Pop" Kolmansberger. "We were playing with a broken Wiffle Ball in the dark and he smacked one, and it got me right in the nose! I was bleeding everywhere. BK thought he had killed me. I told him he couldn't hit it that hard yet! I still have the scar!"

Along with that scar, he, like his wife and every other Nanny and Pap, have countless fond memories of how the game of baseball brought them closer to their grandchildren.

"Tom was always around me," recalled Tom Sr. (Pap), "and when he became a father, Kaden was always around *him*. Sports were just in their blood.

When their grandson's were ten, they all watched them win the Pennsylvania State Championship. When they were 11, they watched them suffer when they lost it. And this past year, they witnessed their grandest experience of all!

"But they're still just little boys!" reminded Marie Walter, Cam's Nanny. "When they were 10 and they were playing for the state championship up in Erie, the whole team came into our room because they found out our room had a hot tub, and all of them jumped in. Then Cam looked up at me and said, 'Nanny, do you have any snacks for us?' So after every game up there, they would have their little party in the hot tub. I thought for sure we were going to get kicked out of there!"

"Well, wouldn't you know when they were up at Bristol this past summer, doesn't Cam come up to me and ask if our room had a hot tub! I told him, no, Cam, it doesn't, but it doesn't matter, you guys wouldn't fit in one any more if we did have one anyway!"

Yes, they certainly had grown in two years, and so did their exposure. "But they stayed true to who they still were," said Bonnie McNaulty, Cole's Grammy. Every time they did an interview or had to give a speech, I was just in awe at how grown up they were, and how humble and responsible they acted. That really is a credit to all those kids' parents; it's a result of good parenting."

"And good grandparenting!" added Memaw Sanders, Kaden's grandmother, who never says anything without a warm, glowing smile.

Gary (better known as Butch) Wagner, Pop-Pop, noted the same thing once the team actually made it to Williamsport, "I remember saying to Bret, 'Bret, are the kids gonna be able to handle the pressure that they'll be under when they play in Williamsport. This is the big stage. There are going to be thousands of people up in those stands and out on that hill.' He said to me, 'Dad, don't worry about the kids, they're fine. It's the coaches that are a mess!'"

"Yeah, they're still grounded, but eventually, at 16, they'll outgrow it. They'll discover cars and girls and they'll put down the baseball," Pop Kolmansberger pondered. "But they haven't yet."

"Well, they're not 16 yet either!" reminded Tom Sr.

For now, these proud seniors can enjoy the youth of their grandchildren and the purity and innocence that they all still possess. It was those same qualities that drew so many people to them and captured the hearts of an entire nation. "We had a man cut down a tree in our yard," said Grandma BAM, "who told me, 'I never watch the news, it's too depressing. And I never watched baseball either. But those boys made me watch both all summer long!'"

They all had stories like that, the ones where total strangers would share their memories that were created by their grandchildren. "We were at Longhorn Steak House," said Pap Sanders, "and these two little old ladies came up to Kaden and shyly asked if they could take a picture with him so they could post it on Facebook. I didn't even realize little old ladies knew what Facebook was!" When it came time to pay the bill, there was no charge. The manager had come over and explained to the family that it was the least they could do to somehow thank Kaden for everything he had done for the community this summer. "And in typical fashion, when we got in the car, Kaden asked, 'Can we go back there again?'"

It seemed like every story they shared re-enforced the concept of virtue and merit. And they all seemed to end with a laugh. "If you had a red shirt on, it didn't even have to be a Red Land one, everyone just wanted to talk to you about the team," said Jessie Sanders, Memaw. "It's like everybody became friends! It was just nice."

Just like the boys. They were just, nice. They carried on the characteristics that many of their parents exhibited. When Grandma BAM's mother passed away, it was Dylan Rodenhaber's father who spoke at her funeral about the friendship he had made with the 100 year old woman who never missed one of her great grandson's (or grandson's) sporting events. "Even in the cold, she'd make every Friday night football game to support Tommy," interjected Grandma BAM. Mr. Rodenhaber jokingly recalled a time when he told the dear lady to meet him at 2:00 am outside the hotel for a "date." "The next day, when everyone got up, she came down to the lobby, saw George (Dylan's father) and said, 'Hey, where were you? I was outside waiting all night!'"

"They just have a way of making people feel really special," said Jessie. "That's what makes them so special. I saw Kaden give an autograph to a little boy one time who was really nervous to ask him for it. The little boy's father encouraged him to go ask, and Kaden heard him say, 'Go ahead, Jackson, go ask him.' So he did. When Kaden signed his card, he said to him, 'There you go, Jackson, thanks for asking.' The little boy turned around amazed and said to his dad, 'He knows my name!' I was not as compassionate of a person as he is already. I hope he never changes."

And there is no reason to believe that he ever will. When another little boy who was in his baseball uniform came up to Kaden and asked him for his autograph, Kaden responded instinctively, "Sure, if I can have yours, too." Grace, kindness, and humanity like that does not erode, not when they are a part of your make-up, your very being.

Nana Kolmansberger tells the story that, "BK stayed with us right before the team went up to Bristol because everybody in his house was sick, and we didn't want him to catch anything. So, we got lucky and he stayed with us. And every night just before bed, he would come downstairs with his blanket and Rufus and just sit on the couch with us and talk. As great as all the memories were from this past summer on the baseball field, that will still be one of my favorites."

"My father passed away this summer," said Butch Wagner, Pop-Pop, "but I'm convinced it was the best summer of his life watching those boys play baseball. Not just Cole. Those boys. That team. *All* of them. They were a special group of kids."

The boys continued to give back and reach out as their status in the community continued to rise. At the Four Diamonds foundation, it was BK who challenged the patients at the Hershey Medical Center with the slogan, "Why Not You?" as a way of inspiring them to overcome their ailments.

And when the games were all over, all of the grandparents wished the same things for not just their grandsons, but for their sons as well. "I was just proud of how they conducted themselves on such a grand stage. I knew that everything that my grandson did that made me proud, was made possible by the way my son raised him. And that made me even more proud," said Tom Peifer Sr.

"And to think this friendship all started up on a hill in Fredericksburg," someone chimed in.

"I remember that hill!" said Pop Kolmansberger. "I remember we used to warn people about parking their cars there. We'd tell them, hey, you might want to move those cars.

Then Butch added, "Move those cars? Heck! We told those people they better move those houses!"

It was a summer of memories. It has been a lifetime of memories, memories that none of them will ever forget—or ever want to. Neither will any of the rest of us.

22

THEIR SHIRTS SAID TOKYO

In the immediate aftermath of the US National Championship, the joy that surrounded not only the players and coaches, but also anybody associated with the Red Land Community could only be described as euphoric. Grown men cried, ladies were speechless, and the only way people could accurately express the jubilation they were feeling was to hug each other—and they did, often.

"THEY DID IT!" quickly transformed to "WE did it!" as so many who felt connected to this team were feeling the same sense of elation the players and coaches were. After taking their picture with the National Championship banner, the boys sprinted out to centerfield to touch the bust of Howard Lamade, a tradition every bit as sacred as the countless superstitions that encompass the Stanley Cup. One by one, they leaped the fence and stretched their arms out to touch the statue that rested beyond the centerfield wall. Ethan Phillips tried to hop up twice, but he was unsuccessful. Eventually, he gave up trying and just turned toward the *Red Sea* and saluted them. They roared back at him and appreciated the fact that he acknowledged them.

Having done that, the boys were able to take one of the most festive, gratifying, and oh, so satisfying walks that will ever be made—the one from centerfield back into the dugout. They looked around, they saw the hysteria that they had created, they floated from the outfield through the infield, pausing momentarily from time to time to wave to the fans, to hug one another, or to point to their teammates at something they saw in the crowd. There was not one among them who was not beaming with pride.

"I was just so proud of the boys, not because they won, but *how* they won. They were like little gentlemen throughout the tournament, throughout the summer. They loved each other, loved playing with each other—*for* each other. And they loved playing for Red Land," said Amy Peifer, who was near hysteria after the game, sharing the joy for both her son and her husband. "The boys deserved to win—not that the boys from Texas didn't, they battled so hard—but our boys' victories weren't any coincidence."

After the game, the boys met with the media on the field and answered their questions. Chayton told Jaymee Sire that his feelings, the crowd, his teammates, were all "Awesome!" Jaden Henline's word was "Amazing!" He used it three times. The entire time the boys were being interviewed, coaches Tom Peifer and JK Kolmansberger cleaned out the dugout in the background—fitting, as usual, they continued to allow the kids to be the focal point of this journey.

The boys finished answering all the questions as respectfully and graciously as they could, and then they just wanted to celebrate. All the nights of practice, all the coaching, all the instruction, all the individual workouts, the buckets and buckets of balls being whisked at them by coaches, dads, friends, instructors—all the sleepless nights of thinking, "Is this all worth it?" "Are we good enough?" "Am *I* good enough?" All of it was now worth it.

The fleeting moments of defeat, the temporary feelings of inadequacy, and the impulsive temptations to quit that were eventually overcome by the desire to persist—they were all worth it! The boys always told themselves that even if they didn't win, it would have been worth it because they got to spend day after day with their friends, who had become more like brothers, and together, they had formed a bond as strong as any family could hope to have.

They always said it was worth it anyway—maybe they were preparing themselves for consolation in case they ever needed it, but now, they did not need it. They won! They were the UNITED STATES CHAMPIONS, and no matter what they would go on to do in their entire lives, they would always have that distinction.

As they came out from under the grandstand, one of the most thunderous ovations they would ever hear in their lifetime greeted them. When they finally got into their van to return to the dorm, the crowd surrounded their vehicle, banged on the windows, and shouted their excitement with roaring approval.

"Is this thing safe?"
"Are we gonna tip over?"

The boys all laughed, nervously, because honestly, they were not sure what the answer to those questions were. But eventually, they were able to get back to their dorms and away from all the chaos—and then they could create a little bit of their own.

They raided their snacks, they dog piled on each other, they ransacked their dorm room—they were boys. They released all the childhood glee they had been taught to hold back to demonstrate respect for their opponents. Now, they could finally celebrate—unfiltered, unreserved, unabashedly. And they cherished every second of it.

Throughout the entire tournament, from districts, to regionals, to states, to Bristol, and then in Williamsport, the boys always had that cloud hanging over them in the form of a question, "What if we don't win?' As they continued to advance, to dominate, that cloud loomed larger, darker, and more ominous. They all saw it, though none would acknowledge it. Now, the skies above them were as clear as the evening of that August 29, 2015 night. There was a purity in the sky, a oneness in the mountains of Williamsport, and a sense of satisfaction the boys, and their coaches, were finally able to enjoy.

As they celebrated, the Japanese players who shared a dorm with them, who were celebrating in a different manner, (their celebration was much more of a sense of relief of having won, than glee) heard them. They were well aware that their dorm mates were victorious, and eventually, they joined in their celebration. There had been a friendship that had formed between the Mid-Atlantic Champions and the team from Japan, which they would face tomorrow. Boys who spend close to two weeks together in close proximity will create either a friendship or a rivalry. These boys from Red Land had won over so many with their good nature, among them the team from Japan, so their relationship was anything but acrimonious despite the fact that the language barrier prevented the two teams from clearly communicating.

Joy is a universal language, and on this night, both teams had a surplus of it. They listened to music, both American and Japanese, and brought it into the common bathroom where the sounds would echo off the tile walls. They sang, though they knew not what they were singing, and they laughed, and danced, and basked in the delight of the fact that they would be playing for a World Championship the following day.

The only problem with the entire situation was that these two teams would be facing each other in that World Championship. To say that fact stifled any of the joy that either team was feeling would be inaccurate. They had a common bond that no other team could understand—they had both felt an amazing pressure to *have* to win, each for its own reasons: Red Land because they were the local team, the chosen ones, the team of destiny, and Japan because that was the expectation each and every team had that came to Williamsport.

The Japanese boys were pieces of a much bigger conglomerate, where baseball was much more like a business than a pastime. They were not even allowed to join the Americans for games like Ping-Pong until they had actually won their first game—their coaches had forbidden it. For them, this was strictly a business trip—difficult circumstances for any 11 or 12-year-old to understand.

They were not only expected to get to Williamsport every year, they were expected to *win* there, as they had in three of the last five years. Failure to do so risked shaming their nation to a certain extent. Their eight-hour sessions that focused on hitting, fielding, pitching, and game strategy were legendary amongst the coaches at the Little League World Series. But neither team felt that pressure of expectation any longer, and that commonality—the fact that they would both return to their homes with the label of "Champions"—allowed both teams to drop their inhibitions and just be kids. It enabled their celebration to reach epic proportions.

Without ESPN, media, or even the looming eyes of coaches, the kids were allowed to be just that—kids. No longer were they ballplayers, or in the case of the Red Land boys, celebrities. They were just children, and for a couple of hours on the Saturday night before the Little League World Championship, that felt to them as good as winning did earlier in the day.

They played endless games of Ping-Pong. The Japanese players became notorious among the Red Land kids for just continuing to play regardless of what the score was. "They never quit. We would get to 11, and they would keep going. We thought, '*Okay, we'll play to 15.*' Nope, they kept going. We hit 21, 25…it didn't matter, they just *kept playing!*"

The Japanese and Red Land players had a home run derby with Ping-Pong balls and paddles, which they named "Dinger Pong" and "Battle Bots." They even invented a professional wrestling / sumo style game the boys created using the boxes their bats were packaged in. They were kids having fun, reaping the rewards that came with victory and a job well done. The fact that they were celebrating with the players from the team they would be competing against in less than 24 hours was inconsequential, and the fact that it was so irrelevant made the moment even better.

◆◆◆◆

Though they had little time to relax, the coaches, too, allowed themselves a brief moment of peace after they won the US Championship. Their respite of choice were episodes of Mountain Men, a series on The History Channel. They had binged on the show during quiet moments in the dorm throughout the tournament. Once, they were caught by one of the Texas coaches who admitted, "Man, we thought you guys were in here watching film on the rest of us, and we all felt inadequate for not doing the same thing!"

They did designate a few hours to familiarize themselves with who their opponents would be the next day, however. Japan's journey was quite unique and dramatic; perhaps that is why their players were so elated that they had made it this far.

After defeating their international rivals, Asia-Pacific, in the opening game, they moved on to beat Mexico. They fell behind to Latin America not once, not twice, but on three separate occasions, the last time occurred in the 8th inning when they trailed by two runs after giving up back to back home runs in the top of the 8th. However, they never panicked, never wilted. They calmly responded by loading the bases on a series of hits, walks, and batters hit by pitches before Yugo Aoki hit the game winning walk off single to give them the dramatic 5-4 victory.

In their International Championship game, Kabu Kikuchi was simply unhittable for seven innings. He scattered four hits and struck out ten over the extra innings, and only threw 77 pitches for the entire afternoon. When Koki Jo beat out a ground ball that Mexico tried to turn into a double play, Japan secured their spot in the final game against Red Land.

The coaches knew their opponent's hitters were a combination of a special speed and power, and they could certainly hit for average. They were not quite as powerful, did not hit for average quite as high as the team from Lewisberry, but they were *dangerous*, and the coaching staff knew that. The unknown was their pitching.

Like Red Land, their ace was unavailable, both Cole Wagner and Kabu Kikuchi would not be able to throw any pitches, having exhausted their pitch counts a day earlier. Adam Cramer was also unavailable, while Japan had every other pitcher able to throw.

Red Land still felt they would be able to do some damage against their pitching staff. The intangibles would be the difference. Japan was amazingly persistent, but the US Champions had all the momentum on their side. They no longer were just representing Red Land, or even Pennsylvania. They were representing the United States of America—no greater honor had ever been bestowed upon the kids or coaches than to be able to represent their nation.

It was a privilege and responsibility that every member of the team, from player to coach, not only accepted, but also welcomed. The more they thought about it, the more they wanted to win it. Although their goal had always been just to win the US Championship, their competitive spirits were ignited at the thought of being able to take it even one step further.

They were well aware of what they were up against; it was almost the traditional literary conflict of man vs. machine as the boys from the town of Lewisberry locked horns with their far superior training facilities and arduously prepared kids from the island of Japan. Nevertheless, they had never backed down from a challenge before, and they certainly were not going to do so now.

◆◆◆◆

The following day, all of the delirium of the night before was forgotten. There was a game to be played, and as much as the coaches and players may not have wanted to admit it, the competitive spirit in each of them wanted to win it. They knew the task was amazingly difficult.

"After all, the name on the back of our shirts said Lewisberry—theirs said Tokyo. How were we going to compete with that?" pondered Lisa Cubbler.

But they *did* compete, and for a brief moment in time, it appeared that not only were they going to compete, they were going to overcome some of the greatest odds in sports.

◆◆◆◆

The *Red Sea* gathered for one last time. Many had found a place to camp out for the evening, whether in the back of their cars (or pickups) or a cabin nearby that was owned by a parent's friend of a friend—who just wanted to help out, as now it was impossible to find *anyone* who wasn't completely overtaken by this group of boys. Others made the trip all the way back home, only to turn around and do it again the next day. As the boys had realized yesterday, it was all worth it. The gas money, the lack of sleep, the what seemed like endless miles back and forth along Route 15, it was worth whatever it took to be directly involved in this atmosphere.

◆◆◆◆

One of the proud members in attendance for this World Championship Game, not of the *Red Sea*, but of the *family* contingency, was Chayt's

"Pop", who showed up unexpectedly. Unbeknownst to anyone, Chayton's grandfather bought a one-way ticket from New Zealand and arrived in Williamsport just moments before the first pitch of the *first* game. As he stood in centerfield, he called his daughter, Pip (Chayton's mom), and began talking.

"Pop, I can barely hear you, what's all that noise in the background?" Pip asked.

"Sorry, love, I'm out in centerfield at a baseball game; there's a lot of people around me," he discreetly responded.

When Pip looked out to centerfield, she saw her father standing under the scoreboard there. Her heart dropped and tears filled her eyes. She had not seen her father for over *four* years. She immediately got her son's attention. Chayton was warming up on the field, and his mom pointed to the outfield under the scoreboard. The young New Zealand native looked out and saw his Pop and Uncle Mark standing in the midst of the *Red Sea*. It was the first sign of just how big this "thing" had gotten. After the game, one of his first questions to Pop Krauss was,

"How long are you staying?"

"Well, til it's over, of course!" was his simplified response. Ten days later, he was still in Williamsport, PA, ready for this final game, and absolutely loving every minute of it.

◆◆◆◆

Those that could not attend still supported the team any way they could. Facebook has made this world a little smaller, and parents continued to be bombarded by messages from long distance friends, some of whom they had not heard from in years. They were flabbergasted to find out they had a small connection to the team.

"Is that your son?" was a frequent question that was asked via a post, a text, or a tweet. Pride radiated through the keyboard when the letters "yes" were put together for a brief response.

The coaches found it impossible to respond to all the well-wishers and congratulatory texts and posts that they received, not only after the US Championship, but throughout the entire tournament. At first they tried to keep up, eventually, they knew they could not.

"It was overwhelming, it really was. There were times when I just had to turn my phone off because it was just a constant presence. I felt bad; I know everybody meant well. I just hope they understood," said Coach Peifer.

Most did. It was just that people had to somehow be able to express their excitement for Tom, JK, Bret, the boys, the team, and the community. Everyone just felt so connected. That is the beauty of a small town. In times of death, folks come together to endure. In times of triumph, the joy is magnified. This was an example of the latter. Now, the ripple they created extended all the way into the waters of the Gulf of Mexico, as the seamen, like Petty Officer Kris Walker aboard the USS Gridley and soldiers from the Pennsylvania Air National Guard 193rd Expeditionary Special Operations Squadron, couldn't wait to tune in and watch the last standing Little League team in America take on the best that the rest of the world had to offer.

◆◆◆◆

The morning of the World Championship, the coaches tried to stick to the daily routine they had created for the past month. The night before, Coach JK reviewed the agenda one last time. Breakfast was at 9:00 am followed by a team meeting at 10:00.

Coach Peifer kept his message simple and consistent. "Take it all in boys; this is our last day together as a team. I'll never forget what we've been through together, and I don't want you to either. Enjoy the day, enjoy the atmosphere, and know that it is because of *you* that all of this has reached the level that it has. This started at a field in Newberry, and look at where we are today."

It was hard for Coach Peifer not to get emotional. Even now, any time he talks about *his* team, *his* boys, he fights back emotions. "Coaching baseball isn't like coaching football," he says, "it's not as intense, as emotional. But I loved that team. I loved those boys. And I was proud to be a part of it." He concluded with, "I'm proud of you, boys. Thank you." Then in typical coach / parent fashion, he dismissed them and told them to go clean their rooms. Coach Peifer still had to be Mr. Peifer, Uncle Tom, and Dad, and the boys had to prepare for their time in Williamsport to come to an end.

◆◆◆◆

After lunch, the boys took their final ride from the Grove, where they had been staying, to the cages. As Coach Peifer had suggested, they looked around and really observed the people and the activity at the complex. It would be their last quiet moment of the day.

Upon arriving at the batting cages, a wave of energy greeted them. It was the first time they were arriving as Champions, and though it may have been a mental difference, there was a *difference* nonetheless. The crowd was every bit as zealous, every bit as excited, but there was less anxiety.

The boys went through their routine, delighted the crowd with the ringing of their bats making contact with the pitches that were thrown in their direction. Cam Walter was serenaded with "Happy Birthday" by the crowd, and it is hard to imagine a 13-year-old boy having a more memorable birthday than Cam. To be playing for a World Championship on the day you become a teenager, well, wouldn't that be every Little Leaguer's wish? The session was still every bit as intense, but it was also sentimental as the boys knew it would be the very last one they would ever have in Williamsport.

The walk to the stadium was more like a Presidential Inaugural stroll down Pennsylvania Ave. than boys going to a baseball game. These boys, however, had a much higher approval rating than anyone who ever resided in the White House! After Texas defeated Mexico to secure third place, it was finally time for the boys to have their final moments.

"No regrets, boys. No regrets. We haven't had any yet, let's not have any today." With that, Coach Peifer sent his team onto the field for the very last time. A roar came up from the crowd and immediately it was different than any previous game. The trademark chant of "WE ARE… RED LAND!" was no longer.

As the boys took the field, the chants of "USA! USA!" reigned down from the grandstands, from the hill, from the second hill. The *Red Sea* had, indeed, showed up again, and today they truly expanded to cover not just a state, or a region, but an entire nation.

On the mound for Red Land was the walk off hero from the previous game, Chayton Krauss. Coach Peifer had no letters left on his initial bracket, which he had created on the bus ride from Bristol to Williamsport, the one that read JCAC. When he originally created it, he knew he would potentially have to deviate from it if circumstances dictated, but up to this point, he had not. When asked what he was going to do if a fifth game were required, he responded, "I figured we would face that problem when we came to it. But I also knew that would be a *great* problem to have."

It was not much of a problem, though. Chayton had pitched well for Red Land throughout the summer, starting three games, winning all of them, and appearing in six. His 0.78 ERA was better than both Adam Cramer and Jaden Henline, and his 18 strikeouts in only 15.1 innings showed he had a similar overpowering arsenal, just as his pitching teammates had. Chayton Krauss was no afterthought. Tom Peifer wasn't *hoping* he would pitch well, he *expected* him to, and was confident that he would come through for his team on the mound the same way he had at the plate less than 24 hours earlier.

Japan had a strong group of supporters, and with them, they brought the traditions of Japanese baseball fans. They had chants, songs, and noisemakers, and they relentlessly cheered their team on for the entire game. For fans in America, sporting events are a place to sit back and relax, but in Japan, they are carefully choreographed opportunities to pledge one's allegiance to a team of their choice. Though they were not nearly as numerous, the parents and extended family members and fans from Japan were every bit as devoted to their boys and their team as the folks from Pennsylvania and made for a festive gathering.

The International Champions drew first blood when Yugo Aoki, who was moved up in the line up due to his phenomenal hitting throughout the series, hit the very first pitch of the game for a single. It was a hunch that manager Junji Hidaka had to flip-flop Yugo and Shingo Tomita at the 3rd to 1st spots in the line up. It was a move that would pay off on both ends of the equation.

After a brilliant diving catch by Adam Cramer that saved another base runner from getting on, Shingo walked on four pitches to put runners on first and second with only one out. As clean up hitter and Japanese pitching sensation Kabu Kikuchi hit a double to left-centerfield, both runners were able to score as Shingo avoided Kaden Peifer's tag off a perfect relay throw from Jaden Henline to put the boys from Japan up 2-0.

Coach Wagner visited the mound. His message was simple, more of a calming influence than anything strategic or instructional. "Throw strikes, buddy, don't let them take away the inside of the plate."

It was a valid nugget of coaching. The Japanese hitters hovered over the inside part of the plate, taking their toes to the very edge of the chalk line that designated where they were legally able to stand. They pushed that limitation. If pitchers were only able to throw to half the strike zone, it gave Japan superior advantage.

Coach Bret wanted to remind Chayton to not allow them to do that. He took his words to heart. However, the next pitch crept inside a little too much, and when he hit Yuma Watanabe, Japan once again had runners on first and second, still with only one out. The coaching staff began to think of what might be their next step.

Notes flew back and forth around the dugout.

"Who's next, just in case?"
"Jaden?"
"Has to be."

In their pregame preparation, the men discussed worst case scenarios, and it was decided Jaden would be used in what they hoped would be a closer role yet again, but since he had only thrown four pitches the day before vs. Texas, he could pitch today without any restriction other than the usual 85 pitch limit. Beyond that, the men would have to get creative, relying on one of their significantly less utilized pitchers.

Chayton was able to gather himself, however, and induce Daiki Fukuyama to hit a well-placed fastball back to the mound. Chayton not only fielded it perfectly, but also turned and threw a strike to his shortstop, Jaden, who was covering second and then threw a perfect strike to Cole Wagner at first. The Patriots had scathed any further damage, only the two runs that Japan initially scored.

The Patriots loved to hit first, and the reasoning was simple. They wanted to inflict as much damage as possible, as quickly as possible. Though there were no knockouts in baseball, mentally, the Patriots had certainly taken out plenty of teams all summer by their devastating displays of strength in the top of the first inning. Japan hoped to do the same thing, but despite the fact they had scored two runs, Red Land had actually stolen some of the momentum by getting a double play to end the inning. They entered the dugout confidently, and the fans were equally as excited as the US Champs got to do what they did best—hit. A 2-0 deficit in the first was nominal, and what was about to ensue may quite possibly go down as the most exciting half-inning in the history of Williamsport baseball.

And it would all start, as it had all season, as everything always seemed to, with BK Kolmansberger, who hustled his way down to first and forced an error by the first baseman. There was nothing BK did not think he could accomplish. It was the same bravado that made him declare only days earlier when the team had traveled to Penn State that he could kick a 30-yard field goal as the Penn State kicker was practicing along with the team. What started as an innocent statement became the focal point of practice when Coach Franklin declared, "If you make that, I'll do thirty pushups. If you miss, the entire team has to do thirty Up/Downs."

The Penn State football players gathered around and started to create a buzz. The thought of their coach doing thirty pushups amused them, and they wanted to give BK as much support as they could. "Come on little man, let's do this!" they shouted. Before any more hype could be created, Braden dropped back in his khaki shorts and game jersey and kicked a perfect strike right through the uprights. The ball had plenty of distance. The next scene was that of a humbled Coach Franklin enthusiastically paying his debt, much to the delight of his Penn St. players and the boys from the Mid-Atlantic team.

It was an air of confidence that was contagious, and his teammates fed off it. When BK got on base to start the bottom of the first, he/they had every reason to believe that this game would be no different than every other game they had played together that summer.

When Cole Wagner came up to bat, it was a complete exhibition of the preparation and meticulous attention to detail that the Japanese coaching staff put into how they would approach what they feared to be their greatest threat. Catcher Raito Sugimoto literally spanned the entire space that is given to Little League catchers. Rather than a traditional rectangle, as is seen in major league parks that allow catchers to move slightly over 3.5 feet left and right, Little League uses a triangular shaped area that extends to over 12.5 feet at its base.

Though Raito never went to the complete extremities of the area, he moved in and out of the area, sometimes nearly squatting behind

Wagner as he stood in the box. They did not disguise their strategy as to how they were going to try to get Cole out, they were going to work him to the inside of the plate—only throwing outside in an attempt to set him up. They were not about to make the same mistake Texas made in the previous two games by allowing him to extend his arms and fling the ball over the left field wall, and they certainly weren't going to flirt with anything over the middle, up, or down in the zone.

As Raito continued to weave himself in and out of the catcher's area, at one point coming out of his squat to almost stand behind Cole for a pitch he wanted high and inside, Daiki struggled to maintain any of his control. Two balls sailed to the backstop, allowing Braden to advance two bases, and after ball four to Cole; Red Land had runners on the corners.

After Jaden also worked a walk and loaded the bases, the Japanese manager went to the mound. He could clearly see that the environment overwhelmed his pitcher and possibly his entire team. Entering the game, his pitchers had only walked three batters in 27 innings and committed two errors in over that same span. In the first three batters that came to the plate, Daiki Fukuyama walked two and first baseman Kengo Tomita had committed an error. Coach Hidaka had to settle his troops. His efforts were unsuccessful.

Chayton Krauss dribbled a ball that went a total of ten feet, but it was enough to plate the Patriots' first run of the afternoon—it would not be their last. His last two hits could not have been more contradictory of each other, but the results were the same, an RBI, one to end a game, and one to start one. Both were met with equal enthusiasm. The comeback was on.

Ethan Phillips singled to left field to tie the game, and then the boy who was never seen on camera without a smile, stood on first base gleaming for having tied the game. He had been struggling the entire ten days with a combination of homesickness and a virus, but as he stood and hopped up and down on first base, there was no sign of either. When it appeared that his only comfort would come from a night at home in bed, another remedy revealed itself, and this one benefitted more than just Ethan.

The bases were still loaded, and there still was nobody out. Coach Hidaka was forced to change his pitcher before his starter even recorded an out. Masafuji Nishijima provided some temporary relief when he stuck out Kaden Peifer, who looked as if he were trying to hit two grand slams with the ferocity with which he swung. He certainly got his money's worth in his first at bat.

"Well, he certainly did not get cheated," observed one of the men who were covering the game for ABC.

The momentary hiatus was over when Jake Cubbler walked, and with it brought in the go ahead run. After a fifth straight ball was thrown, the Japanese pitcher became so desperate to throw a strike that he threw a fastball right down the middle of the plate. That proved to be a colossal mistake.

The last time Dylan Rodenhaber saw a pitch like that, he deposited it into the front yard of Roger and JeriLynn Mease—they still had the mark to prove it. Though there was no house within striking distance of home plate in Lamade Stadium, there was a sea, which had swelled to an ocean, and Dylan quickly plunked that pitch directly into the heart of it out in right field. The carnival atmosphere that was created in Lamade Stadium was nothing short of pandemonium. The delirium that ensued on the bench, in the stands, and on the field as he circled the bases was a memory that every player on the team ranked as one of the most memorable of the entire summer.

He should have taken longer to round the bases. A moment like that should last forever; he should have savored every second that it took to travel the 240 feet from home to first and all the way back to home. The fact is Dylan could not wait to get back to his teammates. They were waiting for him at home plate, and he was the host of the festivities. As the score on the board changed from 3-2 to 7-2, the thunderous chants of "USA! USA!" echoed throughout the hills of Williamsport—and not just the two that were filled in the complex.

The crowd hadn't even settled down a little bit before Adam Cramer took the very next pitch and drilled it into right-center, and as those individuals were still collecting themselves from Dylan's missile, "Ace McSizzle" was standing on second. The boys from Red Land were playing as loose and carefree as they had all summer. When they stepped to the plate, it was as if they were in a backyard Wiffle Ball game where the only question was how far would the pitch be hit. Coming up for the second time in the inning, but this time against a different pitcher, BK followed the lead of teammates and hit a single to right that moved Adam to third—though he could have forced a throw to the plate, Coach Wagner wisely held him at third. Why not? There seemed to be no end in sight to the Patriot Hit Parade, and there was no need, as his son came up for his second at bat.

If they were nothing else, the Japanese kids were resilient. Any other 12-year-old would have disintegrated under the fury of haymakers that they were being forced to endure. However, they continued to persist. They stuck to their agenda. They continued to plug away, as hopeless as it appeared to be. Raito continued to move inside and out against Cole and on five pitches, none of which Cole attempted to hit, Masafuji struck him out.

"Swing the bat, Cole! SWING IT!" He was talking to himself. His frustration was building, and his inability to pull the trigger on any of the pitches that he had just seen bothered him. A migraine that developed late in the US Championship game deprived him of enjoying the triumph with his teammates, but he was baffled at what was preventing him from hitting the way he was accustomed to hitting.

As they had done for each other all season, the teammates picked each other up. When Cole checked his swing on a pitch that was ultimately called a ball, the Japanese catcher took his eye off Braden at first for a split second to appeal to the umpire down at third. When he did, BK took off for second. His brilliant base running awareness provided him the opportunity to put both he and Adam in scoring position. If Jaden could just make contact, put bat on ball, both would be able to score and pad the lead that they had already built. The implosion seemed to be coming in all capacities and the Mid-Atlantic and US Champions did not intend to allow Japan to catch its breath.

Jaden did more than put bat on ball! He took a pitch and deposited it 250 feet away into the shrubbery in dead centerfield that caused a frenzy of souvenir seekers to brave the prickles that came as a result Creeping Juniper.

"What a World Series he is having," declared Karl Ravech, who was witness to the entire Red Land experience that was filled with Jaden Henline highlights. Fortunately, Jaden's father was able to see the entire experience as well, even if he had to risk his job to do it…

◆◆◆◆

It was the day of the very first game, the one that Jody Henline's son was pitching—and he could not get off work. Mr. Henline works at a printing press that runs 24 hours a day. Employees there simply cannot take time off to watch "a baseball game." However, to him, this was not just another baseball game, it was the Little League World Series, and his son was pitching. Vacation days must be requested six weeks in advance, and having no way of knowing, and being compulsively superstitious, Jody didn't dare put in for vacation in advance. So when he requested off a few days before the game, it was denied.

One who is unfamiliar with the magnitude of the Little League World Series cannot possibly fathom the significance surrounding the event. They hear "Little League Baseball" and immediately think back to their own experiences in makeshift ballparks in whatever little town they called home back in their day. Such was the case with the employer of Jaden's father.

His co-workers encouraged him to go anyway, but it wasn't them who would have to pay the price.

"You gotta go. It's your son, it's a once in a lifetime opportunity."

"You can't not be there, Jody."

All of his co-workers were unanimous in their opinions, but at the same time, none of them volunteered to switch their shifts with him—some because they themselves were going to the game.

The day of the game, Jody Henline was scheduled to work a 12-hour shift. He called off. He was well aware of the possible consequences— termination—but he was willing to pay that price, most fathers would be. In what turned out to be one of his most stressful professional and personal days ever, Mr. Henline carried the tension of having his son pitch on national TV, representing an entire community in which he lived and whose hopes and dreams rested on his son's ability to stifle the Midwest hitters, and the stress of not knowing whether or not he would have a job the next day.

ESPN certainly did not help disguise the fact that Jaden's father was in the stands. Cameramen constantly scanned the audience, held up signs asking where the parents were so they could flash to the crowd, and catch the reactions when their son made a play in the field or came up to bat. It was a system that the Red Land parents quickly picked up on, as Scott Cubbler deflected his identity to Aaron Walter during the US Championship game because he was afraid of what he might be caught saying on camera if the result of whatever his son did was not positive.

As Jaden continued to pitch well in the opening game, the camera soon found Mr. and Mrs. Henline. Mr. Henline accepted what he thought might be his predetermined fate upon his return to work.

Upon returning to work the next day, he was greeted by co-workers and management who had seen him on TV the night before. "Jody, we had no idea that was YOUR son and THAT was what you were talking about."

274

"You shoulda said something, Jody," was a line he heard over and over again as his son's celebrity status continued to grow...to which Jody would smile, nod his head, and satirically reply, "Yeah. I probably should have."

For the rest of the tournament, there were never any problems finding people to fill his shift or getting time off. Jody would be at every game, but he would also be at work the next day as well.

Looking back, Jody was glad he made the decision he did and was willing to live with whatever the results of that decision happened to be. He sent a strong message to his sons, Colton, Jaden, and Landon about the importance of family and being there for each other through all of the moments that life presented—the good ones and the bad.

He had seen his son be the winning pitcher in the opening game, saw him stumble vs. South Carolina, only to see him recover to be the hero with the bat rather than on the mound. He saw his son preserve Adam Cramer's masterpiece that gave them the opportunity to become National Champions. Now, he saw the pinnacle of what would become the team's grandest moment—a 10-2 lead over Japan in the Little League World Championship.

◆◆◆◆

The destruction that the US Champions inflicted upon the team from Japan left the Japanese players battered and bruised. After Jaden's home run, the boys went up to bat with a savageness that appeared barbaric. Kyle Peterson commented up in the booth, "Those guys aren't trying to hit singles." He was right. They were following the philosophy that they had been taught and had been so successful with all summer.

"We try to hit the ball as hard as we can every time we step to the plate." Tom Peifer, Bret Wagner, JK Kolmansberger, and extended coaches Kyle Wagner and Aaron Walter, all unequivocally believed in that philosophy. So did the kids. It was a fun way to play baseball, and they displayed that joy openly. It radiated to all those who watched them play. And they got to share in that joy as well. They did not work baseball, they played it—the work they put in was done behind the scenes in an old abandoned warehouse that has been described by detractors as a "Cold War Era Olympic Training Center." However, lions do not lose sleep over the opinions of sheep. They did what they did, and the results spoke for themselves.

And those results were historic.

However, much like when the Japanese players played Ping-Pong, they simply did not stop playing. For a 12-year-old child to have the composure and resiliency to recover from an onslaught like that in front of tens of thousands of people shows a level of maturity and composure well beyond their twelve years. Recover they did—and rather quickly.

In the very next inning, after getting the first batter to ground out to short, the Japanese players put a string of five consecutive hits together—two singles and back to back to BACK! home runs. After the third one, it was the team from Red Land that was obviously flustered, as an error, followed by a single and a double inconceivably made it a one run game at 10-9.

Red Land would never really recover. Muhammad Ali once infamously used the rope-a-dope strategy to wear out a much bigger, stronger, George Foreman. He allowed George to apparently pulverize him in the opening rounds only to completely exhaust him and knock him out in the eighth. Though the beating the Japanese took in the bottom of the first was anything but intentional, and they never were able to really knockout their opponents, it did, in fact, wear out the team from Red Land—physically, emotionally, and now they were beating them mentally.

Japan scored four more runs in the third on a grand slam by the starting pitcher, Daiki Fukuyama, who was not able to get any outs. His blast may very well have been the final blow that Red Land could endure, allowing him to compensate for his ineffectiveness on the mound. And although Braden Kolmansberger tried to initiate yet another rally when he led off the bottom of the third with a double and later scored his ninth run of the series, (completing a record that can never be broken, having scored every time he got on base), it wasn't enough to ever really threaten the Japanese team again—they had usurped control of the game, had repressed and suffocated the home crowd.

In the top of the 6th, after watching Jaden throw his 86th pitch of the afternoon, and his 187th of the tournament, Coach Peifer put his own son on the mound to try to get the final two outs of the game. He knew his son was completely exhausted and had no strength left in his legs after having caught all but the final three innings of the World Series, but as he put it, "I couldn't put somebody else's son out there to withstand what Japan was putting us through."

They had punished Jaden for four innings, unleashing a 13 hit, 9 run onslaught after chasing starter Chayton Krauss after only an inning and a third when he surrendered six runs after being stacked to a 10-2 lead. Now, Tom called on his son to clean up and salvage whatever was left of the magical campaign that the Patriots launched in Williamsport ten days earlier. For now, for this team from Lewisberry—their run had come to an abrupt and unceremonious end. He did, but not before surrendering a few more runs.

When Kaden came off the field to end the top of the 6th, he was wobbling and crying. Just before he got to the dugout, he fell into the arms of teammate Cole Wagner. It was like a heavyweight boxer, who could not withstand even one more punch, collapsing into the arms of his trainer. Except, this was his best friend and teammate, and the boy catching him was every bit as weary as he was.

When the game was mercifully over, the final score was 18-11. They stood on the first base line and showed their respect, politely saluted their fans, and turned their visions to going *home*—though they could not possibly fathom what was waiting for them when they arrived.

23

INCONSOLABLE?

The last pitch was thrown at 6:41 pm on a Sunday evening. After the game, the kids briefly saw their parents before they had to go back to pack up their rooms and load up the bus to go home. When Kaden saw his mom for the very first time, he was in tears. He was exhausted in all capacities—physically, emotionally, and mentally. He tried to stay strong, to hold his emotions in check in front of his father/his coach, and in front of his teammates, but when he saw his mom he could not contain himself anymore. Neither could she.

She consoled her son and tried to give him two weeks worth of hugs in two minutes. It was exactly what he was hoping for. When he finally gathered himself enough to speak, he said, "Mom, I want to go to Disneyworld. And Texas Roadhouse." She started laughing. So did he. Then, they both cried some more.

It was a common scene throughout the complex. Children, no longer ballplayers, were being embraced by their parents, their moms and dads, who they hadn't been able to spend real time with since this journey began 23 days earlier. Now, finally, they were going home.

Home. A place they had not been in nearly a month.

Home. A place where they could get away from the cameras, the crowds, the pressure, the spotlight.

Home. A place that at that present moment seemed so far away it was more like a memory than it was a reality.

Every kid deserves a sanctuary—a church, grandma's house, a playground, or a ball field. Those all could serve as bastions of tranquility momentarily, but they were all a distant second to wherever a child calls…home. People in positions of authority for those entities hold an enormous sense of responsibility to preserve the sanctity of those environments. For these boys, that place called home was nestled in a small town back in Central PA.

From the tournaments for the District, Sectional, State, and Regional Championships, the journey took a total of 62 days, 22 of those were away from home, and spanned over 1574 miles. Finally, the boys would be going...home.

"My son was inconsolable," said Jake Cubbler's father, reflecting back on the moment he saw his son after the last game. "Absolutely inconsolable. I could not get him to calm down; I could not get him to even relax a little bit. I was afraid he was going to hyperventilate. And before I could really even compose him, I had to get him on the bus. When I finally did leave him, it was *my* turn to break down. I wasn't as bad, but I, too, was just so emotionally exhausted. My wife was a mess, too. We all were. Not because we lost—it had nothing to do with the outcome of the game against Japan. It was because it was over. Our journey had come to an end. Just like that, it was over."

And it *was* over—almost. In what seemed like the time it took a Cole Wagner fastball to reach the plate, or a Kaden Peifer home run to sail over the fence, the magical journey that these 11 and 12-year-old kids from Red Land took the nation on was *over*. It hurt in the same manner that it does when a childhood friend moves away, or something you truly believed in is proven false.

Tomorrow, the high school kids in the *Red Sea*, who adopted these players as their little brothers, would all return to school, and the rest of America would go back to work. Mortgage payments, credit card bills, and doctor appointments would become the main concern rather than how many mandatory days Jaden Henline had to rest before he was eligible to pitch again. That was becoming alarmingly real for the boys, their coaches, the parents, and the rest of America who unabashedly bought into everything this team stood for.

Scott Cubbler got in his car and started to drive home. He had to leave before his son saw him become too emotional. His wife stayed behind to help the boys load up the bus so they could be as comfortable as possible for the long ride home. As Scott drove home, twice he had to pull over due to his inability to see clearly through the tears that continued to form in his eyes. Finally, he reached Selinsgrove. He planned to pull over and get a cup of coffee, or a soda. He just needed something to alleviate the perpetual lump that was in his throat.

What he saw blew him away. People were starting to line the street. American flags were everywhere. Red Land signs were being posted; it appeared as though people were getting ready for a parade. A little further up the road, two fire trucks extended their ladders to form a makeshift arc from which a stadium sized flag hung down. The buses, as well as all the passing cars, would have to go under it. Scott quickly called his wife.

"Honey, you've got to see this! Don't go home the back way. Drive through Lewisburg, then Selinsgrove. Don't worry about the traffic, it will be worth it, just trust me." His voice would not make it any further. The words would not take form—they did not do the scene justice anyway.

"Honey, what is it?" his wife asked.

It was useless. He could not talk.

"Scott, are you alright?"

Somehow, he mustered a faint, "Yeah. You just have to see this for yourself. I gotta go." Then he hung up the phone, sat in his car, and cried.

As the rest of America turned off their TV's, made dinner, and then went to bed, the people in small towns all across Pennsylvania took to the streets. They made signs. They painted their faces. They dressed in every fabric of red, white, and blue they could find. They lined the roads, they called the neighbors, they did anything they could to show their support for these children who reminded them about everything that was *still* right in the world.

They came out in the thousands and lined the 97 miles that stretched between Williamsport and Lewisberry. They had to—those kids, those boys, those children, had earned this. They earned it with their smiles, with their intrinsic charisma, and with their dazzling display of sportsmanship that is so rare in modern day competition. They radiated goodness by the way they played while they were off the field and the way they competed when they were on it.

They drew people to them by the way they conducted themselves during their overwhelmingly dominant moments of triumph and their painful, momentary brushes with defeat. In future Little League World Series, there may be teams that will be better (though that will be for the locals to debate), but there will *never* be teams that are more mesmerizing.

Like her husband, Lisa Cubbler found herself having to stop as well—at a Sheetz alongside the road. It was packed. People in the store looked as if they were ready for the 4th of July festival rather than a Sunday night in August. She smiled as she looked around.

As she stood at the coffee counter, an elderly woman approached her.

"Are you going to the parade?" she asked.

"Parade?"

"Yes. For the boys. Those boys from Red Land. They'll be coming through here in a little while. I love those boys. Always smiling. Do you know them?"

"Know them?" She smiled. Almost embarrassed, she answered, "Yes. My son is on that team. Number seven. Jake. He's the right-fielder, or, left-fielder depending on who's pitching or who's up ..." She found herself reliving the memories she had just made of her son running from right to left field from time to time. She smiled as she felt herself starting to ramble. Then she stopped because she felt tears starting to come on.

The elderly lady was just staring at her. "Thank you."

Lisa Cubbler looked puzzled. "Thank you? For what?"

"For letting us borrow your boys for the past two weeks. They are wonderful boys. They brought so much joy to so many people. Thank you for letting us ... all of us ... be a part of your ... family."

Now, they were both on the verge of tears. Their cups were full. They toasted each other. "You're welcome. You're very, very welcome." The older woman put her hand on Lisa's forearm and started to walk away. Before she left she turned around and said, "We are ..."

"Red Land!" Mrs. Cubbler responded on cue.

"Red Land!" The lady almost whispered it. "I loved those boys."

She walked away with a jaunt in her step. Though she was completely out of earshot, Lisa still quietly whispered to herself, "Me, too," and she prepared for the rest of the drive home.

◆◆◆◆

As the night progressed, people lined Routes 11, 15, 22, and 147 trying to somehow express themselves to the boys just how exceptional what they had actually witnessed really was. For those who had been to a game, this was one last chance to be a part of this growing mythical legend that was already forming. For those who had not taken in this team's monumental feats firsthand, it was a last opportunity to salvage a secondhand personal connection with these adolescent icons.

By the time his wife made it to the small towns back home that made up the Red Land area, she was completely in awe of the response people were having to her son's team. Bridge Street in New Cumberland was lined on both sides. This usually only happens for major events such as the Applefest or Halloween Parade, but *this* was a spontaneous celebration of its residents. As the boys drove home, they finally began to understand just how significant what they had done really was. For the two weeks in Williamsport, the coaches tried to shelter them and keep them focused on the task. For the most part, it was unsuccessful. When Cole Wagner starts "trending" on Twitter, people take notice!

Nevertheless, there is a difference between being a "big deal" and being "significant." The boys knew they had become a "big deal," but they could not have possibly comprehended the significance of what they had done. The ride home was the first indication they got as to how much more than just winning baseball games they represented.

"Put your phone away and just enjoy the ride home" was a text that more than one boy received from his parent. They all complied. This was special. They wanted to remember it. They wanted to acknowledge as many of the people as they could who had come out to welcome them home.

Their first stop once back in Central PA was Cedar Cliff, where they would drop their luggage off with their parents and be transferred onto the backs of fire trucks ready to take them through New Cumberland, Etters, Lewisberry, and finally, Red Land High School. Posts on Facebook, Twitter, and Instagram kept the locals updated all night regarding their location and approximate arrival time at various locations—they were all inaccurate. The ride from Cedar Cliff to Red Land should take less than eight minutes; that night, it took well over two hours.

After seeing their children in the parking lot before watching them load onto the bus, the parents decided to gather at Rite-Aide in New Cumberland to watch the first part of the parade. Just after they arrived, an elderly couple pulled into the parking lot and occupied the only parking space that was available—a handicapped spot. Out of the driver's seat, an elderly man slowly got out of the car and popped his trunk. He retrieved two lawn chairs and a walker—for his wife—and set them all up. She meticulously got out of the passenger's side, laboriously moved to the sidewalk, and took her place in the front row to await the boys. Lisa looked at her watch. It was 11:30 pm. She was quite moved. She approached the couple.

"Thank you for coming out tonight," she said to the couple.

"Oh, we had to. These boys deserve it," said the husband.

"I haven't been up this late in years," said his wife. "But this is worth it."

"Thank you so much for coming out tonight. I know the boys will appreciate it."

A gentleman, who stood outside of Rock-It Pizza in Etters, echoed the same sentiment. "When I heard they would be getting an escort home, I wanted to be there. If they would have won, I may not have. But they lost, so I felt as if I had to be there. For them. For these boys who earned my respect, my support, and my admiration. They earned my devotion. And I don't want them to feel as if they let anybody down." He looked around. A sense of pride extended from New Cumberland to Etters, from Goldsboro to Lewisberry. At Red Land High School, over a thousand people were waiting to officially welcome the boys home. There was a DJ, news reporters broadcasting live, and countless fans of all ages. When the team pulled in, it was after 1:30 a.m.

"Do you think we'll get a two hour delay tomorrow?" one of the players asked another.

"I don't know. But this is pretty cool," his teammate responded. "I can't believe all these people are out here this late! They're crazy! They should be in bed. WE should be in bed! I wonder why they did it?"

And with that question, the purity, innocence, and naiveté of the boys was once again revealed. The people came out because they believed in these kids—from the carefree way they played the game they loved, to the selfless way they filled their roles, to the genuine, unabashed manner they carried themselves off the field—and that made an impact. They played not like the selfish, entitled professionals that far too often bombard America with their demands and individual agenda driven propaganda, they played like kids at recess whose only care in the world was not to win, but to play.

In JD Salinger's classic American novel *The Catcher in the Rye*, Holden Caulfield explains to his 10-year-old sister, Phoebe, what he believes is his purpose in life. It's a metaphorical vision of being able to protect and maintain childhood innocence and purity that only children can possess. In a world that in *his* eyes has been oversaturated with corruption, greed, and hypocrisy, Holden desperately clings to the only thing in which he still believes—the authentic spirit, honesty, and the wholesomeness of a child, of Phoebe.

> *"I keep picturing all these little kids playing some game in this big field of rye and all. Thousands of little kids, and nobody's around— nobody big, I mean—except me. And I'm standing on the edge of some crazy cliff. What I have to do, I have to catch everybody if they start to go over the cliff—I mean if they're running and they don't look where they're going, I have to come out from somewhere and **catch** them. That's all I'd do all day. I'd just be the catcher in the rye and all. I know it's crazy, but that's the only thing I'd really like to be. I know it's crazy."*

These boys quickly became America's catharsis. Their optimistic audacity to dream big, despite the fact that they came from a very small town, inspired many. As they advanced, and the stakes rose higher, and the pressure grew greater, so did their smiles, so did their laughter. They became for *us* what Phoebe was for Holden. *Their* field wasn't made of rye, it was a baseball diamond, and it reminded us what a true gift it was to just be a kid playing a game with complete, unfiltered joy. They basked in the spotlight that was cast upon them, and they used their platform not to glorify themselves and their accomplishments, but to reach out to others who desperately needed something to feel good about.

Their intentions were transparent and unblemished. And after their final game, we cried *with* them, not *for* them, not because they lost, but because this majestic journey, the one that they invited so many of us to take with them, was over. And through it all, these children, these boys, reminded us just how special life can be when individual agendas are set aside for the betterment of something greater than one's self.

And Americans, if only for a moment, were brought back to their own childhood when we all played with the same passion and purity that *they* played with. They were kids playing in a field. For a moment, we were able to watch them, be a part of their calling, and we, too, never wanted it to end. Though we were sad, not because they lost, but because it was over, we recognized just how cathartic what we had just witnessed really was. For three weeks in August, and this one night in Etters, we all felt like kids again.

The throngs of people were there because we were reminded of all that was good and right in the world. They were there because people were able to recognize the extraordinary and spellbinding manner in which these boys played a game that so many of us have played in our lifetime. They were there because *these* boys were able to overcome so many of the factors that prevent teams from becoming true teams like this. In a sports world that is polluted by agenda-driven, helicopter parents and entitled athletes who fully expect mediocrity to be rewarded, *these* boys were able to rise above all of that. The community felt obligated to show their appreciation.

The community had become a part of the team, and the team was now an extension of that community—and together, that coalesced into something extraordinary. When they were finally united back in their hometown, the celebration that ensued was something that would become a part of their small town folklore forever.

The boys will move on, as America did, as the Red Land community eventually will do as well. But no matter how old they get, how successful they become, how far away from Lewisberry their paths of life may take them, *these* boys and *this* community will forever be united by the bond that was created in the summer of 2015. And regardless of how far they go, or how big they get, they will always keep a foot in their field.

EXTRA INNINGS

STORIES THAT DIDN'T QUITE FIT IN BUT SEEMED TOO GOOD TO LEAVE OUT

"I Can't Even Write in Cursive!"

It was about three weeks after the World Series had concluded. Kids were back in school, the parades had finally died down, the public appearances were still very much in demand, but now they were not every night. After going up on stage with the Zac Brown Band, getting a tour of Camden Yards and being treated like big leaguers by their Big League heroes that included Manny Machado, Adam Jones, and Buck Showalter, the kids were allowed to live the normal lives of 12-year-olds. This included time with friends playing their video game of choice, practicing for other sports, or just riding bikes.

However, they were not completely away from the game. In neighborhood Wiffle Ball games, other kids were now mimicking their batting stances and idiosyncrasies. Kids would step into their backyard batter's boxes and declare, "I'm Cole Wagner!" and as the boy on the mound would be ready to pitch to him, he would proclaim just as confidently, "I'm Adam Cramer!" A ball hit to the little boy who would be somewhere in the area of shortstop would be fielded with the commentary of, "Scooped up by Jaden Henline, shuffles it to BK at second, who fires it to Chayton at first…DOUBLE PLAY!"

And sometimes the boys themselves got to actually play themselves.

"Go ahead, try and hit it out, nobody's done it!" Ethan Phillips dug in. He was challenged; this was one he thought he would be up to.

On this particular day, the menacing fence was not as far away from home plate as the left or right field in Williamsport, PA, and it was not as high as the famous "Green Monster" in Boston. The fence the kids were referring to was a backyard field in Ridgeview. The fence was the property line that separated the backyard arena from the Storage Unit lot behind it. Protecting the fence, which served as the official Guardian of the Wiffle Ball, was a line of Pine trees that stood now shorter than 25 feet tall. Without this line of Evergreen trees, balls would fly into the Storage Shed Unit, and dozens of balls would be lost. Occasionally, one made it through the branches of the trees and found itself on the wrong side of the fence, but nobody had ever *cleared* the trees.

"Go ahead. Pitch it."

As the neighborhood kids watched, Ethan blasted balls all over the yard, into the trees, reaching sections of the woods that had not been reached before. And then, on a hanging breaking ball that didn't quite catch the breeze the way the pitcher intended, Ethan sent a Wiffle Ball into orbit that easily cleared not only the trees, but the fence, and it landed deeper into the Self-Storage lot than any of the kids ever imagined possible.

"Oh, My GOODNESS!!!"
"You hit that thing a MILE!!!"
"That was awesome! Not even my dad can hit it that far!!!"

As the roar of approval died down, a few of the kids remembered that they had their special Red Land Little League player cards in their collection.

"Ethan, can you sign our cards?"

"Sure, go get them."

The kids hurried back. As excited as they were to have seen him become a backyard legend on Trilee Field, they were even more excited to get his autograph. Soon, the two brothers and their little sister came back with their cards and a Sharpie in hand. They handed them to Ethan, who like an old pro, flipped the card over and signed his name.

"Okay, here's the deal. Three cards, three more pitches. I know I can hit one even farther!"

It was a great deal. They were quick to agree. As he signed the cards, the other kids watched in wonder.

Then, one boy laughed. "Dude, that's not even your name, it's just a bunch of squiggly lines!" Soon, they all shared a laugh.

"I know," replied Ethan, "everybody keeps asking for my autograph, and I don't even know how to write in cursive!"

"But, Honey, What About the Twins?"

I have been sworn to secrecy about who exactly told the story, but anyone who knows the group of grandparents I had the pleasure to sit with, will certainly verify its authenticity....

One night Coach Peifer could be heard in the background of a phone conversation someone else was having, scolding the team for not being ready for bed yet.

"I told you guys to get your showers and get ready for bed!"

"He sounds mad," said the voice on the other end of the line.

"Yeah, he is. He wants us to go shower, but we can't yet, the Japanese kids are in there."

"Oh. But aren't there a lot of showers?"

"Yeah, but..."

"But what, honey?"

"They shower naked!"

There was a moment of silence on the phone. After what seemed like an eternity, Grandma, who was doing her best to understand the dilemma, broke the silence. "Well, honey, how do you boys take a shower?"

Without any hesitation at all, and with almost a hint of annoyance in his voice from having to answer such a silly question. "In our bathing suits."

"Oh. Okay. But, honey, what about the twins? When do the twins get their bath?"

"Grandma, I have to go…"

Click.

"Bret, Just Call a Dentist!"

It was a night in the summer of 1995. Kyle was catching with the Single A Boise Hawks in the Northwest League in Idaho. At the same time, brother Bret was pitching for the AA Arkansas Travelers in the Texas League. Back home in Pennsylvania, Butch and Linda did their best to keep up with their sons' minor league progress. Late in the evening, Linda was awakened by a phone call from her son, Bret, who was on the road in Texas and was complaining of a terrible toothache.

"Bret, just call a dentist. What would you like me to do; I'm 500 miles away? Make an appointment with the dentist tomorrow and have him take a look at it. That's all I can tell you." With that, she hung up the phone and tried to go back to sleep.

An hour or so later, again the phone rang. This time, it was Kyle. "Mom, I hate to call you this late, but I wanted you and Dad to know I have to have surgery tomorrow. I got two of my teeth knocked out tonight when there was a malicious collision at the plate. I'm alright now, I'll be alright after the surgery, but it was a nasty crash at the plate."

His mom was stunned. Kyle and Bret never spoke to each other that night; neither knew what the other was going through. But the esoteric bond that is said to exist between twins was never more apparent than on that night in 1995.

"You'll Never Make It as a Pitcher"

In his junior year of high school, Bret and his brother went to Veteran's Stadium for a showcase with the Phillies, and once he got there, he was unsure if he should go with the hitters (to the left) or with the pitchers (to the right). He put his arms up in the air, turned around, and looked at his father. "Dad?"

His father responded, "Go with the hitters, you'll never make it as a pitcher." So, like any kid would, he shrugged his shoulders— and listened to his father. A broken leg suffered entering into his senior year forever altered the path that Bret envisioned for himself. He was still every bit as athletic, could still destroy a baseball with his bat, but he was never really the same in the field, so he focused on becoming a pitcher.

"Did the Boys Win While I was Gone?"

Chayton's mom, Pip, works as a Physical Therapist in a Rehabilitation Center. She had been working with an elderly gentleman who became very interested in the team, and he kept updated on their progress throughout the summer. While Pip was in Bristol with the team as they clinched their spot to Williamsport, the man suffered cardiac arrest and was pronounced dead after being unresponsive to efforts to resuscitate him. Miraculously, after 14 minutes, the man came back to life!

When Pip returned from Bristol and again began working with that same man, the first question he asked her was, "Did the boys win while I was gone?"

She smiled.

"Yes, sir, they won the Mid-Atlantic Region Championship. They will be playing in the Little League World Series in Williamsport!"

"Good. Then I'll have to make sure I stick around a little longer so I can see how things turn out."

When she returned to work after the boys won the US Championship, she went to that man's room and saw all the #WhyNotUs and GO RED LAND signs the man had there. It seemed the boys' quest had provided him with a sense of purpose to continue living.

When he did his rehab, his favorite shirt to wear was his #WhyNotUs shirt. "I want to work as hard as those boys do," he would explain to Pip.

After the World Series, Pip took Chayton to meet the 90-year-old man who used the team as his inspiration to keep living. Before they left, Chayton grabbed an old baseball, autographed it, and brought it to the man.

"Sorry it's a little old and beat up," Chayton said as he handed the ball to the man.

"That's okay, son. So am I. It's perfect. Thank you."

"We Called Him Hopper"

Luke knew just how hard Cole worked to become the ballplayer that he now was. There were countless numbers of nights they spent together at their father and uncle's facility, just the four of them, trying to perfect Luke's skills and trying to build Cole's. "We called him '*Hopper*' because he didn't run right," said Bret, thinking back to where Cole was as compared to where he currently is with his baseball skills. "We couldn't decide if he was left-handed or right-handed 'cause he really wasn't any good with either of them. Luke was the athlete, Cole was the scholar."

However, Bret Wagner was not ready to concede that his son was not going to carry on the family tradition of being a ballplayer. "Bret, you were relentless with Cole," said brother Kyle. "Re-lent-less. But you were only relentless because Cole never stopped wanting to be good. So Bret kept working with you [speaking to Cole], driving you, and never once lowered the bar. [Turning back to Bret] You never once said, 'Well, maybe he just won't be that good.' You just kept pushing... because Cole wanted to be pushed."

"Sometimes, it feels like we're raising the other one's kid," says Bret. "Because baseball always came so naturally to me, just like Luke. And Kyle, Kyle had to work a lot harder, really hard, more than I did, but he was always willing to do it—just like Cole. I mean, Luke, if you were my kid, we probably … we probably wouldn't do much!" More laughter, more applause, more reminiscing. Baseball provides another bonding moment in the life of the Wagner family.

The two boys have pushed each other to get better in the same manner that their fathers once did. But the transformation was neither smooth nor easy—especially on the mound. When Cole was 11, after a debacle of a performance in the Ripken Experience Tournament in Aberdeen, his father announced to the entire family and anybody else who was in earshot at the time that, "The Cole Wagner pitching experiment is *over!*"

As Butch remembers it, the first inning went really well. "Cole, you were humming the ball across the plate and by the batters! Strike One! Strike Two! Strike Three! You struck out the side without so much as a foul ball! I thought to myself, 'Oh man, he's pretty good. He's going to make a great pitcher.' Then in the second inning, not so good. Ball in the dirt. Ball outside. Ball behind the batter. Ball over the backstop. Walks the bases loaded, walks in a couple of runs. And there went Bret to pull him. I thought to myself, 'Oh man, he's got a lot of work to do.'"

As Cole explains it, it was not that he could not find the strike zone as his father claims; it was that his arm always hurt. "I mean, I was hurt a lot of the time. I was hurt when I played with the 9/10 team, I only pitched one inning. I was hurt when I played with the 10/11's, I only pitched one inning. This was the first year that I actually really pitched. Before this year, I only ever pitched one year 'cause that's all *you* could really stomach!"

An uproar of laughter echoed across the room because there was more truth in that statement than his father would probably care to admit. From "… that's all you could really stomach!" to arguably the best 12-year-old pitcher in the nation, the work that was done by Cole only added to the tradition that the Wagner name holds.

"We Thought the President was Coming!"

The Sheetz in Selinsgrove became an official rest stop for many of the travelers who were journeying between the Red Land area and Williamsport. Fans would congregate there, fueling up and freshening up. The night after the game with Japan provided a number of remarkable stories of people and how they prepared for the boys' journey home.

It has been well documented just how patriotic Route 15 looked as townspeople brought out anything they could to decorate the road that the boys would travel on to return to Red Land.

While at Sheetz, a Canadian couple approached Stephanie and Jody Henline. "Excuse me, but do you know what's going on? Why are all these people out here this late on a Sunday night and decorating the highway? It's been like this our entire ride up 15."

"Oh," Stephanie tried to explain to the foreign couple, "the team from Red Land that won the Little League World Series yesterday is coming home tonight. I guess everybody just wants to congratulate them. They won the US Championship."

"Ohhhhh," said the Canadian woman. "We thought the President was coming to town. We don't like him much, so we were going to get out of here as quick as we could. But if it's kids that are coming, we'll stay and watch the parade!"

The Henlines never identified that their son was a member of the team.

The Rickey

It was 1991, and the Red Land Varsity team was preparing for the PIAA State Playoffs. The team was loose, their confidence was high, and their mood was good. At the same time, Rickey Henderson was 32 years old and playing in what probably would be his last game as an All-Star. Rickey would lead the American League in stolen bases that season and was known for his "snap catches" in the outfield as a way of making routine fly balls far less mundane. Rickey would position himself directly under the ball, await its arrival into his glove, and instantaneously snap his glove onto his leg. Then, he would jaunt back into the dugout and wait to hit. With ESPN's Sportscenter a staple now in American homes, this highlight was seen repeatedly. Soon, baseball players all across America were trying to do "The Rickey."

Bret Wagner had mastered it. During batting practice, he would stand in centerfield and shag fly ball after fly ball, and each time he would work to perfect his version of "The Rickey." The key to a good "Rickey" was to time the snap so the glove was already in the downward motion when the ball was actually caught, and nobody timed it better than Bret—at least most times. As the balls continued to be sent in Bret's direction, the 18 year old phenom, who would have been a sure first rounder straight out of high school if he hadn't broken his leg in a football injury earlier that year, got more and more daring (reckless).

CRUNCH!!!

He snapped too soon. The glove was moving toward his leg before the ball reached it, and that sound was the ball smacking Bret Wagner square in the teeth. The mayhem that ensued was a combination of teammates scrambling to find his two front teeth, hiding the steady flow of blood that was now pouring out of his mouth, and doing it before Coach Brandt Cook ever saw anything.

"What's going on?" Coach Cook hollered. "Stop messing around! In fact, Bret, get outta here and go throw before you get hurt!" Bret Wagner was all too willing to obey. He raced from the field, covering his mouth the entire time, and hid in the bullpen area until his mom could come bail him out. Legend has it, he's the only player Coach Cook ever threw out of practice.

"I didn't miss any games. I guess that's why Coach Cook didn't kill me."

"Do We Have a Deal?"

Word around the dorms was that the asking price was an unused Easton MAKO bat. That's what Isaac Sanchez wanted in order to trade his customized Rolin ® baseball glove with the Little League World Series patch on it. It certainly was a prized item, possibly the grand pick of them all, and *if* he were going to trade it to somebody, it was going to cost.

One of the great traditions amongst the players in Williamsport is trading. Normally, the players will trade pins with each other representing their region or country, but sometimes, the trades get very unique. Adam Cramer was able to get a boomerang from one of the players from Australia in exchange for one of the Mid-Atlantic Champion pins that were becoming increasingly valuable with each win the team earned. Japanese shirts were a popular item, as were batting sleeves from Mexico.

Pins, however, were the most sought after item. And it was not just for the kids on the participating teams. Tents were set up around the complex inviting *all* kids to come in and barter with other children for what it was they were seeking and what they had acquired. Dylan Rodenhaber got an Oriole team pin from one of the kids from Texas in exchange for three Oakley pins. Braden Kolmansberger accumulated so many pins in the deals that he made that he had to start an album to be able to keep track of all the loot he had collected.

Nobody was able to land something as authentic as the personalized gloves that the players from Mexico had—but Ethan Phillips wanted to change that.

"I heard a lot of kids were offering him a bat for the glove. Then I heard that he wanted a brand new one, one that did not have any marks on it at all. I wanted to sweeten the deal a little bit, so I offered him two bats."

Isaac was intrigued.

Ethan had a sound reasoning behind why he was willing to offer such a steep deal. Both he and Cole Wagner did not use the Easton MAKO bats that were so prevalent throughout the World Series. They both used Anderson bats, and though they had used their MAKOs in batting practice, they were not *game* used. That meant the wear and tear on them was minimal.

When the boys started their run through districts and regionals, Bret Wagner had called a representative from Anderson and told the rep that his son and a few of the other kids on the team preferred the Anderson bats to the Easton's and asked him if he would be willing to donate a few bats to the boys to use in the Mid-Atlantic Regional tournament. The salesman did not bite. "We can't do it. We wouldn't want to set a precedence," he responded.

As the team progressed through the tournament, and after both Ethan and Cole showed their feats of strength in their opening game, the sales rep quickly called Bret back and said, "Let me know what size they want, and we'll overnight them." That made the boys' donated Easton bats obsolete, so Ethan was willing to trade them.

"Two bats. Come on, nobody else is offering you *two*," Ethan tried to persuade Isaac.

"I know. But they're used," Isaac retorted.

"I know. But one of them was used by Cole Wagner."

"Good point. Deal," agreed Isaac.

With that, Ethan Phillips acquired the most prized trade item of the 10-day period, a customized Rolin ® baseball glove with the Little League World Series patch. He was so excited, he used it in the game against Japan, and ABC zoomed in on it while Ethan was in the dugout, and they pondered, "I wondered what that cost him?"

"No telling…"

Ask Ethan. He will tell you it was the best deal he ever made.

"FIVE! FIVE! FIVE!"

When Bret was at Wake Forest, he played centerfield when he was not pitching. One series, when the Demon Deacons were playing the Georgia Bulldogs in Georgia, Bret Wagner was having a really tough day at the plate. To say he was struggling would be an understatement; he had struck out four times and was not really close on any of them. As the game progressed and moved to the last inning, Bret was due up fourth. In the confines of the dugout, in a corner all by himself, he secretly prayed for a 1-2-3 inning. It did not happen. With one out and a runner on first, the third batter of the inning stepped into the box.

"Let's roll it up!" the Georgia manager screamed out to his infield.

"NO!!!!" responded the Bulldog student section who was earnestly awaiting Bret Wagner's fifth at bat. "No Double Play! No Double Play!" The Georgia faithful knew that Wagner was on deck. Bret refused to step into the on-deck circle. He hovered in the shadows of the dugout, hoping for some reprieve. This only served as a catalyst for their calls. "C'Mon, Wagner, we know you're in there! Get on out here and take your medicine!"

At this point, his teammates were howling. To say they were having as much fun with the moment as the student section of the opposing team would be most accurate. When the batter in front of Bret hit a harmless pop to first, the fans got their moment. "Wagner's coming up!!!"

So Bret, the career .332 hitter, who hit .355 his senior year at Wake, looked down the bench at his teammates and said with a smirk, "Wish me luck!"

There was not a fan in his seat by the time he strolled to the plate. "Five! Five! Five!" came thundering down from the grandstand. They all wanted that fifth strike out. After the first two pitches, Bret was staring at an 0-2 count. On the third pitch, Bret made contact and hit a one-hopper back to the pitcher. The disappointment in the folks from Georgia was palpable. Bret ran out the dribbler to first, but, surprisingly, as he turned back toward the dugout, he was grinning from ear to ear.

In the parking lot after the game, Kyle did his best to be the good brother and warn Pap and Bret's mom and dad, who had been in the stands and witnessed what had happened, of how Bret may be feeling when he got to them.

As Bret emerged from the locker room and approached them, he had that same grin on his face as when he turned back from first base. "Well, that was one heck of a performance, wasn't it?" Bret asked.

"I don't know, Bret, that last swing looked kind of defensive," responded his father.

"Dad, I was just trying to get the bat to somehow actually *touch* the ball. Of course, it was defensive!"

"He's Still My Little Brother...Part 2"

"I've never seen him so happy," said Hollis. "My favorite moment was when he scored the winning run in the second game against Texas to win the National Championship, and the look on his face was pure joy. He was running to his teammates, trying to get to Chayton to give him a hug, and he just had this huge smile on his face. Pure joy. I was so happy for him."

"We all had moments like that, just watching our little brothers play a game that they loved to play but play it really, really well—and watching everybody fall in love with them while they did it. For me, it was watching Adam pitch that first night against Texas. He was just amazing. I was so proud of him. This whole experience really has brought us closer together. I gained a lot of respect for just the way they were able to handle everything that was going on around them so gracefully," said Lindsay in a very approving big sister kind of way.

Upon returning to Etters, it did not take long for the big sisters to be able to remind their little brothers exactly where they ranked in the hierarchy of the family totem pole. "One day," said Hollis when asked how long it took until she had to remind BK that he was the *little* brother. "The day after they came home and we had that late night parade that ended at Red Land, he came walking downstairs with nothing on but his underwear and a stuffed animal. My dad and I immediately looked at each other, and I said, 'There's your National Champion, America.' I think I embarrassed him a little because he immediately went back upstairs and put some clothes on."

There were still some adjustments that had to be made by the older siblings, though, as their brothers' new celebrity status had some unexpected ripple effects that made for more than a few awkward moments. "Yeah, I had to get used to my friends coming over and asking if my brother was home. One day the UPS guy asked if this was the Kolmansberger's house of 'that little guy' who won the World Series. But it was kinda neat to see them having their moments as celebrities."

The girls handled their brothers' new community status with the same grace and patience that their brothers had shown just two weeks earlier. "Until we saw them sitting in the front row of the *Red Sea* at the football games, and there we were sitting behind them! I didn't like that at all!" joked Hollis, and Lindsay quickly agreed.

"It could not have been worse!" added Cheyenne. "I'm just a freshman, so I was all the way in the back, and there Ethan was—front and center! He doesn't even go to Red Land yet!"

Through it all, though, the girls were able to form tighter bonds with their brothers as their protective instincts gave them the inclination to want to shield their younger siblings from all the demands, attention, and pressure. "I don't think we ever really took them or the run they were making for granted, but I think we all really missed the experience we had of going through all of that together."

16 Candles

It was going to be a long day for them in Philadelphia. Their son had a travel tournament scheduled, but the weather did not look very promising. A co-worker had asked her if her family might stop by her daughter's 16th birthday party that night, "if you get the chance." She commented as to how much it would mean to her daughter if somehow her son could "just stop by."

She promised her co-worker that she would *try* to stop by if the circumstances allowed them to do so. They certainly did not commit to going, but they did say they would try. As fate would have it, the weather allowed them to go. "I am so glad we made this a priority. The impact that these kids have had on so many is just so inspiring.

Her husband agreed. "We are very fortunate to have healthy kids who have embraced the positive impact they can have on others."

The young lady whose birthday it was had had a tough year. She had been suffering from Parry-Romberg Syndrome, which is a rare degeneration of the tissues beneath the skin affecting the neurological, ocular, and oral systems. After many months of battling, she finally appeared to be on the road to recovery—and on this particular day, she was turning sixteen years old. Truth be told, she was thankful just to be able to have a Sweet 16th birthday party to celebrate.

When the family arrived, the party, already festive, became even more cheerful. Though he was younger than most of the invited guests in attendance, he fit right in. His mom was astonished at how mature and comfortable her son had become at making public appearances. It was an observation that many of the parents had made about their children. "It seemed as if these boys had been in the spotlight all their lives. They can look strangers in the eye, shake their hands, and be totally at ease," observed Lisa Cubbler after seeing her son being interviewed by the local media upon his return from Williamsport.

When the young lady brought out her cake, the guests sang the traditional "Happy Birthday" and the candles were extinguished with a wish. One could only imagine that the wish was to be able to do the same thing next year. What followed was anything but traditional.

Behind the girl was a candelabrum that consisted of sixteen candles that were specially designed for sixteen significant people in her life. One by one, she took the candles and presented them to the sixteen most significant people in her life—her mother, her father, her best friend.... and then, she presented one to the boy who played on the Red Land Little League team.

"I thought to myself, 'Oh, my God, if we would have had baseball, we might not have come," reflected the boy's mother. "I'm so glad we made this a priority."

When she gave the candle to the boy, the girl explained that while the team was making their run in Williamsport, he "just made me smile." Like so many of the Four Diamonds families had shared with the team, their moments of joy were limited, and they cherished whatever reasons they could find to escape their illnesses. This team provided that much-needed escape. Most times reality was too cruel, too distressing, but when this young lady watched the boys play, she forgot all of that. Every time she saw them play, her spirits were lifted because they just always seemed to be so *happy*.

They were always smiling, always loving the moment that life provided them. She wanted to love life like that, too. She vowed that when she got healthy again, she would love her life in the same manner. This was her chance to thank the team, through him, for those moments.

So, she gave the boy from the Red Land team one of her candles. Had she had the opportunity, she probably would have given one to each of the boys. Many others would have as well.

People believed in these boys, who, to them, symbolized wholesomeness, contentment. People wanted to live life the way these particular boys played baseball—with joy and innocence that radiated to all who watched them—and by doing so, it enhanced their lives and made them smile.

They were just boys playing a game that they loved, and they played it well. Here's hoping that they, and we, will always approach life's challenges in that same manner—with a purity of spirit, joy in our hearts, and a smile on our face—as the boys in the field did.

THANK YOUs

My first thank you would have to go to the very first teammate I ever had, my mom. Through every battle I have ever fought, she has always been by my side. In victory or defeat, the strength of her character and passion in her convictions has inspired me my entire life. She has always been my hero.

To my father, who every time I heard a story for this book about a son and his dad, I recalled one of my own memories that I harbor in a special place in my heart of the times we shared together throughout my childhood. From playing catch in Gilroy, California, to following in his footsteps to Virginia Tech, I hope he is as proud of me as the fathers on this team were of their sons by the way they conducted themselves on the biggest stages of their life.

To my sister, who has accepted me for who I am, despite the fact it is so different from who she is. The beauty of a team is the individuals of which it is made. There are so many qualities and attributes about you that I admire, that I wish I had, but I appreciate the understanding and patience you have shown with me throughout every phase of my life.

To my extended family—Thank you for fully accepting me into your family and for always making me feel as if I were welcomed, valued, and appreciated.

The Coaches, Tom-Bret-JK, Kyle and Walt. You guys took a chance on me. You had a story to tell and trusted me to tell it. The faith you put in me to capture the essence of the team you created, and the accomplishments you achieved, was a mammoth responsibility. My greatest motivation throughout this process was to meet your expectations. It is easy to see how you inspired these boys to become National Champions because you did the same thing for me. And to Mitch, who believed in me before this project ever even began.

To the Boys in the Field: You know not what you did, nor how you inspired so many, myself included, not by the games you won, but by the manner in which you conducted yourself as you competed. Your work ethic, your spirit, your camaraderie amongst your teammates was inspiring and refreshing. The enormity of what you accomplished, the positive energy that you created amongst your community can never accurately be described, but it will never be forgotten. But as a member of that community that was truly overtaken by what you did in the summer of 2015, I simply say, "Thank You." Your humbleness and innocence as you told your stories was everything that I hoped they would be. May what you have already achieved serve as motivation for everything else you will accomplish in your lifetimes.

To the Parents of the Players—Your sons are a reflection of you. They are humble, kind, and generous. I appreciate the trust you all put in me with your truly heartfelt stories.

To the Red Land Community—Nobody deserved the joy and elation that was created last summer more than this community. Red Land is a special place because special people live here, and I want to thank you for your support through the many endeavors that I have embarked upon WITH you, FOR you, and BECAUSE of you. What the nation saw on those hills of Williamsport was everything that is right about this community.

To Nancy Zimmerman who, when I first approached her about being a part of this project, simply asked for a copy of the book in exchange for all of her photographs. Her kindness, generosity, and talent epitomize so many aspects of this community. And thank you to the professionals that helped me along the way to make this idea a reality—Marsha Blessing, Phyllis Wheeler, Anne Gallaher, Lucy Gnazzo, David Small, and so many other people who supported, encouraged, and provided invaluable insight to move this project forward.

To My Former Teammates from Another Sport—The bond that we created, the tradition that we established, the battles we fought, the struggles we endured, created a bond that will never be broken. The trust that Tom, Bret, JK, Kyle, and Walt had in each other made me miss the times when we prepared, competed, and triumphed…together.

To My Former Players & Students on ALL levels who have believed in what we tried to create on the fields of competition and in the classroom. Thank you. You are the reason why I love what I get to do professionally on a daily basis.

To my teammates who I feel privledged to call my friends. My life has been enriched because you all have been a part of it. Thank you.

To my teammates with whom I work with on a daily basis. The work you do as teachers on a daily basis, the reasons why you do it, is a true inspiration not only to your students, but also to me. My professional goal is to be as good as so many of you. Thank you for the examples you set for our students and your colleagues.

And finally, I would like to think that my grandfather, Papa, who along with my father, took me to my very first baseball game, would have enjoyed this book, and would have loved this team.

When I think about all the people I have to thank, and all the blessings I have to be thankful for, I truly am a lucky man. The Lord has blessed me with a life far greater than what I deserve, and for that, I thank Him.

Thank you.

Scott

ABOUT THE AUTHOR

Scott Slayton has lived in the Red Land community for all of his adult life. After graduating from Virginia Polytechnic Institute and State University (Virginia Tech), he became an Instructor of English at Red Land High School in 1998 and has been there ever since.

Whether referred to as Mr. Slayton, Coach Slayton, or Coach Scott, he has worked with Red Land kids of all ages, both in the classroom and on the fields of competition. From Varsity to Elementary, PIAA State Playoffs and a District Championship, to Summer Camps and Tee-Ball, Scott has committed himself to helping Red Land kids excel both academically and athletically.

His fondness for the Red Land community is matched only by his love for baseball, specifically the New York Mets, the United States of America, and children. Scott so believes in the purity of childhood that he has been an active member of the St. Jude Children's Hospital running team, and has completed three marathons for St. Jude that have raised over $5000.

Together, he and his wife of 15 years, Kelly, have built their own "team" that provides each of them with their greatest joys in life.

CPSIA information can be obtained at www.ICGtesting.com
Printed in the USA
BVOW01s1853120916

461903BV00019B/115/P